SEATTLE PUBLIC LIBRARY
0 01 00 0103305 8

D0971500

# BOONE

# BOONE

T. Boone Pickens, Jr.

Houghton Mifflin Company · Boston · 1987

AUTHOR'S NOTE

This book recounts many conversations held over a long period of time and reconstructed from memory. In each instance the substance and tone of these conversations is accurate; the dialogue is as precise as memory permits.

*A Richard Todd Book*



*Library of Congress Cataloging-in-Publication Data*

Pickens, T. Boone (Thomas Boone)
Boone.

"A Richard Todd book." — T.p. verso.
Includes index.
1. Pickens, T. Boone (Thomas Boone) 2. Mesa Petroleum Co. — History. 3. Industrialists — Texas — Biography. 4. Petroleum industry and trade — United States — History. I. Title.

HD9570.P53A3 1987 338.7'6223382'0924 [B] 86-27648
ISBN 0-395-41433-4
ISBN 0-395-43290-1 (leather)

Printed in the United States of America

D 10 9 8 7 6 5 4 3 2 1

Dedicated to my wife,
*Beatrice Carr Pickens,*
to my father,
*Thomas Boone Pickens,*
and to the
memory of my mother,
*Grace Molonson Pickens*

# Acknowledgments

Like all my accomplishments over the years, this book was a team effort. It wouldn't have been possible without the help and advice of many talented people and I would like to acknowledge their contribution.

Among my colleagues at Mesa whose reading and criticism were essential are David Batchelder, Sidney Tassin, Andrew Craig, Ron Bassett, Warren Vieth, and Ralph Whitworth. Others from Mesa whose labor and advice I depended on were Trixie Lee Slife, Jeri Williams, Mary Stein, Becky Lemoine, Sally Buford, and especially Frances Hibbs.

The wonderful memories of my old friends Lawton Clark, Wales Madden, Harley Hotchkiss, Jerry Walsh, Jim Upchurch, Bob Stillwell, and Ed Watkins helped bring the story alive.

Jim Conaway moved into our home to collaborate with me on writing and structuring the book. My agent, Bob Lescher, gave me valuable insight into the business aspects of writing and publishing. I enjoyed working with all the professionals at Houghton Mifflin. The patience and talent of my editor, Dick Todd, were key to refining the book. I also want to thank Luise Erdmann, Austin Olney, Sandy Goroff, Marly Rusoff, and Louise Noble.

The book would not have been possible without the encouragement and support I received from my family. I am indebted to them for their sacrifices and understanding during the year that I spent an overwhelming amount of my spare time writing and editing.

*Amarillo, Texas, 3 December 86*

# Contents

## *Four / The Big Cat Walks*



## *Five / The Long View*

# *Up Front*

This is the story of a man who turned a $2,500 investment into America's largest independent oil company in thirty years and along the way discovered that something is terribly wrong with corporate America. Mesa Petroleum is the company, and I'm the man.

I have been called a corporate raider, a greenmailer, a communist, even a piranha, by men at the top of much larger corporations with whom I have battled. There is a revolution going on. You may not have heard of it yet, but we are beyond the skirmish stage, and before it's over big business will be changed forever.

If you are a stockholder, the chances are that one way or another, most corporations are misappropriating your money. It is legal under the system; every day this respectable crime is perpetrated in corporate corridors across the country.

I know because I have been there. Some people with things to hide threatened and cussed; I have also been praised and heartily thanked by a neglected minority — the shareholders.

Along the way I have enjoyed some great privileges. I have made a lot of money for myself and other people, and I am proud of it. I want others to have the chance to do the same.

I'm a conservative, born in Oklahoma, and now an adoptive Texan. I made it on my own, having the good luck to be born in America, where starting with nothing doesn't mean you have to end up that way. I believe the greatest opportunity lies in a free marketplace. There are powerful forces afoot trying to restrict that freedom in the interests of the vested and already wealthy. I am talking about a relatively small collection of corporate executives who would use the engine of American commerce for their own narrow ends.

It may seem strange to hear this from a successful entrepreneur who values large companies enough to spend a lot of money and time trying to acquire them. The struggle is an important one. The new leaders will probably not be found among politicians, but among this country's next generation of businesspeople who have rejected the arrogance of big corporations. In such young entrepreneurs lies the preservation of this great land.

How I got from a little town in eastern Oklahoma to the towers of Wall Street is an exciting, unlikely, sometimes painful story.

And, if you're young and restless, I'm hoping you'll make a journey similar to mine.

# BOONE

# *Prologue*
## July 1983

The Monday morning after the Fourth of July weekend I paused in the hallway outside the boardroom of Mesa Petroleum, in Amarillo, Texas, preparing for a difficult task. I had to meet with the operating committee, and we all knew we had serious problems. The boom times brought on by OPEC were over. At one point Mesa had as many as fifty-one rigs working, including five expensive jack-ups in the Gulf of Mexico. We had put most of our eggs in one basket, and we were not finding the oil and gas we expected. Meanwhile, we were spending $500,000 a day to keep the Gulf operation going.

We had a fleet of boats servicing the rigs, and helicopters were shuttling crews back and forth; it was like financing a war. Two of our latest wells had cost $75 million to drill and complete, but they produced far less than expected. And the price of oil would soon be headed south.

Mesa had made a lot of money — in the United States, Canada, and the North Sea. But we were overstaffed, with too much management and too many support troops. We had begun scaling down our activity in 1982, but we would have to do more — much more.

The price of oil would collapse if the Saudis opened their spigot. I had been going around like the Ancient Mariner, telling anyone who would listen that "this thing can't last. It's hanging by a thread — the Saudis. And we can't depend on the Saudis."

I walked into the boardroom, greeted by the expectant faces of five men I knew well. We had gone enthusiastically into the Gulf of Mexico in 1970, but our results were inconsistent. In short, we had blown it.

We had some options now, but whatever we did, we would emerge as a radically different company. There were two who wanted to go for one more big oil or gas field. And two others wanted to cut back and return to being a smaller company or maybe even sell out. Then there were two of us considering another alternative, the one I was about to announce.

"Boys," I said, "this is it. We've got to figure out a way to make $300 million, and we've got to make it fast. We've lost too much money in the Gulf of Mexico. We can't drill our way out of this one. A field goal won't do it — we need a touchdown."

They were apprehensive. Not only were we slashing our budget, but we were about to embark on a new course that would make Mesa either a major force in corporate America or a has-been.

I was used to having my back against the wall. But $300 million was a lot of money — more than half of Mesa's net worth. You don't find that kind of money under a rock. We were about to enter a risky game that would make us famous, and in some circles infamous, initiating deals involving corporations much larger than Mesa: Gulf, Phillips, and Unocal. We would identify the undervalued, mismanaged companies and then make a huge investment in them. We would try to force the managements to do something for their stockholders, including us, and if they refused, we would try to take over the companies. These were high stakes, carrying a high risk, and I'll admit it was a little scary.

I went back to my office and stood at the window, looking out at the city and the big country beyond. Amarillo sits on the high plains of Texas, 3,600 feet above sea level. It enjoys long, dramatic vistas and fine, dry air — it's a great place to live. I had learned most of what I knew here on the Texas plains, knowledge that was about to be tested in a new way.

# *One*

# EARLY DAYS

· 1 ·

# *Welcome to Holdenville*

I grew up "where the pavement ends, the West begins, and the Rock Island crosses the Frisco." That was Holdenville, in eastern Oklahoma, a railroad town, a speck in the grand sweep of the Great Plains that includes the Texas Panhandle, Kansas, Nebraska, and parts of Colorado and New Mexico. Space was what we had the most of in Holdenville. The open land surrounded us like an ocean — vast, rolling, the sky meeting the horizon in some far-off place that I could only imagine.

At night I lay in bed listening to the freight trains shuttling through, wondering where they had come from and where they were headed. During the day I could walk out our back door, go a quarter of a mile, and be alone in endless country.

There weren't many houses on our street. All you could see at night were dark and ominous-looking trees and all you could hear was the wind and the occasional howl of an animal; it could feel quite eerie. Sometimes, coming home after dark, I would suddenly begin running, my imagination conjuring up a horrible fate that awaited me behind a dark tree. Other times I saw myself as a conquering hero.

The space made those of us in Holdenville grateful for what we had: a handful of brick churches, two square blocks of offices, three drugstores, and a hardware store — that was "downtown." There were the respectable institutions, like the hospital and city hall, and some just as essential, like the Manhattan Cafe, where we ate out. On Friday and Saturday nights they'd open up the back room — the Blue Room — and there in the dim light is where we first went dancing to jukebox songs like "Elmer's Tune."

There was also the Turf Bar. Sometimes I would stand in the back, folding papers for my afternoon route and watching as the bartender chalked up the baseball scores on the blackboard. Some men sat at the bar drinking beer, and others played dominos and "pitch" at tables in the dim light. My mother didn't approve of the Turf Bar; she called it "the Bucket of Blood."

But there was very little crime in Holdenville, just the frailty of human nature and some gossip that turned malicious, some heavy drinking that turned to alcoholism, some infidelity, and the occasional public scandal. As in most small towns, there were few secrets. That helped create a sense of community that bound the townspeople.

The desire to connect to the larger world, which is part of the psychology of any small town, surfaced in funny ways. Everyone in town could recount some personal encounter with Dizzy Dean, the baseball hero who grew up near Holdenville; the kid down the block from me used to claim kinship with Pretty Boy Floyd, the infamous bank robber.

When I was twelve, my dad gave me a .22 rifle and taught me to shoot it. I hunted with the Jones boys for squirrels, rabbits, possum, and anything else we could find.

I was a shy kid. In the fourth grade, my schoolmate Joy Elaine Phillips had to read my homework aloud for me in class because I couldn't bear to do it. In the winter I often had ear infections and sometimes had to be driven to school. My father had a streak of good luck one year and in a wild moment bought a bright yellow Pierce-Arrow, an unusual sight in Holdenville, to say the least. I was embarrassed to ride in it, and when my mother drove me to school, I would ask her to let me out down the block. Then I would hide in the bushes until the yellow car was out of sight.

My father was in the oil business. A "landman," he would ferret out landowners willing to lease their mineral rights and then "turn" — sell — the leases to an oil company.

The discovery of the big Seminole oil field the year before I was born was a sign of the future, both for me and for the country a hundred miles around. It turned sleepy little Seminole, just up the road, into a boom town. Its resources were outstripped by the influx of people — many reputable, some not — all itching to get in on the action. The population, which had never been more than 5,000, shot up to 20,000. The boom brought an increase in crime and a decrease, at least temporarily, in the level of morality; in those days, where there was a boom there was also a whorehouse or two. I remember my father telling me about Seminole: overcrowded streets, tent cities on the edge of the town, and oil rigs jammed together so closely they practically touched.

Holdenville was no boom town, but it did experience the effect of the oil fields, just as it had been affected earlier by the building of the railroads. As towns like Holdenville have struggled, Americans have tended to idealize them. There may be some wishful thinking in that vision, but, looking back, I believe that Holdenville was an ideal place in which to grow up. Parents could raise their children in a relatively free environment, and a young person could establish a set of values that would last for life.

During the Depression, my father had plenty of work. At the same time, many people from our state were forced to migrate west. Insulated by its oil economy, Holdenville largely escaped that kind of hardship

The whole area paid a price for our prosperity. The natural beauty of the country, with its rolling hills and placid streams, was marked by pockets of ugliness, all of them the handiwork of man. I remember the trees lining the creeks along the road to Seminole. By the time I was five or six, they were all dead. My father explained that it was because the salt water that came out of the oil wells was just dumped into the creeks.

"Well then," I asked, "why did they do that?"

"Because that was the easiest way to get rid of it."

"But," I persisted, "couldn't they do it another way?"

My father changed the subject. I was learning at a young age that you didn't buck Big Oil.

I was always competitive, though I can't say exactly why. Winning seemed important from the time I was a small boy, and I clearly remember playing football on the corner lot with the kids on my block, scrapping for the ball and devising a passing strategy at the age of eleven with Bobby Lee Loftis that would defeat the team from two blocks away. They were bigger than we were, but our brains and spunk usually combined to carry the day.

When I was twelve, I had a small paper route — only twenty-eight houses, about half the size of the other routes — and I got a penny for every paper I delivered. When the route next to mine opened up, I talked my supervisor into letting me have it, too. A few years later, the route on the other side became available, and I got it as well. I was delivering 125 papers a day and making more money than I could imagine.

My route started one block from the newspaper office. This was handy because I could be throwing papers three minutes after leaving the office. I would place two bags strategically on my bike so that as I emptied one I would be able to pick up another full one and keep throwing.

I would leave the newspaper office at high speed, go up Broadway of America, down Creek Street, back up Echo, criss-crossing the streets, cutting through yards, jumping curbs. Not all the papers hit squarely in front of the door; I can remember demolishing three bottles of milk one time on Mrs. Cordell's porch.

As I finished throwing the last paper, I slipped into something like a skier's tuck and began the two-block ride to the newspaper office. I would come flying into the finish as though I had set a new time that would be forever etched in a record book somewhere. It didn't hurt to dream a little.

Another of my jobs was to deliver newspapers to the bus station every day, and I would drape the mailbags over the bike's handlebars and back fender and start down the hill, hoping for the best. The mailbags made braking a problem. One day I couldn't stop and went flying through the swinging door, colliding with a bench. The mailbags broke open and the bicycle ended up in the pile with me; I broke a rib against the handlebars. Some Indians sitting in the waiting area never even cracked a smile; it was the most excitement they had seen in Holdenville in years.

The newspaper office gave me my best glimpse of the outside world. I used to stand over the teletype machine and read all the news stories about the war in Europe. Lord Mountbatten was one of my heroes. I read every word about the HMS *Hood*, the battle cruiser sunk by the German battleship *Bismarck*.

The war seemed very close.

An important rule that was instilled in me even before I knew it was the desire not to let anyone down. I know where it came from — my mother. If a person depended on me to do something, I would be damned before I failed him.

My mother ran the Office of Price Administration (OPA) for the three-county area surrounding Holdenville. The OPA was charged with rationing gasoline and other goods that were in short supply during the war. Rationing offered opportunities for petty corruption. Some OPA administrators were simply incompetent; others were competent but helped their friends get more gasoline than they were allowed. You can be sure that never happened at the Holdenville office.

I was thirteen when America entered the war. Sometimes I would go to Mother's office after school and ride home with her. One day a gas station owner named Ray Smith came into the office with a sad story. He had accidentally left a nozzle on the ground with the pump on and had lost several hundred gallons of gasoline. I had worked at his Sinclair station on Hinckley Street one summer, as a "tire-buster," and he had been good to me.

He pleaded with my mother for more gas. She listened politely until he finished, then told him that she was sorry to hear about his misfortune but that he had already received his ration for the month.

After he left, I said, "You should have given him the gas."

I got the same look she had given Mr. Smith.

The only reason she had listened to Smith's story was because he had been nice to me. Mother had a great sense of integrity. If she said she would do something, you could consider it done. She taught by example. I had a real problem if I promised to do something and didn't deliver. Once, breaking the rules, I went hunting with my friend Gene Jones without telling my mother. It was a blustery fall day that turned from clear to gray and then blew up into a sleet storm. We had ridden our bikes out to the lake 7 miles from town. The storm forced a lot of ducks to look for cover and we were knocking them down all over the place. Gradually I became aware of a car horn in the distance. It was my mother. She said very little, just made me tie the bike onto the front of the car and told me to hold it and sit on the fender while she drove the 7 miles home — through the storm! I could hardly straighten up when we got home. My mother was a no-nonsense person.

Living next door to us were my maternal grandmother, Nellie Molonson, and my aunt Ethel Reed. My grandmother, aunt, and mother saw things pretty much the same way and reinforced the same values. I sometimes felt I had been hit with a triple whammy! My aunt Ethel was a widow and had one son, Billy Bob, who was four years older than I. Billy Bob was the closest thing I would ever have to a brother.

My grandmother, whom I adored, gave me advice, most of which centered on the idea that the best life was "a life of moderation." Grandmother was a great believer in the old-fashioned virtues — hard work, thrift, forthrightness. She owned four rental houses, and one summer she asked me if I wanted to make some extra money by mowing the lawns.

I said, "Sure."

She asked me to make an offer for the summer.

"Grandmother, I'll mow them once a week for 10 cents a lawn."

"Fine," she said.

Within a week, I realized I had sold out cheap, and I thought Grandmother would let me off the hook.

She turned me down. "This will be good training for you," she said. "Next time, you'll think a little longer about what you're committing to before you jump into it."

Although her decision was final, she tempered it by offering to sharpen the mower blades at her expense.

I lived next door to my grandmother for sixteen rewarding years. One Saturday, when I was on my way to town with 50 cents, she asked me what I planned to spend the money on.

"A haircut, the picture show, and a bag of popcorn," I replied.

Her response was to the point: "Remember, a fool and his money are soon parted." I didn't know then that it was an old saying — it hit me with real force.

She had some other phrases, expressions of homespun philosophy such as that well-known Oklahoma expression "Root hog or die," meaning, "Get in and compete or fail." If she felt you were asking for too much help, she would say, "You have to learn to sit on your own bottom."

Aunt Ethel was my schoolteacher in the fourth and fifth grades. Though I always did well in her classes, she would not give me an A. When I complained, pointing out that my work was at least as good as that of the kids who received A's, she had a stock reply: "They are working up to their potential, and you're not."

This response could bring me to the verge of tears, but my aunt wouldn't bend. When my mother asked about my inability to get an A, she got the same answer.

My mother was the disciplinarian in our family, but that description implies a harshness that she lacked. She sometimes spanked me, usually after I had made some wisecrack, but her discipline involved more than mere punishment for my childhood shenanigans. Mother made sure my free time was spent in ways she considered productive. I was involved in sports, Boy Scouts, working at a job or practicing my clarinet. She didn't believe in my wasting time.

Fortunately, my musical career was short-lived. Floyd Crumm, my teacher, recommended thirty minutes of practice each day. At my mother's standing order, I was to come in from baseball or basketball thirty minutes before dinner and practice. This practice period coincided with the time that Dad read the evening newspaper. The two activities were not compatible, but for a while my mother's wishes prevailed.

Then, one evening when I was supposed to be practicing, my mother came from the kitchen to find me reading the sports page. My father was in his favorite chair, the cigar smoke rising from behind his paper.

"Why aren't you practicing your clarinet?" my mother asked me.

"I'm taking a break."

"You've only practiced for five minutes. Now if you're not going to practice, we'll give the clarinet to Bill Howell."

It was a threat. The Howells lived five blocks away, and their son, Bill, was two years younger than I.

Mother went back to the kitchen, and I resumed my screeching. My father interrupted, asking me, "Didn't you hear what your mother said?"

"What?"

"She said that if you aren't going to practice, we're going to give the clarinet to the Howells."

I just stared at him.

"So if you don't want to practice," he continued, "then take the clarinet to the Howells'."

Without a word I boxed the clarinet and took off for the Howells'. Emma Jane, Bill's mother, answered the door. "Here's the clarinet," I told her.

She looked dumfounded, and I didn't wait for an answer. "My father told me to bring my clarinet to you for Bill to play," I added, then hurried home.

Five minutes later, I was reading the sports page again. Mother came into the room and asked, "Why aren't you practicing? Where is your clarinet?"

I hesitated, waiting for my father to come to my rescue. But his paper stayed up. Finally I said, almost inaudibly, "I took it to the Howells'."

"You did what?" she asked.

I stammered, "I took it to the Howells'."

At that point the paper dropped, and my father said, "Dammit, Grace, you told him if he wasn't going to practice, we would give the clarinet to the Howells. So he did."

My mother hesitated, then walked back into the kitchen. The clarinet was never mentioned again.

She hated to give up on the possibility that her only child

would be a musician, but she had already been told by a talented friend, Dode Funk, that little Boone would never make it as a clarinet player.

It was Mother who had decided I should be called by my middle name, Boone, instead of Tom, like my father. No child likes to be different, and I was no exception. It was embarrassing to have to repeat my name two or three times before people would understand, and I was afraid that kids might make fun of me. I had been mistakenly called Booner, Ben, Bobby — even Jerome!

My mother saw things differently. "Once people understand your name," she said proudly, "they won't ever forget it."

My parents had very different personalities, but they loved each other, and each influenced me in different ways.

As a child, I never thought about growing up to be an oilman. Like those of most American boys, my childhood fantasies revolved around becoming a Hall of Fame baseball player like Dizzy Dean or Carl Hubbell, two major league pitchers who were both from Oklahoma. The flamboyant Dean was a local hero, but my favorite was the more businesslike Hubbell.

I knew the oil business offered a real option. It was a good way to make a living. After all, my father made his living in the oil business. Everybody in town liked Tom Pickens. Friendly, unflappable, generous to a fault, he was a wonderful storyteller — maybe the result of being a preacher's son. His father, the Reverend A. C. Pickens, had served as a Methodist missionary to the Indians and performed the Lord's work wherever the need arose, so he had spent his youth moving from one small Oklahoma town to another. The West offered plenty of opportunity. But Tom Pickens was too much a man of the world to follow his father's example. He loved cigars, cards, a hearty drink, and a night out with the boys.

My father, almost ninety now, likes to tell the story of being out of college on his own and sometimes staying up all night playing poker. He returned to his boardinghouse at dawn and saw a light in his window. He found his father sitting in the room, in a straight-backed chair, smoking one of Dad's cigars. He had come over by bus from Tecumseh, 40 miles away, and had sat up all night reading, as he often did.

"Where have you been?" my grandfather asked.

"Playing cards." Dad was glad to see him, but a little nervous. He tossed his winnings on the bed and said, "Here, take what you want."

He thought his father would take $20 or so, but he took it all. The First Methodist Church in Tecumseh was about to get its best collection ever.

"Son," his father said, "this money has been working for the devil long enough. Let's let it work for the Lord for a while."

By the time my father got to Holdenville, at the age of twenty-five, he was a lawyer, having earned his law degree from Cumberland University, a small school in Lebanon, Tennessee. He accepted a position with the Holdenville firm that soon became Crump, Hall & Pickens, but he found that law was not as exciting or rewarding as the oil business and soon left the firm. Buying and selling leases required many of the skills of a lawyer, and my father was good at it.

Landmen spent a lot of time at the county abstract office, where the land titles were kept. Not long after getting into the oil business, my father met a young woman who worked in the abstract office. Slight and pretty, Grace Molonson managed the office. After a year's courtship, she and Tom Pickens were married, in 1923.

Dad's office, on the top (second) floor of the Benson Building, was open to anybody who came along. My mother sometimes criticized him; she thought he gave too much time to "ne'er-do-wells."

My own relationship with Dad was simple: we were pals. We shared an interest in sports, which he encouraged: he took me to ball games and made sure I had plenty of balls and bats. Wherever we went, we usually had a good time.

My father's passion for card playing did not diminish with time. He sometimes played all night, and he loved to say in the shank of the evening, as he raked in the big pot, "The big cat walks just before daylight, boys."

Dad did well, but business was never going to captivate him the way it would me. Playing poker, making a few bets, hunting, fishing — now that was fun.

I remember a time, in the fall of 1939, my mother went to Memphis, Tennessee, to see an eye doctor, on the Rock Island's Memphis–California. Dad and I put her aboard, and the train had just pulled out when Dad said, "We're going to take a trip, too."

We headed south in his new Chevy. We drove all the way to Waco, Texas, to see Baylor and Oklahoma A&M play football. It was a Friday, and we barely made the eight o'clock kickoff. We grabbed a couple of hot dogs and hurried to our seats. Billy Patterson was Baylor's quarterback and helped carry them to victory. I'll never forget the unexpected excitement of that game.

Little did I know, but this adventure was just getting under way. After the game we headed for Dallas. We stayed overnight in a motel on the highway, because every hotel room in Dallas would be filled. The next day was the traditional game between the University of Texas and Oklahoma University, and when we hit Dallas, the first thing I did was to get the sports page and find out where the Oklahoma University headquarters was. Dad and I then went to the Adolphus Hotel to meet some friends from Oklahoma.

We headed for the stadium early. Dad hailed a cab that took us to the front gate of the Texas State Fair Grounds. The stadium was next to the State Fair, which was in full swing — I couldn't believe it. The Texas-Oklahoma game, then the fair, all in one day!

Texas had a great little running back, "Jackrabbit" Crain, from Nocona, Texas. They called him the Nocona Nugget, but he was stopped by the Sooners that Saturday afternoon. OU beat Texas, 24–12.

On Sunday, Dad appeared in no hurry to leave Dallas. He asked me, "How are you doing in school?"

"I'm doing just great."

"Well, I've got some work I could do in this area." There was a pause, and he added, "The Southwest Conference championship game's being played in Fort Worth next Saturday, between Texas A&M and Texas Christian."

I couldn't believe what I was hearing. Was he actually planning to stay over for that game?

He made a couple of calls in Dallas and Fort Worth during the week, then we took care of the serious business. Dad wanted to get a bet down on the big game, so we went to check "the line": two or three bars would always book the games. Dad compared the odds and made a $300 bet on A&M. In 1939 we weren't blessed with syndicated bookies. Each bookie handicapped the games with no help from experts like Jimmy the Greek. The $300 bet was "full"; if we lost, we had just enough money to buy gas to get back to Hughes County, Oklahoma.

I knew this was a week I would never forget. I was already uneasy about playing hooky. And $300 was a lot of money. I asked myself, "Can we get away with all of this?"

We had good seats for the game. In the first five minutes, TCU's great end, Don Looney, made a circus catch in the end zone, and we were down six points. I thought, Oh, God. We're gonna lose $300.

Dad said calmly, "The game's just getting started."

Well, after an exchange it was TCU's turn to punt, and A&M's safety fielded it right in front of us. He streaked down the sideline for a touchdown.

Dad said, "Now, how do you like the way this ball game's going?"

A&M won, 20–6. I was so happy I was left-handed, as the saying goes, and also relieved, but as soon as we got in the car and headed for the bar to get our $300 I started to worry about what was in store for us at home. I thought they had probably sent the Federales out after me for missing a week of school.

Dad said, "You always start worrying too early."

It's a habit I've overcome.

*

By the time I got to high school, in 1943, basketball was the most important thing in my life. Fortunately, I was well coordinated. I wanted to be good, so I practiced shooting baskets in the backyard for hours at a time, in both winter and summer. I played in every pick-up game I could find — at the expense of my studies. I had visions of a state championship, of last-second winning baskets, of being carried off the court by my delirious teammates, of being a star.

I had the same dreams as just about every other school kid in America. Only five feet nine inches tall, I wouldn't have made ball boy today, but I came along at the right time for short basketball players. Our coach, John Daugherty, liked me. He also taught the Oklahoma history course, which I took, spending almost every class period shooting baskets in the gym.

"All you have to know," he told me, "is the five civilized tribes of Oklahoma — Cherokee, Creek, Choctaw, Seminole, and Chickasaw." It was the first time I saw the payoff for athletes.

Once, just before a history test, the coach asked me in the gym who I thought the most important governor of Oklahoma had been. I mentioned one governor, and he said, "Hell, no. He was a crook. The most important governor of Oklahoma was Alfalfa Bill Murray." When I sat down to take the test, I saw that the first question was: "Who was the most important governor of Oklahoma?"

Sometime in the late 1930s, the search for oil in the Seminole area had begun to run its course. More to the point, my father had begun to run out of luck. Instead of playing it safe with land deals, he started investing in wildcats, which had a much greater potential payoff than lease sales — and a much greater risk.

As it turned out, my father was better at assessing risk in a game of five-card draw than in looking for oil. By the time the war was under way, the family was pinched. The yellow Pierce-Arrow was long gone, and the Chevy wasn't new anymore. Dad took a job as a landman with Phillips Petroleum and was assigned to its office in Amarillo, Texas. He went because he had to, not because he wanted to. Before, it had never taken my father long to adjust to a new situation, but now it did. This was the first time in his life that he had not been self-employed, and the transition to the corporate world was difficult for him. I don't think he ever really made the adjustment; he had lived in the wild too long. He didn't like Phillips — but he wouldn't have liked Mobil or Shell, either.

In the summer of 1944, my parents told me we were moving to Amarillo. This was the first real setback of my life, and I didn't handle it well.

My mother, however, quickly adjusted to the idea. She would miss her mother and sister and all her friends, but she looked on the move as a great adventure and more opportunity for all of us.

I hated the idea of leaving Holdenville, where I was about to become a big shot. My first day at Amarillo High School was a real shock. Holdenville High had had all of 200 students; Amarillo, with a postwar population of 50,000, had more than 2,000 students in its one high school, a huge and intimidating place. I went home not to our familiar house but to a second-floor apartment.

Moving to Amarillo was probably the best thing that ever happened to me, for I discovered I could compete on an equal footing without feeling inadequate. But before I realized that, I would seek refuge from the big city by hitchhiking the 300 miles to Holdenville once a month to hang around with my old friends for the weekend. I would stay with my grandmother, trying to convince her to let me come back and live with her.

"No," she would say firmly. "Your parents live in Texas now. Your place is with them."

When I got back to Amarillo, I would start in on my parents, pleading with them to let me live in Holdenville. I pushed my mother to the limit.

"If you want to move to Holdenville, you may," she said, her voice full of steely resolve. "I've talked to your grandmother, and she's agreed that you can live with her. But if you go, that's it.

You can't come back here during the school year." She added, "You just can't stand the competition in Amarillo."

I went to my room and thought about it. I returned to the kitchen and told her I had changed my mind.

"Okay," she said. "If that's the decision, I don't ever want the subject brought up again."

That quickly, Holdenville became part of the past.

· 2 ·

# Coming of Age

By the time I was a senior at Amarillo High in 1947, I had found a new life. I had been a starting guard on the basketball team for two years. We had reached the semifinals of the state championship against Thomas Jefferson High of San Antonio, a much bigger and stronger team, which was ranked number one in the state. It was led by the great Kyle Rote, who later became an all-pro running back for the New York Giants.

Nobody gave us much of a chance. But with thirty seconds left in the game we were ahead, 38–37. Everyone in the gym was standing, rooting for us, the underdogs from Amarillo. Well, almost everyone. I was inspired to play the game of my life. Years later, I would look back on that game and compare it to my business life. I don't want to make too much of it, but I've always done best as the underdog. Fortunately, I've always had a few people cheering me on from the sidelines.

The Amarillo team won a moral victory that night, but a moral victory only. We lost the game on a last-second shot and it was my fault: I let Rote knock the ball out of my hand. I fouled him after he got the ball, he missed the free throw, and Benny White, Jefferson's big center, made the winning basket. It was a terrible blow.

My coach, T. G. Hull, said, "Don't worry about it. You played a good game." Coach Hull was an important influence on me and his lessons served me well throughout my career, mostly his simple, no-nonsense philosophy. Time and time again I found that if I was thinking clearly, I would have to agree with whatever he said. He later told me, "Play every game for all you're worth. But when it's over, it's over."

I went to Texas A&M after graduation, hoping to be a basketball star, but I was a little short and slow for college basketball. I was going with the prettiest girl in the junior class at Amarillo High, Lynn O'Brien. Petite and shy, Lynn came from a fine old Panhandle family. Our on-again, off-again love affair had started while I was still in high school and continued after I went away to college.

The next year I transferred to Oklahoma A&M at Stillwater, where I decided to study geology, at my father's insistence. In February 1949, Lynn and I decided to get married. Our parents wanted us to wait a few years, but we wouldn't listen.

My mother used to say that she never saw anybody grow up as fast as I did after getting married. By the end of 1949 we had a baby daughter, Deborah — and Lynn and I were both full-time students. Our parents helped us financially — I never felt good about that. I worked as a tutor for some of the weaker geology students. We rented a house for $60 a month and sublet one room for $40 (breakfast included) to a friend. And that, sports fans, is entrepreneurship.

Lynn and I jockeyed our courses around so that we rarely needed a babysitter. It gave me an opportunity to get to know Deb and to play a large part in her early upbringing. I did a lot of the feeding and morning baths, as they fit my schedule better than Lynn's. It was a thrill — and quite a learning experience — for a new father.

My grades during the first two years of college were about as unimpressive as they had been in my last two years of high school. I wasn't serious about becoming a geologist, and that was the way Dr. V. B. Monnett, head of the department, saw it. Better known as "Ole V.B.," he was one of those formidable figures, like Coach Hull, whom you appreciate much more in later years than when you see him every day.

When I was a sophomore, I asked Dr. Monnett about job prospects when I got out of school, and he said, "Pickens, they're not even hiring the good boys."

My last two years I did well and was on the dean's list.

By the time I graduated I had mowed lawns, delivered papers, worked on a pipeline crew, and roughnecked, one of the toughest jobs in the oil patch. I had also been a fireman on the railroad and had worked in a refinery. I knew something about work, and I'd had my share of experiences.

The oil industry was in one of its slumps; 1951 was a tough year to be starting out as a geologist. I went to Bartlesville for an interview with Phillips Petroleum — my first interview in a coat and tie. My earlier jobs had been fine for a student, but now I was on my own and had a family to support, and only one out of seven of my classmates got a job.

I expected a personnel manager to be friendly, but this guy was something else. He was bored, and I was nervous. He looked at my letter of recommendation from Dr. Monnett that I thought would put me on the inside track and said, "Dr. Monnett says you have all the training to be a good geologist, but that sometimes you lack motivation."

"I'm ready to go to work, sir," I said.

Two weeks later Phillips offered me a job. Not long after that I was also offered a job with Humble Oil, the giant Texas oil company that was part of Standard of New Jersey. I much preferred Humble, but its job wouldn't be available until August and I could start at Phillips as soon as I graduated, in May. Given my situation, the decision was easy. My starting pay was $290 a month.

The company's founder, Frank Phillips, was one of the original wildcatters — flamboyant and larger than life. As legend has it, Phillips was born in a log cabin, and at an early age he saw a barber wearing a pair of flashy striped pants. "I made up my mind," he later said, "that I wanted to earn enough money so I could afford to wear striped pants even on weekdays."

In fact, he started as a barber, then became a bond salesman, and finally, just after the turn of the century, he got into the oil game. He and his brother moved to Bartlesville, one of the earliest of the Oklahoma boom towns. Their first three wells, all dry holes, put them close to bankruptcy.

Frank Phillips decided to give it one more try, vowing that if the fourth well was dry he would get out of the oil business and start cutting hair again. You can guess what happened. Not only was the well a gusher, but, as the story goes, Phillips completed eighty oil wells in a row. In 1917, he consolidated all his oil interests in one company, which he based in Bartlesville and named for himself.

By the time I was hired, Frank Phillips had been dead for two years and the company he founded was one of the twenty largest corporations in America. With 20,000 employees, it had chemical and plastics divisions, an international operation, refineries, hundreds of gas stations across the country selling Phillips 66 gasoline, two dozen exploration and production offices, and a large staff of bureaucrats.

I spent an uneventful summer there in 1951. Our life was simple, as you might imagine, but there was excitement in my vague plans for the future. I rode a bicycle to work, which brought a few snickers, but it was sure easy to park. For recreation I played softball on the department team a couple of nights a week and hunted squirrels in the Caney River bottom early most Saturday mornings. I had learned to hunt squirrels years before in Holdenville.

We ate everything I brought in. Once Lynn asked if I couldn't shoot some younger, more tender squirrels.

I was waiting for my assignment to a division exploration office, which was the destiny of a junior geologist. One day I was surprised by an invitation to have lunch with Dr. G. L. Knight, a regional exploration manager. I had known him in Amarillo back in 1946, when I was parking cars for Phillips in the old Rule Building garage.

Dr. Knight took me to the Bartlesville Country Club for lunch, and I was about five minutes late getting back to my desk. My supervisor called me into his office and closed the door. His first comment was, "Why were you late?"

I told him about the lunch with Dr. Knight.

The supervisor was a full-fledged bureaucrat. Where did we go for lunch? Why did Dr. Knight invite me? How long had I known him?

Finally I said, "Look, I was only five minutes late, and we've taken thirty minutes finding out what I had for lunch. I'll stay over and make up the time."

Being late wasn't the real issue; he wanted to know about my relationship with Dr. Knight. He fired back, "That's another thing you don't understand. You are to be out of the office by five-fifteen. Nobody stays in the building after hours, and you have been staying sometimes until six o'clock."

Once I went to work without a tie. I wasn't used to wearing one, and sometimes I wouldn't put it on until just before leaving the house. The day I forgot my tie, the supervisor told me I had to go get one. I could see it was damned important to him. I rushed downstairs and signed out with the security guard, which took several minutes. I went across the street to a men's store and bought my first and only clip-on tie, for a dollar, and ran back, stopping to sign back in. By the time I got to my office, I had wasted almost an hour — all for a tie!

The supervisors seemed rigid and distrustful. A bell rang at five minutes to eight every morning to get you to your desk, just like grade school. Yes, we had a five o'clock bell, too. It was amusing to see people start easing to the door five minutes before the bell sounded. It gave them a real thrill to make the first elevator.

Some old-timers had what was called "the Bartlesville twitch"; they were always looking over their shoulder, afraid they would be caught doing something wrong. I got an early introduction to this paranoia when a fellow worker asked me to meet him in the restroom. He had something important to tell me. Curious, I agreed, and in the restroom I asked, "What's up?"

"Shhh!" He put his finger to his lips and pointed toward the stalls.

I glanced underneath the doors but didn't see any feet.

"They stand on the seats," he whispered. "Sometimes they stand there all day, trying to get information."

I can't remember what he told me. The incident was absurd, but the message came through loud and clear.

A week after I had lunch with Dr. Knight, my boss told me I had been assigned to Corpus Christi, where the small South Texas division was located. I was to leave the following week.

"Can I leave right now?" I asked.

That surprised him. "Sure," he said, glad to get rid of me.

I went to the personnel department and picked up an advance to cover my moving expenses. Then I pedaled home with the speed of a former paperboy and broke the news to Lynn.

Lynn, Deborah, and I were on our way to Corpus in Lynn's old Oldsmobile 88, a gift from her father. We found a nice place, a stacked duplex, for $65 a month while we were on standby for company housing. A few months later we got a three-bedroom house in the company camp for only $16 a month.

I was at work on Monday morning, having left Bartlesville on Friday afternoon — maybe the fastest transfer in company history. At about the time I arrived, the division made its first significant oil discovery in years, a successful wildcat drilled in Copano Bay, about 40 miles north of Corpus and just a few miles from Rockport. I was assigned to B. C. Phillips (no relation to Frank), the geologist who would develop the new oil field.

Development takes place after the field has been discovered. If exploration geologists are considered the elite of the oil business, then a development geologist is the equivalent of a down lineman in football. He does the gruntwork. The exploration geologist gets to be the running back.

After a summer in Bartlesville, I was eager to go anywhere and didn't care what kind of work they gave me. Being a well-site geologist sounded great to me; I even got a company car, a '48 Chevy, the oldest car in the office. It was my first car ever and I was glad to have it, for our house was 5 miles from the office — quite a bike ride.

B. C. Phillips, known as "B.," trained me to do well-site work the old-fashioned way. On most of our jobs we were the only representatives of Phillips. Nobody in Corpus or Bartlesville would know if we got to work early or if we stayed until everything was done.

Our work required many hours in the field but was not very challenging. We spent a lot of time waiting for something to happen. Well-site geologists often play a lot of cards, and B. and I were no exception. I usually won, which really upset him; it was humiliating to lose to the junior geologist. I was glad to have the few extra dollars, so I tried to keep a straight face when he got riled over what he called bad cards.

"Are you some kind of tinhorn or something?" he'd ask, throwing the cards down. "I'm going fishing."

After a while he would come back. He had a habit of jerking his pants up and stuffing in his shirt. "Get the cards," he'd say. We'd play another game and he would lose again.

Once he got so mad he threw the deck out the window. "Now we'll see if you're gonna beat me again," he said. "The cards are gone!"

Sometimes I thought that if well-site work was going to be my future, I had better take up needlepoint as a pastime.

Then B. was transferred to Bartlesville. My boss came to Copano and told me my training was over and I was being moved up to B.'s spot. If I did a good job at Copano for a year, he added, he would bring me into the office and make me an explorationist.

It was good news, but the division geologist didn't deliver it with a smile. "If I ever come back up here," he said, "it will be to fire you."

I was picked green for the job, but I was determined to do it and made sure he never had to return to Copano. I was responsible for four rigs, sometimes five, and averaged twenty-five days a month in the field. When any new well was drilled close to my area, I jumped at the opportunity to look after it.

My boss gave me the authority to make small decisions, which I appreciated; I think he saw me as a comer, and he often gave me career advice. Most of it boiled down to the wisdom of my sticking with him.

When Bartlesville wanted information about the Copano development, he would call me into his office and have me scribble down the answers to their questions. He was good at making it sound as though the information came right off the top of his head. A year later I was promoted to exploration work, just as I had been promised. I was proud of the job I had done at Copano and felt that it was great to be working for Phillips.

During my time in Corpus, however, I had begun to see things that bothered me. Maybe I was naive, but I couldn't understand why a big company like Phillips put up with things that were wrong and that weren't good for business, either.

I noticed the petty graft and corruption first. At Copano, it was hard not to notice. Phillips was leasing drilling rigs and boats that were in poor condition, and nobody was concerned. You knew there had to be a payoff somewhere.

Then there was the company grapefruit grove. In order to get the oil and gas rights to a particular tract in the Rio Grande Valley of South Texas, Phillips had to buy the surface rights as well, which happened to include a grapefruit grove. It was common knowledge that the division landman was making a few bucks on the side from the sale of the grapefruit. I couldn't believe that a big company had such a ridiculous operation going on. And my boss was unhappy because he hadn't been cut in on it!

At about this time I was working on a well that caused a real problem. We had cored the prospective pay zone and run logs, and when I looked at the data I was sure that the amount of oil the well would produce would never justify the cost of completion. When I told the division geologist over the telephone, he said, "What do you want to do?"

"Let's plug it," I said.

He told me to come on to Corpus so he could see the data. It didn't take him but a few minutes to come to the same conclusion: he agreed there was a small but noncommercial pay zone. But Bartlesville decided to "run pipe" — to complete the well — a decision that would cost around $300,000.

"The ivory tower just came down with another one of its red-hot decisions," said the division geologist, his voice heavy with sarcasm. He added, "Our neck is stuck out now."

I hadn't even realized we had a problem; now it was us against them. The two geologists closest to the situation agreed that the well should be plugged. What was the point of having us if Bartlesville was going to overrule us on a decision as basic as this one? It was a tip-off about how the organization was run.

I watched closely as the well was being completed. It started off at a pretty fair rate, which came as no surprise. We knew it had a pay zone, but it was very thin. Bartlesville was quick to point out what a fine well we had, though we had predicted a good initial rate. Within two weeks, the production fell off to practically nothing, also as predicted, and this time not a peep was heard from Bartlesville.

I had been around long enough to know that completing the well was not just an opportunity to undermine a decision made in a division office. The department could also claim a "producing well" and put it in the win column, even though the small amount of oil wouldn't pay for the casing. This was consistent with Bartlesville's decision-making. Avoiding the category of "dry hole" was worth $300,000 anytime, even though the well would never recover its cost. In a big company, a lot of mistakes can be buried.

In September 1953, I was offered a transfer to Phillips's Panhandle division, in my hometown of Amarillo. I accepted because Lynn and I decided that the high, dry climate of the Texas Panhandle would help Deborah, now four, who had asthma. We were right about that. But in most other respects the Amarillo transfer was a disaster: I was back at the bottom of the totem pole.

The Amarillo office was more than twice the size of the Corpus office, and I saw some things I hadn't seen before.

The production superintendent had a nice fringe benefit. Salesmen regularly called at the office, selling everything from pipe to the mud used in drilling wells. The superintendent had established a routine for new salesmen: they would come into his office holding their hat and an envelope of $20 bills. They would place their hat and the envelope on the corner of his desk. The men would shoot the breeze for a while, and the salesman would pick up his hat as he walked out, leaving the envelope behind. Now he was in line to do business with Phillips.

At last the superintendent's demands became so blatant that

even Bartlesville couldn't look the other way. He was transferred and told to cool it — but I'll bet it was a short-lived cooling-off period.

I sometimes thought about leaving Phillips — in fact, I had been offered a job back in Corpus — but around this time I became worried about my health. During the previous year I had developed a real problem with fatigue. I first noticed it as a college basketball player: exhaustion would overtake me long before the game was over. The coach started putting me in for five minutes at a time, then taking me out to rest. Years later, at Phillips, I noticed that the problem was getting worse. My doctor diagnosed it as a damaged liver, although the many tests that were run were inconclusive.

I became alarmed. I was running a low-grade fever and slept at my desk during the lunch hour to help get through the afternoon. After standing over a drafting table for an hour, I had a hard time straightening up without pain. I went to bed most nights by seven o'clock. My bones were so sore that if Lynn's foot touched my shin during the night, I would come up yelling.

Then the doctor told my father-in-law that he didn't think I had long to live. At the same time, the doctor admitted that he didn't really know what was wrong. My mother had been telling me that as a child I had been diagnosed as having an enlarged spleen. Finally I reported this to the doctors, though I didn't have much faith in that old Holdenville diagnosis, but it turned out to be true. I went to a specialist in Dallas, at what was then Southwest Medical School. He confirmed that it was a spleen problem, and in April 1954, my spleen was removed. Thanks to my Phillips insurance and because I let the medical students poke around on my stomach, the tests and hospitalization cost me all of $44.

After the recovery I was a new man. We often give ourselves a lot of credit for the bold things we do, but at times like that I realize how much depends upon good health.

Six months after I came to Amarillo, in the winter of 1953, Phillips was drilling a deep well through a series of porous granite wash formations. That doesn't mean much unless you're in the oil business, but every time the bit reached one of the porous zones, the drilling rate increased; that's called a "drilling break." It's not an indication that the well has penetrated a productive zone; however, it is a possibility. The way to find out if the zone contains oil or gas is to run a "drill-stem test," a time-consuming and expensive procedure, during which all the pipe is pulled out of the hole and then put back in with the necessary testing equipment.

I remember a cold, windy day when it was obvious that we would recover only salt water if we ran a drill-stem test on this zone — a waste of time and money. I knew that, and so did everybody else on the rig, including the "weevil" roughneck who had been there only a week.

It was not my decision, however. I called the division geologist, who had never done well-site work, to decide if we would test. He had the Bartlesville twitch — and a stomach ulcer, to boot — and was afraid to make a decision that might get him in trouble. The safest course, he said, was to run a drill-stem test, and so we did.

More salt water, of course. When I would sarcastically report the results, he would instruct me to call him the next time I had a break. We would drill for about half a day and, sure enough, there would be another break — and another order to run a drill-stem test. It was a real morale-buster. A drill-stem test took twenty-four hours to complete and it was winter in the Panhandle. The crew was wet, cold, and fed up. It wasn't right to put them through this kind of ordeal just to protect a weak-kneed division geologist.

The next time I was in the office, my boss asked me how things were going. I couldn't hold it back. "I'll tell you how they're going," I said. "Why don't you take the money you're wasting on drill-stem tests and spread it around with a few raises?"

He told the division manager what I had said, and I was called on the carpet. "We don't need any more suggestions like that, Pickens," he said.

Several weeks later, one of the executives from Bartlesville with whom I had played softball visited the Amarillo office.

"How's it going?" he asked me.

"All right, I suppose. But I'm sure getting tired of well-site work." He nodded sympathetically. Then he said, "I'd like to give you a little advice. We heard good things about you, but if you're ever going to make it big with this company, you've got to learn to keep your mouth shut."

It was many months before I faced up to the fact that I would be happier on my own. I decided I wasn't going to stay around for twenty years and then find myself bitter because I had pissed away my productive years.

Subconsciously, I must have been preparing for the day when the urge to leave would be too strong to ignore. I was taking note of human behavior in business. For instance, although I was a geologist, I realized that I did not have a geologist's temperament. Geologists generally have a tendency to be overly optimistic because of the nature of their business. You can get a string of dry holes that could destroy some guys, but you can't give up. You have to think that the next one is going to hit a big field for you.

I am usually more conservative than people want to believe. In the oil patch I often saw enthusiasm that turned out to be misplaced, and I became leery of perpetual optimists.

In November 1954, the division geologist announced that he had a new project for me. Phillips had agreed on a joint exploration program with another company, Pan American Petroleum. I was to be paired with one of Pan American's geologists, and together we would recommend to our respective managements where we should drill several exploratory wells in the Oklahoma Panhandle. This was a good assignment for a young geologist. Then my boss made a little speech about how he wanted me to do sand studies and be finished with the preliminary work in a year.

I knew I couldn't last a year. The night before, I had been complaining to Lynn about the bureaucracy, and she had said, "If you're unhappy, why don't you quit?" I don't think she meant it seriously; she was just tired of my criticism, and I didn't blame her.

I told my boss, "I'll bet that Pan American geologist and I could pick a location this afternoon." I was exaggerating, but I knew it didn't take a year to figure out where to drill a well.

"Oh, no," he replied. "We've got to have the studies before we can move forward, and that will take a year."

"In that case," I said, "you'd better find someone else to do it. I won't be here a year from now. In fact, I'm resigning today." It just popped out; I couldn't believe I had said it.

He panicked. He knew his superiors would ask why I was leaving, and he didn't want to explain.

"Now wait a minute," he said. "Hold on. You better call your wife and talk to her about this." He thought Lynn would talk me out of it, but I didn't give her the chance.

He saw that I wasn't going to change my mind, and he literally ran to the division manager's office. About five minutes later, the manager called me in. After I talked with him briefly, he called Bartlesville. Once the regional exploration manager was briefed, the division manager handed me the phone. I listened as I was offered a $25-a-month raise and a vague promise of no more well-site work. I was sitting in the office, but I was gone, gone from Phillips, already thinking about setting up my own office. I had saved a little money and made a few contacts, but I hadn't done any of the things most people do when they're preparing to quit. Fortunately, I was long on confidence. "Thanks," I said, "but what I really want to do is leave."

I immediately became the enemy in the company's eyes. A draftsman was sent to check my map rack, to make sure none of the maps were missing. "If I was going to take anything," I said, trying to laugh it off, "I wouldn't have stolen a map, I would have copied it." But it hurt a little that they were suspicious; after all, I had been a loyal employee for three years, five months, and twenty-one days.

"I want your car keys and credit card," the division geologist said. But the division manager made an exception for the unemployed person I had become, and he let me use the car to take my things home. I was back in a half hour and told everybody good-bye.

I walked out into the sharp November wind blowing off the high plains of Texas and headed for the bus. I was twenty-six years old and on my own. Although it scared the hell out of me, I felt as though somebody had taken his foot off my neck.

Lynn was home when I came in the front door, having run the two blocks from the bus. We had two small daughters — our second, Pam, was just eight months old — and another baby on the way; Christmas was just around the corner.

I told Lynn I had quit.

She looked at me for a moment. "Boone," she said, "what are you going to do now?"

· 3 ·

# *Over the Fence*

The wind blows a lot in the Texas Panhandle. It's part of the landscape; people work around it or through it, cussing the blue northers that hang icicles off the cattle's noses in January. But generally the Panhandle has the best weather in Texas and that exhilarating feeling you get in high, dry climates.

Not long after leaving Phillips, I was standing in a roadside phone booth a hundred miles northeast of Amarillo making a deal. It was just another day, but for some reason — one of those quirks of memory — I can see it as plain as yesterday. The wind was hot and loaded with dust. It was the kind of dirt that works its way into your mouth and nose. I had a sinus infection, but I also had a well drilling 10 miles away. It was nearing the pay zone and I had to get to it. But first I had to wrap up a good prospect I had working on some leases two counties away. It was like pulling two pieces of rope, tugging to get them close enough to tie a knot. I had become an independent oilman, which meant a life of difficult decisions, personal risk, and grueling hours. Independence meant you were free to drive a couple of thousand miles a week, eat when you could, and try to outsmart leasehounds, big oil companies, the weather, and the geology. I thrived on it.

I jumped into my 1955 white-over-blue Ford station wagon and took off. I had made a down payment on it with the $1,300 I had saved in the Phillips thrift plan. Now it had a few miles as well as a few dents. I didn't know when I bought that Ford how much I would come to love it. It provided transport, office space, even a bed. Many times I had fallen into an exhausted sleep stretched out across the front seat.

The West Texas oil patch was a no man's land, with plenty of opportunity if you could get financing, keep your health, and hold on to your sanity while juggling a dozen different deals.

I used to shave in service stations and soon became an authority on roadside restrooms in the Panhandle. Humble had the best, without a doubt: clean, bright, and warm! Phillips had the worst. Not only were they filthy and freezing, but apparently the operators hadn't gotten their annual allotment of toilet paper.

When I walked out of the Phillips office that windy November day in 1954, I knew the warm-up was over. I needed to make a deal, and fast. My immediate objective was to get a "farmout" — a common transaction, whereby a leaseholder in effect sublets his acreage to someone willing, and financially able, to drill a well. I had no money and no leases, but no debts, either. That's the last time I can remember being out of debt, but I was still broke. My back was against the wall. If I could find a good prospect and sell it, I would get some cash and maybe a piece of the action.

I had a prospect that I thought would be an easy sell, and Phillips owned the leases. Phillips had never shown much interest in the area, and the leases were about to expire. I took the deal to a local independent, Walter Caldwell. He liked what he saw, and the rest was easy: he would drill two wells on the Phillips farmout, and I would get $2,500 for putting the deal together. Both wells were small gas producers, and Caldwell tagged me "boy geologist."

He also let me do the well-site work for $75 a day plus expenses. I got ten days' work, which came in handy. Walter knew I needed the money and let me have a few extra days, and I never forgot it. I had been on my own for about thirty days. My foray into the oil business as an independent was off to a good start, and I knew that we would have a good Christmas in the Pickens house.

The success of those two wells ended any doubts I might have had about leaving the corporate umbrella. This was what I was born to do. It became clearer once I was actually out there on my own, putting deals together. The most important thing is that it was just plain fun. Feeling the pure joy of work and success — jumping out of bed in the morning charged up to accomplish something in the day ahead — is necessary for an entrepreneur.

I didn't go into the oil business with the idea that it would be a straight shot to wealth. Of course I wanted to be successful and to live comfortably. And money has frequently been a motivating force in my life. It's quite a thrill to make money.

But I was never one of those kids who at the age of ten was struck by the realization that he wanted to be rich. While a lot of the oil industry's intrigue and romance is the potential it offers to make somebody a millionaire overnight, I somehow never thought that would happen to me.

The oil business was getting tougher than the back end of a shooting gallery by the mid-1950s, and the instant oil millionaire was becoming an endangered species. If there was a single image that symbolized the oil industry in the public mind, it was the gusher. Almost everyone has a mental picture of a gusher: a well that has just struck "black gold" and is raging out of control, oil blowing over the derrick the way steam and water spew from a geyser, while a handful of delirious, ecstatic oilmen drench themselves in this shower of wealth. "Wildcatters" — people who went after oil in new, undiscovered reservoirs — were the popular heroes of the oil business.

Neither of these images — the gusher or the wildcatter — was created out of whole cloth. There were plenty of gushers in the early days of the oil business, as one giant oil field after another was discovered. The reason for the gushers was that the technology had not been developed that would prevent the oil from flowing uncontrolledly to the surface. And there were plenty of real, rough-and-tumble wildcatters in those days, too — men like H. L. Hunt, Sid Richardson, Hugh Roy Cullen, and Jimmy Owens, larger-than-life figures who made and lost fortunes during the fabled boom times of the 1920s and 1930s.

But the heyday of the gusher and the legendary wildcatter was already coming to an end by World War II. The boom times were pretty much over by then, not only in Oklahoma, Texas, and Louisiana but everywhere in the United States where huge reservoirs of oil and gas had been discovered. The get-rich-quick mentality that helped make the boom times such a wild era was fading.

The price of oil was at best stagnant, which made overnight wealth difficult to achieve. Gradually, it became clear that finding oil was a lot harder than it used to be and required new technologies and expertise. Yet no matter how quickly and effectively the industry responded, it could not offset the declining quality of the prospects.

The independent oilmen were determined to stay, despite diminishing opportunities. Bob Anderson, the chairman of Arco, once said, "You can do anything to an independent oilman but eliminate him."

Independents have always found more oil and gas in the United States than the major oil companies. And many of these independents have been every bit as flamboyant as the first wildcatters. But by the 1950s the industry was becoming cautious and more technically oriented, less free-wheeling, and dominated by the large, mature corporations that had grown out of the boom times. It was becoming more bureaucratic and less entrepreneurial, but because of the purity of the risks there will always be more entrepreneurs in oil than in any other industry.

The success of that first farmout gave me confidence in my ability to make deals. But there was plenty left to learn, and mistakes would help me. I just had to avoid making the same mistake twice. Fortunately, I have a good memory. I was more productive in making my own deals than I had been as a cog in a corporate machine.

Confident that I was on the right track, I set up shop. Lynn's uncle, a local cattleman named John O'Brien, let me use a small, one-room office in exchange for a few hours of geological work each month. I set some modest goals for myself. I wanted to make $12,000 in 1955, of which $5,000 would cover overhead and expenses. The rest would equal about what I had been earning at Phillips. In addition to well-site and consulting work, I wanted to participate in several wells that would be drilled on my geologic work. It was easy to see that I could make more money by putting together deals than by doing well-site work. Three deals for the first year seemed a reasonable expectation.

By all measures, 1955 was a poor time for anyone to get into the oil business. In the course of my career, the industry has faced three severe depressions: the current and worst one, which began in 1982; the early 1970s, before the OPEC embargo; and the mid-1950s. That slump reached bottom in 1956, when the Hughes rotary rig count — which tracks the number of active drilling rigs and is therefore a key measure of the industry's health — sank to its lowest level in several decades. In 1955, oil was about $3 a barrel, where it had been for more than a decade. The major oil companies were slowing down their activity in the United States and had begun producing new fields in Saudi Arabia and other countries. The number of independent oilmen falling by the wayside seemed to outweigh by far the number who were making a go of it. So going out on your own was considered risky at best. I had three and a half years' experience under my belt and had seen a lot of action for a young geologist. I was still green, but I was sure that could be offset by hard work.

We had three children by this time; Mike had been born the year before. When I left Phillips, I was twenty-five years younger than any other independent geologist in the Panhandle. I can't recall anyone who gave me a prayer of succeeding except my dad and mother. Only a few people were as blunt as my wife's uncle Pete. "Boone," he told me soberly, "you don't have a chance. You don't know anything. How could you? You only worked for Phillips for three years."

As business psychologists often point out, entrepreneurs have a high tolerance for risk. Thus their own perception of the odds they're facing doesn't always square with the grim reality of the situation, which helps explain why they drive forward where more cautious souls would not. So it was with me. Although times were tough, I knew what had to be done and I wasn't going to look back. I had enough confidence to know I could make it even in the bad times and enough youthful naiveté to delude myself about how bad things really were. Sometimes — and this was one of those times — it's better not to know.

My office was on the fourth floor of the old (1921) Amarillo Building. The floor had collected a few other entrepreneurs, in oil and cattle and any other commodity they thought they could trade. I made some good friends there; we had some amusing times between deals.

I could sometimes pick up a hundred bucks in a card game, which I did without regret. I've always enjoyed gambling and make no excuses for it. Card playing is a skill, and in its own way a demanding one. The pleasure comes not from taking someone's money — although that is fun, too — but from testing your memory and reflexes. You can learn a lot about a person by playing cards with him, and the people you enjoy knowing, you will enjoy more in a card game.

We had other bets, some of them pretty funny. Charlie Osgood, whose office was next door, bet me $5 I couldn't eat chili for thirty days straight in the old Arcade Cafe. I won that bet. (Though they had good homemade chili, I almost threw up the last three days. It was quite a while before I could eat John Lilly's "bowls of red" again.)

Things were pretty slow in Amarillo in those days. People were scraping by, and that included the Pickenses. I never lost my resolve, but sometimes, looking out the window toward the flat, open country, I had my doubts. It was a tough business I had chosen, and you needed more than brains and hard work to make it — you had to have some luck.

I made money any way I could that year — selling deals, wellsite work, and consulting. Whatever came in helped; it all looked the same on the deposit slip. On the road, I always poked around to see if there was any way I might be able to make a few extra bucks out of the trip. The average deal brought in about $1,000, but to make $2,000 was a real victory.

I made contacts every chance I got, just as I do today. I haven't changed much over the years, and I find that other people don't change, either. They just get older. If they were smart to begin with and can control a few bad habits, they generally get real smart.

I was a sole proprietor: I had no employees and even did my own typing. I didn't have a letterhead — just typed it on. I looked younger than I was, which didn't help. People picked up on my friend's label of "boy geologist." I was a good hustler, and I learned as much as possible about the Panhandle oil business. I knew who owned the acreage and who drilled the wells. I tried to distinguish the players from the tire-kickers. Whenever I was in Dallas or Houston, I would stop by the offices of people who sometimes drilled wells in the Panhandle and leave my card. That yielded some contacts, including one with the Hunt brothers. The reason for my getting the work was price: I was cheap and fast.

After finishing a job, I headed for home. When you're out of town as much as I was, you're subjected to a lot of temptations. There was always a bar and some good-looking gals inside, and it wasn't hard to get some action if you wanted. I am as weak as the next guy, and so I decided to limit my exposure. I still practice that and encourage my people to "head for the house when you get through."

The key to making deals was for me to develop "drillable" ideas. I would return to the office at night, after the kids had gone to bed, and work on my maps, looking for places where another well might be drilled or a farmout negotiated. Once I had a prospect, I then started looking for an investor to drill the well.

It wasn't an easy way to make a living, but hell, I didn't know any better. My family didn't miss anything that counted. During the winter we went skiing in New Mexico. I didn't hesitate to reach down and pull a few bucks in from somewhere or even borrow whatever I needed to see that my children had the same opportunities as other kids. At the end of 1955, I compared my performance with my goals. I did not make $12,000, but I came within a few hundred. I'd been involved in seven drilling deals — four more than my plan. On balance, I thought that 1955 was a success.

But I was also starting to realize that I wanted to do more than scramble through life as a one-man operation. There had to be a better way.

*Two*

# RAISING THE ANTE

## · 4 ·

# *Serious Business*

It was time for me to redefine my idea of success. I wanted to expand my business and hire someone to help carry the load, to handle some of the details. That was the first step toward what became my larger dream: to build a real company.

When this dream takes hold of you, it's incredible what sacrifices you'll make. As I was about to discover, the sacrifices aren't always sensible. Opportunity came soon, and in a way I had never expected. In the summer of 1956, a casual acquaintance named Eugene McCartt dropped by the office. He was a big man in his late thirties; his family owned several local supermarkets, and, like many businessmen in the Texas Panhandle, he invested in drilling deals on the side, without much success. He said he had been following me and had heard good things, and he wondered if I would do some geological work for him.

He came back for a second visit and told me he was tired of drilling dry holes, and he had a feeling I might be able to come up with deals that had better odds of producing oil and gas. Did I have any ideas? Well, I had plenty of ideas. I suggested that we form a company that would develop some good prospects. He said he'd think about it.

Within a week he was back to say that he was ready to go, but he wanted to bring in a friend as a partner. The friend turned out to be my wife's uncle John O'Brien. I supposed McCartt was checking me out and had told O'Brien about our discussion. I knew O'Brien a lot better than McCartt and was happy to have him in on the deal.

We quickly worked out the details: O'Brien and McCartt would each put up $1,250 for half the stock; I would put up a $2,500 note for the other half. I would be the president of the company, running the day-to-day operation. As co-owners, McCartt and O'Brien would be board members and pass on major decisions.

The most important part of the agreement was that McCartt and O'Brien would establish a $100,000 line of credit for the new company. This would be our working capital, so we could make bigger deals than I had been able to do on my own. In return, I agreed to have McCartt and O'Brien off the line of credit within five years; otherwise, they had the right to take over the company.

I rented office space in a small, new building on the edge of the downtown area. We christened the new venture Petroleum Exploration, Inc., or PEI. Maybe the name lacked imagination, but it accurately described our business. I hired a landman and a geologist, and in September 1956 we opened for business. The three of us got our pictures in the newspaper, with the headline THREE YOUNG OILMEN FORM NEW COMPANY and a generous description as "well-known Amarillo oilmen."

I continued to learn the game by trial and error. Looking back on the formation of PEI, I can only shake my head at how naive I was. For openers, I thought it would improve the company's balance sheet if I held back my salary! I had budgeted myself only $12,000, about the same amount I had made the year before. For six months I didn't draw a dime because I still had consulting fees coming from my work the previous year. Finally O'Brien took me aside and told me that withholding my salary wasn't going to help because we had to accrue it anyway. I think he saw how sincere I was about wanting PEI to succeed, but he must have thought the leader had a lot to learn.

Not long after we got going, I was trying to persuade someone to invest in a deal. I said, "If you take this deal, we'll have your money back to you in three years."

This guy was a veteran investor in drilling deals and knew all the advantages and disadvantages. But he couldn't help smiling. "Boone," he said, "let me give you some advice. Don't ever use that line again."

"Why?"

"Why would I want to give you my money just so I can get it back in three years? I've got my money now."

From then on I used phrases like "three-year payout" or "annual return" or something equally impressive that essentially meant the same thing.

A more serious mistake involved the distribution of the stock. When I hired the landman and the geologist, we all agreed that they should receive stock options as an incentive. But McCartt and O'Brien convinced me that the stock options should come out of my 50 percent. Had I known what I was doing, I would have insisted that the options come from everyone's stock so that our respective ownerships would remain equal.

Three months later, the landman was gone; it had become apparent that it was going to take a lot more than a stock option to motivate him.

I informed McCartt and O'Brien that I was going to fire the landman, and they decided that we should pay him $10,000 for his stock option. I was surprised. How could the stock be worth that much after only three months? They outvoted me, two to one, and graciously said I could buy the option back personally if I wanted to. I couldn't, of course, because I didn't have that kind of money, and they knew it. I went to the bank, borrowed the money for PEI, paid the landman, and put the stock in the treasury.

Boy, were they giving their young executive some real schooling. McCartt and O'Brien now owned a majority of the stock, and if any dispute arose among the three of us, they had the controlling vote.

I might have been only twenty-seven years old, but I knew something about the oil business and I had incentive. I had to get my backers off the line of credit or lose my part of the company — and as it turned out I did get them off, in two years instead of five.

They could see that I was determined to make PEI go, though McCartt was never sold on me. He told a mutual friend that I would never make it because I was a dreamer. Of course, he was not entirely wrong. I admit it, I was a dreamer, but I was a lot more realistic than McCartt gave me credit for.

While I did have my share of setbacks during that first year, I was blessed with a few lucky breaks as well. Trixie Lee Slife came on board as secretary and unofficial office manager. She was with us for nearly thirty years and set the standard for professionalism in the office life of both PEI and Mesa. Then, on July 5, 1957, Lawton Clark walked into my office to interview for the position of landman. Tall and thin, with a quick smile and an engaging manner, Lawton had started his career much as I had, with a large company, Union Oil Company of California. (He had worked with PEI's geologist, Dick Parker, who had come from Union Oil, so when our first landman was fired, Parker told Lawton about the job.)

Lawton didn't know me from Adam. He was reluctant to leave Union Oil for a venture as speculative as PEI, but at the urging of Parker he came to Amarillo for a look. We did a lot of talking that weekend; by Sunday night I had offered Lawton the job and he had accepted. Lawton turned out to be not only a good landman but also a great friend and collaborator. Even now, I can't imagine a better person with whom to share the frustrations and rewards of building a company.

For the next twelve years Lawton was in on everything I did. He saw me at my best and at my worst. When you work close to someone for twelve hours a day, you get a good feel for his strengths and weaknesses. In that small office at Fifteenth and Taylor streets, all of us elbow to elbow and the walls so thin we could hear every phone conversation, it didn't take long before we all knew each other very well. In a struggling company, you can't hide your weaknesses the way you can in the giant bureaucracies we had all come from. God only knows, we didn't want to fail and have to go back.

Lawton and I made a good team. He was older and more mature. I was feeling my way, working as much on instinct as anything else. I knew the people in the office were counting on me to keep the company going. Every move I made was magnified by our very smallness, and I couldn't afford to make many wrong ones.

One of the instinctive things I did in those days was write "mad" letters. Poison pen letters, Lawton called them. After some deal had gone haywire, I would dictate a strong letter to the dimwit who had blown it (if it wasn't me) and, with great pride of authorship, hand the letter to Lawton.

"Pickens," he invariably said, "do you really want to send this thing?"

"Hell, yes!"

"Why don't you put it in your desk drawer until tomorrow and see if you still want to send it."

The next day, having come to my senses, I would look at the letter briefly and chuck it in the wastebasket. Eventually, I stopped wasting my time. I later learned that Harry Truman used to write letters like that and stick them in a drawer — even when he was President. At least it was a good way to let off steam.

PEI began by doing the same things I had been doing when I worked alone, the things I knew best: "geological consulting services, exploration and developing of new leases and farmouts, reservoir evaluation and leasing service," as the newspaper so grandly put it. The only thing that changed was the scale: with $100,000, we were ready to buy our own leases and do bigger deals.

An oil company lives or dies on the cash it has to invest. In a typical deal, we would get a few thousand dollars when we sold the prospect and would retain a "back-in interest," a percentage of any profit the well made in three, four, maybe five years. The upfront cash paid the bills but didn't provide enough capital for us to drill our own wells. I soon realized that selling deals to other companies was not the way to build PEI.

The solution was to raise additional equity from outside investors so we could put money into our own prospects. Frequently done as a limited partnership, this new equity would allow us to participate in our drilling success much faster. This was how a lot of independents raised money, but there was one drawback: none of us had ever done it before.

It was up to me to find the investors. Asking people for money is the most essential skill for a young dealmaker. I quickly realized that it did not come easily, especially when the investor knew nothing about the oil business. It was as hard as anything I had ever done. But if I hadn't done it, no one else would have. That feeling of having it all come down to what I could do was kind of scary. If there is one moment that I can identify as the origin of my kinship with stockholders, this was it. I still feel personally indebted to those first drilling participants who bet on Boone Pickens.

Those first investors were not the so-called mullets from the East, with a lot of money and not much savvy. I made a few trips to New York in search of money but struck out. There were so many other people doing the same thing that I never really had much of a chance. Our first investors were mostly Amarillo people who were willing to give a local boy a shot. Some of them still thought of me as a skinny kid who had played guard on the best basketball team Amarillo High School ever had. But I pulled out my maps and showed them where we could find some oil and gas, and by the time I handed them PEI's brochure, they were usually pretty well convinced that I might be able to do the job.

I must have made ten presentations for every investor I signed up. After seeing all those people and making my pitch, I was grateful to those who did invest and even to those who just listened.

Because my investors were local people rather than strangers living miles away, I couldn't hide if I failed. They could stop me in the grocery store or corner me after church or catch me at the office, and they did. In a city as small as Amarillo, it wouldn't be long before everyone knew the results.

O'Brien and McCartt were putting their money into the drilling programs and encouraging others to do likewise. McCartt had the idea to name the programs for respected townspeople whose credibility would help draw in other investors. Those people — businessmen like Jess Latham, Weldon Howell, George Morris, and Dr. Don Marsalis — would help our sales.

Our first program was small, a trial balloon. Our second fund was much larger. Formed in March 1958, it consisted of fifty-one investors and a pool of $500,000, enough money to drill sixteen wells. A year later, eight of the wells were producing gas, one was an oil well, seven were dry holes, and PEI was estimating that they would produce revenues in excess of $2,250,000, or "an investment return of four to one," as we proudly noted in one of our 1959 reports.

That turned out to be conservative. The return was closer to six to one; one of the gas wells is still producing today, some twenty-seven years later.

Six months later came the Marsalis program, named for the local doctor and businessman. "Doc" Marsalis was a wonderful guy and became a good friend of mine. He would come by the office religiously once a week to talk about the drilling program or just to shoot the bull. (When Mesa Petroleum was formed in 1964, he and Jess Latham were two of the original directors.) The Marsalis program — fifty-two investors; a total of $475,000 — drilled thirteen wells, of which only four were dry holes. "Total net revenue . . . is estimated to be in excess of $3,000,000 or an investment return of six to one," proclaimed our report.

I've never thought of myself as a "workaholic," then or now. I put in a lot of time at the bench, but from the start I always made sure that any call from home would be put through no matter what I was doing. I believed in good planning, and if I could accomplish as much in ten hours as someone else could in twenty, that really made me happy. I made sure to set aside a little time for outside activities; I played basketball until I was in my early thirties. Then I took up golf. And, like my parents, I played cards: I belonged to a regular Tuesday night poker game for years. During hunting season, I shot dove, quail, duck, geese, and pheasant.

We didn't have a very complicated social life, and I spent a lot of time with my family.

By 1958, I had been married nine years and had four children. (Thomas Boone Pickens III, who goes by Tom, like my father, was the last, born in 1957.) I loved my children, but my marriage was in trouble.

Lynn and I had different interests. That was easy to overlook when I was a high school basketball star and she was the prettiest girl in the class. But after ten years looks became less important than compatibility. I cared passionately about my work and wanted her to take a greater interest in it. I had a sense of humor and admit that I was sarcastic at times. But instead of laughing at my jokes, Lynn disapproved of them. I believed strongly in the kind of discipline I had received from my own mother and applied it to the children. Lynn often disagreed with me.

Most troubling of all, she often just said nothing. I remember nights at home after the kids were in bed when I would try to start a conversation about something that had happened during the day. She would say, "That's interesting." She was unhappy — maybe she didn't know how unhappy. I probably should have forced the issue.

One night about this time, Lynn and I went over to see some friends and eat Mexican food. After dinner, they wanted to play bumper pool. I wasn't much of a player, but after several lucky shots, I had won a few dollars.

I remember looking over at Lynn. Every time I made a shot, she winced. When I missed, she quietly smiled. Unfortunately, that summed up what our marriage had become.

We stuck it out for the sake of the children, which was probably a mistake. Lynn and I seldom fought in their presence, but there was a constant tension they must have felt. I made it a point to be home for dinner and tried to instill the respect I believe children need. I wish I had been perceptive enough to see that staying together wasn't helping any of us. Our relationship caused me to focus more on the company and what I wanted to accomplish.

*

Oilmen had been exploring in Texas and in nearby Oklahoma for more than fifty years, and thousands of wells had been drilled. In the four years since PEI had entered the competition, we had made some nice discoveries. But there wasn't what you would call a big discovery in the bunch. There were no gushers and nothing even close to a "company builder."

The industry has always had a deep psychological need to believe that there are still huge fields to be found, the kind that can turn a small company into a major one overnight. After all, the legendary wildcatters lived to find the "big one."

One such Dallas wildcatter, Jake Hamon, Jr., who was worth several hundred million dollars, once told me that the reason he kept going to the office every day was, "I still want to find that big field! It's hard to explain. You just . . . Goddamn, you want to find an East Texas field! You want to find a Spindletop!"

In 1959, PEI was doing fairly well. But we too were hungry for a "big one." I heard about a deal that sounded too good to be true. An old high school friend, Walter Kellogg, had married Mumzy Cowden, from one of Midland's more prominent families. Their wealth, like that of most ranch families in West Texas, came not from ranching but from the tremendous oil and gas production that had been discovered on their land. Walter told me that there were several promising tracts on the ranch that might be available, one of which was very close to a recent Mobil discovery.

I certainly was interested, and after looking into the situation I became even more so. The Mobil discovery was significant. But the prospect would require a deep and expensive well. It was a tough decision, but the rewards seemed too great to pass up.

I went to Midland on a dust-blown day to see the prospective location. I will always remember two things from that trip: Andrews County was so dry, the jackrabbits carried their lunch; and there were more millionaires in the lobby of the Scharbauer Hotel than in any other spot in the world.

We took the Cowden deal and did the necessary seismic work, bringing in two geophysicists to interpret the data independently.

Soon after we got the leases, two major oil companies tried to buy into our deal. It looked like a cinch — and that should have scared the hell out of me. My experience today would have told me that there are no cinches in this business.

We couldn't find anybody who doubted that we were about to drill a good well, and I was as excited about the Cowden prospect as any dreamy geologist I had ever met. I was so sure that this was the deal that would put PEI on the map that I turned down the offers from the two major companies. We were going for broke on this one.

The Cowden well went to 15,000 feet. After four months and $500,000, all we had was a dry hole and a flat pocketbook. If I had been anything but a geologist, I would have realized we were damn near busted.

Doc Marsalis's comment was: "All sickness isn't death, boys."

I couldn't help adding: "But some sickness comes awfully close."

According to oil field optimism, it isn't a dry hole until you plug it. We plugged it. Then we had to figure how we would escape from the trap we were now in. We had to get something going; there was a limit to how much money we could raise, and we didn't have contacts outside our area. We had a lot of competition. It seemed that most companies, big and small, were trying to line up drilling funds.

Since our area was getting picked over, I decided to look elsewhere. I traveled to western Canada with Lawton to see what it might offer. We couldn't afford to do anything more than take a look for the time being.

In late 1959, we formed a company that would operate exclusively in Canada. We raised $35,000, most of which we put up ourselves. The rest came from the original PEI backers, McCartt and O'Brien. This time, however, McCartt and O'Brien were minority shareholders, with 25 percent of the stock. They were pissed off by the split, but I wasn't about to give up control a second time.

We opened an office in Calgary and named the company Altair Oil & Gas Co. I was the president and major stockholder. It was an unusual time to start operations in Canada. The oil industry there was in a slump, and at the Calgary airport you could see more oilmen leaving than coming in. But I was beginning to understand something about myself: I often did better in a down market. There was less competition, land prices were lower, and drilling was cheaper.

It was easy to see why some oilmen were bailing out. The price of oil in Canada was lower than it was in the United States, and the market for natural gas was poor. But to a geologist who had been operating in an area that was picked over, Canada seemed almost untouched. The oil industry had developed later in Canada, and there were vast expanses of unexplored land. We could sometimes lease thousands of acres for only pennies an acre.

That was the case in the Hoosier area of Saskatchewan, where we filed on 350,000 acres. Two years later, we had a lease rental of $35,000 and didn't have the money. I took the prospect to D. D. Harrington, Amarillo's best known and most successful entrepreneur. I knew my time would be short, so I gave him only the blood, guts, and feathers and said, "I need $35,000 to make the rental."

Harrington said, "It's a good prospect and I'll pay it." We shook hands, and as I left he said, "Boone, when you get to the point that you don't have to make a deal, you might make a good one."

In 1963, we made our best discovery on some of this Hoosier acreage.

Lawton and I were elated over the Canadian prospects. The economics were sometimes marginal, but the potential was unbelievable. We were able to build our files cheaply because everybody else was pulling out and anxious to sell.

We knew where we wanted to go. The next step was to raise some drilling money. It wasn't long before we were making contacts again in New York and elsewhere, searching for anyone who might be a prospect for our deals. Looking back, it seems as though I have spent my whole life raising money for a deal. One thing you learn fast: you may not find money, but you're sure to meet some interesting people.

On one trip to New York, we met with a fellow named Milton C. Nuroc. Nuroc walked confidently into the room looking as if he had dressed in the dark: he wore a plaid coat and striped pants. He apologized for being late.

"Gentlemen," he said, "I'm sorry, but I missed the bus. My wife took me out to the highway, and I just missed it."

"Where the hell did you come from?" I asked.

"Camden, New Jersey."

Lawton and I rode buses, but we'd been told that this guy was a big operator!

Nuroc wanted us to put up our reserves as collateral in return for Gulf Oil's advancing us $3 million in drilling funds. Gulf would then receive 50 percent of whatever we discovered, and if we didn't find anything, Gulf could take our reserves. Nuroc, of course, would get a piece of the action for having brought us together.

The one thing Nuroc failed to mention was that he was not an agent for Gulf, or anybody else.

As it turned out, we got lucky on that same trip, and it was about time. I'm a firm believer in luck, but I also believe you make your own. We were desperate for leads, so we ran them all out. Lawton had heard about two guys interested in raising drilling funds. We had followed up a hundred similar leads and gotten nowhere. But we were in New York anyway, so why not ring another doorbell?

The two guys were Ed Wylie and Nate Shippee, a real pair to draw to. Wylie was the quiet one, an in-house counsel for a small corporation. The more flamboyant Shippee controlled the patent on blister packaging. At the time we met, he was making his living selling cardboard boxes. They wanted to moonlight as money-raisers for oil deals. They planned to concentrate on Greenwich, Connecticut, and were looking for a good company to work with. But Wylie and Shippee, it turned out, knew very little about the oil business.

It was an unusual meeting. We would start to explain how a drilling fund operated, and Shippee would jump out of his chair, filled with enthusiasm. "This is great!" he would say. "Just great!" I could see why this guy sold a lot of cardboard boxes.

Then we'd explain the tax consequences, and he would jump out of his chair again. "Intangible drilling costs! The oil depletion allowance! Boy, is this gonna be great!"

We'd tell them about the million-dollar drilling programs we had put together. "Chicken feed!" said Shippee. "We can raise a lot more money than that. A lot more money!"

When the meeting ended, I said to Lawton, "Ten to one, we never see those guys again."

I was wrong. Shippee and Wylie called us, asking all kinds of questions, and a few months later they came to Amarillo. Then they formed Prudential Drilling Funds. It took a year and a half from the time we met them, but their first drilling program raised nearly $2 million.

Shippee thought of himself as a mystic who had the answers to the deepest questions of the universe. Every Christmas he sent Lawton and me a pamphlet he had written for the year, revealing the truths he had discovered in his search for knowledge. It was utterly incomprehensible. He said we could have as many as we wanted. Lawton always ordered a gross for fear we would hurt his feelings.

We were doing whatever it took to survive and we were learning. By the early 1960s I had enough experience to start doing some interesting things. They didn't approach the scale of what came later, but it was good training and tested the same instincts. I was preparing for something, but I could not have imagined what.

In 1962, playing it safer than we had on the Cowden dry hole, we drilled ninety-eight successful wells in an old field in Hutchinson County, Texas. Basically, we couldn't finance that much drilling, so we had to be creative. Each well cost $28,000 to complete. We "turn-keyed" the wells to individuals and companies for $40,000 apiece, usually retaining a 25 percent interest, with the guarantee that the wells would do 60 barrels of oil per day on a production test.

I went to the contractors and service companies and arranged to defer payment until six months after the completion of a well, thereby getting, in effect, a short-term, interest-free loan. Our 25 percent interest served as collateral for the debt.

We were developing existing reserves with new completion techniques. We had no gushers, but no dry holes, either. And our unconventional financing allowed us to drill many more wells.

After ninety-eight wells, PEI had made close to $750,000, and our investors had also done very well. We had 23 employees, where there had once been only three, and more than 300 investors, where there had once been two. Along with my growing assurance as a businessman came a newfound confidence in my ability to manage the enterprise and to lead a group of people.

I started to think about adding reserves by acquisition as well as discovery. I didn't want to miss any possibility. Our million-dollar drilling programs would undoubtedly bring us reserves. But the process was slow, and costs were going up all the time. When all was said and done, the chances were slim that any one strategy would ever make us a major player. We needed to fish with more lines out.

Merging with or acquiring a bigger company could do for us what those eighty-three gushers had done for Frank Phillips fifty-odd years earlier. It would be like finding a giant oil field already developed.

I learned years later that the trick wasn't hooking the fish, it was getting the fish in the boat, and too big a fish might sink it. But back then it was difficult just getting one to bite. This was before anyone had devised strategies for tender offers, and I thought there was only one way to merge or acquire. First, the combination had to make sense; second, you had to make contact.

The minutes of some of our board meetings are full of merger references involving Juniper, Cardinal, Austral, Equity, Aztec, General Crude, Eason, and others. What the minutes fail to say is that most of the time the merger "possibility" was little more than a dream. The few times we got to the negotiation stage it didn't last long, but I never lost heart. I knew that the theory for growth and the analysis of the companies were sound; all I had to do was overcome some giant egos in order to make a deal.

I remember one real long shot in early 1963, when I approached Harold Dunn, the head of Shamrock, an independent oil company based in Amarillo but many times larger than PEI. We had two dozen employees, and Shamrock was the largest employer in town. I thought the two companies would make a natural fit. The way I analyzed it, we had plenty of ideas but not much money, while Shamrock seemed to have more money than ideas.

I called on Mr. Dunn and showed him my plan, but I thought he wasn't taking me seriously. I knew he wasn't when he took out a big cigar and leisurely lit it.

After a couple of weeks, I called on him again. "What do you think of my idea, Mr. Dunn?"

"Pickens," he said, "you don't have enough whiskers to make this deal."

We later tried to sell Shamrock some of our Canadian deals, and I made a couple of trips to Calgary with Mr. Dunn on the Shamrock plane. I'll never forget those trips as long as I live. Dunn was a short, overweight, balding man. Always in a three-piece suit, smoking his ever-present, king-size cigar, he looked like a caricature of a capitalist. But I liked him. Harold had a quick wit and was a good card player; he was a man's man. But he could sometimes be arrogant.

He always brought an entourage on the trips to Calgary. Soon after we were airborne, the gin rummy game would begin, and Harold would tell one of his subordinates, "Get me a bourbon and branch water."

After two or three drinks, he would start feeling good. Here he was, the head of an oil company, an important man in Amarillo, flying in the company plane. He would take a puff from his cigar, smile a self-satisfied smile, and declare, "Boys, Shamrock Oil and Gas ain't no chickenshit outfit."

I thought he was funny. But I knew that wouldn't be my style if I made it.

· 5 ·

# *Going Public*

Undercapitalization afflicts 90 percent of the new businesses in America, and we were all too typical. Every time we got a little cash something would happen, and we'd be back at the starting line.

First, it was the Cowden dry hole; next, a bombshell dropped by our partner Gene McCartt. One Sunday morning he called me with bad news: he was seriously ill — probably cancer of the pancreas — and he assumed his time was short. He wanted to get out of PEI and his price was $350,000. Naturally I was concerned — both for McCartt and for the company.

We were already carrying a half-million dollars of debt — a real load for a company our size. Lawton used to say that we could survive one big mistake, but back-to-back mistakes would probably bust us. It occurred to me that we might be lining up for a second big mistake.

But Lawton and I both decided we should acquire McCartt's interest, and we convinced ourselves that we could haul the debt. McCartt, meanwhile, realizing that we were concerned about the payments, said he would do what he could to ease our burden. We signed a three-year note. He assured us that if the company was unable to make a payment, he would stretch things out for us.

Unfortunately, that understanding turned out to be pretty weak. McCartt did give us an extension on our first installment, but that was it. When we asked for help the second time, he issued a demand letter calling the whole note. If we defaulted, he'd take over the company. We realized that that was exactly what McCartt wanted. For the lack of a $50,000 payment we could have lost it all, and there would have been no Mesa Petroleum. It makes me think of all the promising ventures that have gone down before they ever had a chance. We finally were able to scrape up the payment, but we were now pinched worse than ever. (McCartt's problem with his pancreas must have been a false alarm; he is still around today.)

I had to adjust my dreams to fit reality — or could I somehow change reality to match my dreams? By late 1963 we were facing another $50,000 payment to McCartt, with no chance of an extension. We had our backs to the wall again, but the pressure was getting easier to handle, maybe because we were getting so good at working out the problems. It was like an obstacle course, and we just kept going.

My ability to come up with ideas actually improved when the heat was on. The more I rolled things around, the more confident I became that I would find a solution. Gradually I began to see a logical way to get our collective ass out of the crack and increase our cash flow as well. The solution was to take the company public.

When I talk about it today, going public seems obvious, but in 1963 it was unusual. More important, it was almost unheard of to take a small oil company public by pooling the interests of the drilling participants. But that's what I had in mind. When it became common fifteen years later it was known as a "roll-up."

Issuing stock for capital is the most fundamental service Wall Street provides. This classic stock market function has given rise to the great Wall Street firms — and, for that matter, to America's industrial might. Entrepreneurs need more capital than banks are willing to lend — to expand, to build new plants, or just to get started — and they can find that capital by selling their ideas in the equity markets. In return for assuming the financial risk, stockholders *own* a percentage of the company — a fact that has been forgotten by too many executives.

When a company goes public, there is excitement for both

the founders and the new stockholders. In the hot "new issues" market of recent years, analysts issue glowing predictions about a company's future, and the founders often become "instant rich" — multimillionaires overnight.

In 1964, it wasn't that way for us. There was no Wall Street excitement, no analysts writing glowing reports. We simply exchanged stock for the interest that investors had in PEI's various wells and drilling programs. It was more than a year before brokers traded us "Over-the-Counter."

And I wasn't the classic founder who became instantly rich; our deal was too skinny for that. My salary was $24,960 that year. Although I had a substantial interest in both PEI and Altair, the stock didn't have much value.

Looking back, I realize I should have asked for a substantial option, which would have rewarded me if I was able to increase the price of the stock. (Shareholders should insist on management's having stock options; almost the only way they become valuable is if management is successful and the price of the stock increases.) Our deal was fragile, and it wouldn't have taken much to upset it, so I didn't ask for an option. I now see that I was probably a little too sensitive and lacking in confidence.

We began work on a prospectus, which had to be filed with the Securities and Exchange Commission for the offering. Such a document is largely the work of lawyers. I went to the Houston law firm of Baker & Botts and dealt with Baine Kerr, who assigned us to John Kirkland, one of the firm's best young lawyers, and an equally bright younger associate, Bob Stillwell. We hired Arthur Andersen & Co. to be the auditor for the new company; Randal McDonald, one of its smart young men, was assigned to us.

Kirkland, Stillwell, and McDonald were good teachers. Stillwell, who was plenty smart but temperamental at times, has been on our board since 1969. Bob has been one of my closest advisers for years and became a key member of the merger team we put together in the 1980s. Arthur Andersen is still our auditor, and it has helped with many transactions through the years.

At one of our first meetings, I told the group that we were

going to stop every time I didn't understand something. "You're paying us by the hour," Kirkland said. "This could get expensive."

"It'll be a lot more expensive if I don't understand it now," I replied.

By February 1964 we had given our new company a name, Mesa Petroleum Co., after the picturesque, table-topped lands that rise out of the stark plains of the Texas Panhandle.

Through the years, I have found that many CEOs could care less about the mechanics of a deal and depend almost totally on their lawyers and investment bankers. They don't ask questions because they are afraid of looking stupid. I would rather look uninformed at thirty-six than stupid forever after.

Although in time we became good friends, Kirkland and Stillwell were skeptical. The odds were against our doing a roll-up. I was getting experienced at trying to pull off tough deals. But I kept plugging along, and that helped win the lawyers over. At some point, it seems everybody starts to pull for you.

The two younger lawyers had a hard time believing I was on the up-and-up. I wasn't getting any cash out of the deal, and I had no free ride on the stock. Since they thought no one could be that dumb, they assumed I must be very clever. I had to be working some angle; they just hadn't figured out what it was.

A couple of weeks after we began work on the registration statement, we were in a meeting when Stillwell and Kirkland excused themselves from the room. When they returned, Kirkland gave me a serious look and said, "We've got something here that we need to discuss with you. The Altair stock book didn't balance by five thousand shares, and we see where you issued a stock certificate to bring the book in balance. Where is that stock?" His tone was accusatory.

"Oh, that went to Perry Dave Williams," I said.

Kirkland wasn't impressed. "We know that, but who the hell is Perry Dave Williams? Your brother-in-law?"

"No, he's our production engineer in Calgary. When I realized we had a problem, this was how I balanced the books."

"You *what?*"

"Well, Dave had been working very hard. So I gave him a cheap option as a reward and he exercised the option. I like the key people in the company to have stock ownership."

The two lawyers shook their heads in disbelief. They had both heard their share of goofy stories, but never anything quite like this. They left the room to make the phone call that they thought would shred my story.

When they returned, Kirkland said, "Boone, I can't believe it, but your story checks out. You really did take care of Williams." He broke into a wry smile. "I think we'll do this job for you after all."

"What do you mean?" I asked. "We've been working for weeks."

"That's true, but we hadn't really made up our minds about you until now."

We got along fine after that. Even today, we may not always agree, but we have never questioned each other's honesty.

What made the deal difficult was not the preparation of the registration statement but persuading a lot of people to do something they were disinclined to do. We were asking them to trade their ownership in income-producing properties for stock in a new company, and convincing them to do it rested squarely on my shoulders.

If we could roll-up the properties for stock, it would provide us with the cash flow to do some bigger things. The oil and gas reserves would give the newly formed corporation a strong balance sheet, allowing us to borrow as much as $2 million. A less profound but no less significant issue was keeping track of all our investors, knowing who was in what drilling program and how much they got each month — an accounting nightmare in the precomputer age. Once, when Lawton was talking about the future, he put his hand to his forehead, like an Indian scout peering into the distance, and said, "If we keep having drilling programs, we're going to have bookkeepers as far as the eye can see." The roll-up ended the programs.

The amount of stock distributed to each participant would depend on how large and successful he had been in the programs.

PEI had some 300 investors, about two thirds of whom lived in the Amarillo area. Not all of them had to agree to become shareholders to make the deal work, but we had to have at least two thirds of the property values. I could tell that Kirkland, Stillwell, and McDonald had doubts that I could get the investors to convert.

We couldn't offer any cash in the transaction because we didn't have any cash to offer. What could we offer? In terms of hard numbers and solid projections, not very much. The only concrete thing I could tell my prospective stockholders was that the deal would be a tax-free exchange. I stressed that all of us had the commitment to make the company succeed. And that was about it.

Ultimately, all I could guarantee was that I would work hard and do my best to make money for the stockholders. It was almost a replay of 1957 and 1958, when we formed those first programs. Now, as then, I was asking them to believe in me.

And so it began, day after day, week after week: meeting with investors and painstakingly going over our plan, showing them what I thought we could do and why it was in their best interest to convert from drilling participants to stockholders.

The yes votes came, but they came slowly. Just as in the early programs, I felt an intense loyalty to the people who agreed to become my first stockholders. Is it any wonder that I later talked so much about stockholders' being the backbone of the free enterprise system? This was not some impersonal public offering sold by Wall Street brokerage firms. These were my neighbors, friends, and associates. I knew every stockholder personally.

Not everybody said yes. One large investor blew up after I explained the deal to him. "I don't understand why you're angry," I said. "I'm just making you an offer, and if you don't like it you can turn it down."

"What you're offering," he replied, "is insulting." It was always tough to take remarks like that.

I may have saved the deal by not taking either personal stock options or founder's stock, thus eliminating any suspicion about my own motives. The stock I received came from my participation in the drilling programs, along with my interest in PEI and Altair. I was about to own 15.8 percent of this fledgling company.

The offering was scheduled to close at the end of April 1964, and I could see that it was going to go right down to the wire. Doc Marsalis had signed up early, and that helped bring in some of his friends. John O'Brien also brought a group in. I got a big boost when Wales Madden, a well-known Amarillo attorney, came along.

Although Wales was about my age, we were not close friends. He had been president of the University of Texas student body in his college days, which automatically keeps a person in politics forever after. He was now serving on the board of regents at the university, one of the most prestigious political appointments in the state.

Wales and his wife, Abbie, had been in several PEI drilling programs over the years. Wales came on the Mesa board, and our friendship grew over the years. We traveled together on many business trips, and Wales became an adviser and confidant, a role he plays to this day.

As we got closer to the deadline, some of the investors realized how crucial they had become to the success of the offering and tried to cut special deals for themselves.

One man told me, "I'm your swing vote."

"Well, you are pretty important," I replied.

"If you make a deal with me, it's going to have to be a better one than you're giving everyone else."

I wouldn't do that, I told him, so he bowed out. It eventually cost him $3 million.

By mid-April we still weren't over the top. The one person who could do it for us was a longtime drilling partner, R. H. Fulton, who owned a pipeline construction company in Lubbock, Texas. One of our biggest investors, he really had become the swing vote.

R. H. Fulton was one of the most difficult personalities I ever dealt with in my thirty-five years in business. He was always slow to pay; he either had an excuse or just refused to pay on time. He seemed to enjoy delaying his payment while you sweated. It was a sick game.

When I first approached him about our offering, he made a comment that pretty much summed up his philosophy: "I can't believe you would want to run a publicly owned company. I wouldn't stand for any son of a bitch calling and asking why I did something."

Months before the offering closed, he had promised to convert his properties into Mesa shares. I wanted a board of directors made up of the largest stockholders, so I asked him to come on the board. He seemed pleased and accepted.

But as we got closer to the deadline, it was apparent that he had lost interest. We'd send the documents to him for his signature, and he wouldn't return them. Lawton, meanwhile, knowing how important it was, pressed me to get Fulton signed. This had been going on for nearly three months, and time was running out.

One Sunday morning in late April, I called him at his ranch, about an hour from Amarillo. He sounded sleepy. I asked if he had signed the papers, and he said no.

"I need you to sign right away. Today, in fact," I said.

There was no answer.

"R.H.," I said, "I'm coming out there with another set of documents." I hung up and went out to his ranch.

I knocked and rang the bell, and when nobody answered I let myself in. I found Fulton still in bed. I started toward him, papers and pen in hand. I had made up my mind that he was going to sign them.

"Ready to sign, R.H.?" I asked.

He didn't answer. I tried to hand him the contract, and he ducked under the covers.

"Come on, R.H., we've been going around on this thing for months."

He didn't respond. I was exasperated, but I couldn't miss the humor of it: the future of Mesa Petroleum depended upon a pipeline contractor hiding under a blanket!

"R.H., you can't stay under there all day. And I'm not leaving without your signature."

After a pause, I heard his muffled voice: "Give me the damn papers."

I passed them under the covers; he passed them back with some illegible scribbling just above the signature line. That was good enough for me.

The lawyers couldn't believe the story and asked me to repeat it twice. "Did you actually see him sign?" asked Stillwell when he looked at the signature.

"No," I replied. "But I can give you an affidavit that says I handed the papers to him under the covers unsigned and when I got them back they were signed. I don't see any other way it could have happened unless he signed them."

Stillwell nodded.

We were home free.

On April 30, 1964, PEI and Altair ceased to exist and were replaced by Mesa. In all, 239 investors became stockholders, and we issued 420,052 shares of stock. There was a ten-minute pause while the staff shook hands and gave each other a pat on the back.

During the time I had been trying to persuade investors to become stockholders, my good friend and next-door neighbor, Bill Neel, offered some solicitous advice. "Now, Boone," he said, "you know I'm with you all the way. But it takes time. So don't be too disappointed if you lose money the first year."

Our first year was right on target. We had revenues of $1.5 million and a net income of $435,310. We paid a dividend that first year and for the next twenty-two years. It wasn't the *Fortune* 500, but it was a good start.

One of my sales pitches to investors had been that, as shareholders, they would have more liquidity than as drilling participants. A drilling participation is essentially illiquid because there is no market for such a small interest in a multitude of properties. Shares of stock in a public company can be bought and sold quite easily — if there is a market.

With 239 shareholders and very little interest in the new company, there wasn't any market for the stock. I had to make the market myself, essentially providing free brokerage service to anyone who wanted to buy or sell, matching one with the other.

R. H. Fulton attended only one board meeting and decided he was not interested in Mesa: he was the first to sell out, for $6 a share. We were neither surprised nor disappointed.

I worked out a deal with him. I offered the block to the employees and directors, and what they didn't take I did — about half of the stock. Three years later, at the time of our last payment to R.H., our profit was more than $1 million; ten years later it was five times that amount. This was accomplished with no equity, 100 percent leverage.

I handled other blocks of stock that way, offering them first to people associated with the company and then looking for buyers or buying it myself. But this was a pretty inefficient way to make a market.

My father often says, "Son, it looks like you shot at the house and hit the barn." That's about the best way to describe what happened when we bought a small Utah mining company called Standard Gilsonite.

I examined almost every deal that came in the door, and Standard Gilsonite looked like the best of a poor crop. It had about 2,200 stockholders, and that *did* get my attention. If we could get that many stockholders, our stock could be traded over-the-counter. If Standard hadn't had all those stockholders, I wouldn't have spent fifteen minutes on the company; but I convinced myself that we could make a go of it in the gilsonite business. Mesa issued about $500,000 worth of our stock to Standard's shareholders in a stock swap.

Gilsonite is a shiny black mineral that is almost a pure hydrocarbon. In the United States it is found almost exclusively in Utah, and it's used for several things: as a base for paint and resin and as a coating for telephone poles. Gilsonite is one of the ingredients used by Halliburton, the major oil service company, to lighten the cement slurry when well casing is being cemented in place.

Standard Gilsonite's problems were bigger than we thought. Its mining costs were so high, they were barely competitive, and the mines were pathetic. This was all confirmed when I finally took a trip to one of the mines of American Gilsonite, our main competition. Where we had one guy digging with a hand pick 200 feet underground, American had a guy sitting on a bulldozer, strip-mining the stuff. Where our vein was about 2 feet wide, its was about 50 feet. Need I say more?

But Standard Gilsonite did provide us with enough stockholders to create a market for Mesa stock. By 1966 we were ready to raise debt capital, and that would have been impossible without an active market for our stock.

The following year we were listed on the American Stock Exchange — a real milestone. I thought it was more exciting than going on the New York Stock Exchange two years later.

It was 1967 when the first New York analyst found us. His name was Charles M. Northrup, and he worked for a small New York brokerage house, Hoppin Brothers and Company. Northrup came to Amarillo, a trip hundreds of analysts have made since. Analysts seldom get in to see CEOs. But by being accessible I could not only create good will, I could also learn a lot about other companies.

Northrup's report was published in February 1967. "In our opinion," he wrote, "the Mesa Petroleum Co. of Amarillo, Texas, is a company that has proven its ability to compete successfully while growing during its relatively short history. . . . We feel that Mesa has been overlooked in today's market where the common equities of so many small oil companies with less impressive and often unprofitable records are so popular with investors."

There was one line in the report that I'll never forget. It was almost a throwaway line, buried in his four-page analysis: "In addition to internal growth, management is also considering acquisitions in the petroleum industry."

Well, yes, as a matter of fact we were.

The people who became shareholders back in 1964 and stuck with Mesa over the years made the right decision. They have made a lot of money — fifty times what they would have made by keeping their drilling fund properties. Employees did well, too. John Boros joined us in 1964. He left, as vice president and secretary-treasurer, twenty years later, several times a millionaire.

I can go to the Amarillo Club today and see people whose investment in a PEI drilling program has been transformed into millions. One of the biggest winners is John O'Brien, whose original $1,250 investment is now worth more than $7 million — a dramatic contrast to the $350,000 that Gene McCartt got back in 1963.

# · 6 ·

# *Little Fish, Big Fish*

Our revenues for 1968 were $6.2 million, up from $1.5 million at the end of our first year. And our profits had grown to $1.4 million. During the first five years, more things had gone right than wrong. Our cash flow had grown steadily, and we had increased our reserves every year. We now had 62 billion cubic feet of gas reserves, thanks in large part to our success in Canada. We had accumulated these reserves in a period when oil prices were stagnant and the industry depressed. (Statistics later revealed that half the independent oil companies went out of business in the late 1960s.)

Furthermore, our stock price had risen significantly. The stock that R. H. Fulton had sold for $6 a share in 1964 was now trading on the American Stock Exchange for $35 a share.

But we had a long way to go. Our growth was steady but slow, and I was impatient. I wanted to make a discovery that would catapult us five or ten years ahead of our time. But I knew that unless we got lucky and found something big — and I could count on the fingers of one hand the number of companies to which that had happened — there was only one other way to take the giant step — acquisition.

Acquisitions were fairly common by the late 1960s — it was the era of the conglomerate — but most were friendly deals.

I was intrigued with the relationship of a company's market price to the underlying value of its assets. Many people, including some managements, like to view the stock market as an irrational mechanism. My analysis was the opposite. Over the long haul, the market reflects management's ability to make the most out of its assets. So the price of a company's stock is like a report card. Mesa's stock has almost always traded near or above the appraised value of the assets. A going concern should sell for at least the value of its assets, and something more if it has good management. If a company has poor management, the price of the stock will suffer, usually selling substantially below the appraised value.

In early 1968, I found a good prospect for acquisition, the Hugoton Production Company of Garden City, Kansas. It turned out to be a diamond in the rough. Hugoton had been in the news because of several abortive merger efforts. Originally part of the Panhandle Eastern Pipeline Company, Hugoton had been spun off in 1948. It owned a substantial part of the Hugoton gas field, in Southwest Kansas — the largest gas field in the United States. The company's gas reserves were huge: 1.7 trillion cubic feet compared to Mesa's 62 billion cubic feet.

But Hugoton was making no effort to replace its reserves. Management seemed content to deplete the reserves slowly and thus liquidate the company. A depleting reserve base can be an albatross around your neck; in effect, you are drawing down inventories (reserves) to pay dividends.

Hugoton's largest stockholder was the Clark Estates, Inc., a New York money management firm. One of the firm's officers, Mike Nicolais, also served as the president of Hugoton. With this one exception, the company's fifty or so employees all lived in Kansas.

When we examined Hugoton, we found it was receiving an inferior price for its gas, and we could see that an aggressive management could get a lot more mileage out of the assets. Once we concluded that Hugoton was worth a shot, Wales Madden and I went to New York to see its president and try to get something going.

Nicolais was a knowledgeable investment adviser, but he wasn't too impressive as the head of a big gas producer. Early in the meeting, he admitted that Hugoton had called off three previous mergers. He added that they were not averse to trying again under the right circumstances. He listened attentively as we explained our plan — it was nothing like the brush-offs I had received from other company presidents. At the conclusion of our meeting, I invited him to Amarillo, and he accepted.

In Amarillo, Wales and I took Nicolais to dinner, and we had a good discussion about our respective companies. The following day Lawton and I gave him a tour of our operation, taking pains to point out our phenomenal growth since 1957. My relative youth — I had just turned forty — seemed to bother him, so we tried to show that we had considerable experience. As I drove him to the airport, I said, "I hope we convinced you that Mesa and Hugoton would fit."

He nodded, but cautioned that he had to discuss it with his board. As I drove away from the airport, I felt we had a good chance of making this one. A week later, Nicolais called to give me the bad news. He was polite, but said they had no interest in a merger.

I didn't do much the rest of the afternoon. I sat in Lawton's office for a couple of hours, slumped in a chair. Lawton later told me I was as down as he had ever seen me. He tried to cheer me up, but I was deep in thought.

In the past, I had backed off when we were rejected. But this time it was different. We had a young, experienced management and a strong record of making money. Hugoton would bring huge reserves and good operations but no prospects for the future. "Dammit, Lawton," I said, "this would be great for both of us. We would be their future."

If only we could be given a chance. I didn't understand why the Hugoton board didn't see the potential. By late in the afternoon I had made up my mind: we were going after Hugoton. Mesa's first takeover battle was about to begin. Lawton and I felt like Orville and Wilbur Wright. Would this thing fly?

The Hugoton battle was the forerunner of things to come. We

were the minnow trying to swallow the whale. But what we lacked in size, we would make up for in creativity and tenacity.

The Clark Estates owned 11 percent of the stock, which put us at a disadvantage. For in any takeover battle, ownership is the key. You can make some noise at 5 percent and a lot of noise at 15 percent and you can rock the boat at 25 percent, but when you get to 50 percent it's all yours. Hugoton's bylaws said that two thirds of the stockholders had to approve any merger; this meant that 34 percent could block a deal.

We took a small position in Hugoton's stock, about 2 percent, at a cost of $1.3 million. Since we didn't have the money to buy a lot more stock, our best option was to make an exchange offer of Mesa securities for Hugoton stock. Unsolicited or "hostile" exchange offers are almost unheard of today because they are so time-consuming, and their complexity makes them easy to defend against. They weren't common then, either; we were flying without instruments.

We offered one share of a newly created Mesa preferred stock (with a market value of about $85) for each share of Hugoton common stock, and we would take "any or all" that was tendered. The shareholders would have the right to convert each share of preferred stock into 1.8 shares of Mesa common stock for five years. In just a few weeks, our actions upgraded the market value of Hugoton from $77 million to $137 million, an all-time high.

The key was our offer to pay a $2.50-per-share dividend on the preferred stock. For years, Hugoton's main attraction was its $2 dividend, and we counted on its cash flow to take care of most of the $2.50 dividend that we were offering. It would be up to Mesa's management to make up the difference. We were confident that we would not have to pay the dividend for long. We counted on upgrading its gas contracts and sales and knew it would be reflected in the price of the stock. And once the price went up, holders of the preferred would convert into our common stock and we would be free of the dividend.

In late September, we had our strategy set and the registration statement prepared for the Securities and Exchange Commission.

The offer was to be filed the following Monday. Wales and I returned to New York and met with Nicolais. I didn't think he would go for the deal, but I thought we owed him the courtesy of telling him about it.

We gave him a copy of the registration statement. "If you have any interest in merging the companies," I told him, "we need to know now."

He said he was going on a two-week vacation; I said we were going to file the following Monday. We both did what we said we were going to do. The meter was running; it would take at least thirty days to clear the SEC.

Almost everything about hostile takeovers was different in those days. The regulatory attitude was different, since the government was developing some of the rules under which takeover battles would be fought. Even the nature of the battle was different; it wasn't total war, as it usually is today.

If Hugoton's board had been willing to play tough, they could have delivered a serious — perhaps fatal — blow. All they had to do was cut the dividend. It was easy for us to see the predicament we would be in if Hugoton did not pay the dividend: we wouldn't be able to pay the $2.50 on our preferred stock that we were exchanging for their common. But I had gotten to know Nicolais and felt there was no way he would cut the dividend.

We mailed our offer and waited for the Hugoton stock to pour into our exchange agent in New York. Trickle was more like it. When some of the brokers called Hugoton's big stockholders, they discovered that we were not being taken seriously. The stockholders were suspicious of a small, little-known Texas company that was trying to take over a much larger company like Hugoton. By mid-October, however, we had accumulated 17 percent of their stock. We were now their largest stockholder and getting ready to rock the boat.

On October 23, Hugoton announced that it had agreed to merge with a Los Angeles company, Reserve Oil & Gas. I had thought it would run for Cities Service or possibly Standard of Indiana (now Amoco), but Reserve Oil & Gas? If I had been asked to pick our favorite opponent, that would have been it. We had just gotten the break of the decade!

We had more to offer than Reserve did. I don't recall reading one analyst's report that said Reserve would be a better choice than Mesa. Some analysts questioned our size, but not our record. Reserve had a real problem with both its size and record.

Our stock performance was far superior. And Reserve's 1968 earnings were only 34 cents per share compared to our $1.83. We were finding more oil and gas than it was. And it was offering only a $2 dividend compared to our $2.50.

One of my jobs was to see that the deal was well publicized and our story told, and time was short. Hugoton was trying to garner the two-thirds vote needed to approve the Reserve merger. Meanwhile, with 17 percent of the stock, we needed to persuade another 17 percent to join us in order to block their deal.

It was time to contact some of Hugoton's directors and large stockholders informally. Our plan was to get our ducks in a row so that we would be ready to go once their deal with Reserve died. So I was back on the road, doing the same thing I had been doing since 1957: trying to convince people that what I had to offer made good economic sense.

I flew to New York and met with one of Hugoton's directors, James B. Alley, a partner in the law firm of Hooker, Alley and Welden who had considerable influence on the Hugoton board. He was a gentleman and gave me plenty of time to tell my story.

I focused on Mesa's strong points: our good earnings, successful exploration, and stock performance. I explained in detail what Mesa would do with Hugoton's properties and personnel if we acquired the company. It was my kind of deal: I was on the right side of the issue and was prepared to present my case.

A year later Alley told me he had made one telephone call to Amarillo. Apparently he had an old acquaintance who could give him an opinion on Boone Pickens. His friend had said, "I don't know much about Boone, except that he's the only oilman in town who still works on Saturday."

I was busy talking to reporters and analysts. It was the first time we had done anything really newsworthy, and this was my first exposure to reporters. I was too critical of Hugoton's management and board but otherwise did all right. I seldom refuse to talk to a reporter; it just goes with the territory.

As Thanksgiving approached, I had a gut feeling that we were going to win. Hugoton and Reserve had not made any further announcements, which probably meant they had received negative responses to their merger. I was finding that as I met with the large Hugoton stockholders and explained our offer, their doubts went away.

There was one stockholder, a Virginian named Fred Robinson, who I had heard was opposed to our offer. Alley called him on my behalf and Robinson consented to see me, but only if I could make a 9:00 A.M. meeting at his farm the next day. I headed for Washington, D.C., and arrived around midnight. Very early the next morning I was on the road, winding my way through the Virginia countryside. I was thirty minutes late and running scared. Then I got a break: I saw a tall, elderly man in a muddy field trying to get fourteen cows into a pen. I was sure it was Fred Robinson. I realized he didn't have a prayer of gathering the cows by himself.

I hurried out of the car and climbed over the fence. Herding the cows was not easy. It was even muddier than I thought, and I slipped and fell a couple of times. After about half an hour we finally got them into the pen. As we walked to the house, I tried to wipe some of the mud off my suit.

Robinson was polite and listened closely to my story. After a two-hour meeting he said, "Boone, I'm not going to intercede on your behalf. But I'm not going to vote against you, either."

The prospect for victory was starting to move from possible to probable. Robinson and his wife together owned 5 percent of Hugoton's stock, and I knew that Nicolais had counted this block in his stack. It was a real shot in the arm.

There was no doubt that our efforts were tying Hugoton in knots. Although we didn't have enough stock to take over the company — we weren't even close — we were blocking Hugoton's merger with Reserve. In an attempt to break the stalemate, Nicolais agreed to my coming to New York for a meeting with the Hugoton board. We had done well with Alley and Robinson, so why not with the board? I couldn't wait.

The next morning, Wales and I were in Hugoton's offices. Finally, after waiting for forty-five minutes, we were invited into the meeting. I was surprised when I walked into the room and saw John McMillan, the president of Reserve Oil & Gas; he was neither a director nor stockholder. As the meeting proceeded, Alley was quiet — too quiet. It seemed as though everybody was against me. But I was confident that I could sway them to my side. After all, we were Hugoton's largest shareholder.

I sat there in the paneled boardroom and listened to these men who knew very little about the oil business ask hostile questions. I answered them calmly and politely, but it was getting harder with each question. Then one of the directors, John E. Bierwirth, the head of National Distillers, rose. He was overweight, red-faced, and very arrogant. "I'm leaving," he said. "I'm not going to waste any more of my time listening to this guy."

"Mr. Bierwirth," I said, "how much stock in Hugoton do you own?"

He barked, "The National Distillers' employee pension plan owns 10,000 shares."

"I didn't ask you about the employee pension plan. What do you own personally?" There was a long pause, and I could see that his temperature was at the boiling point when I said, "Let me help you. Hugoton's proxy material shows that you own a hundred shares."

Bierwirth was so mad, I thought he was going to bite himself. But he didn't argue. He just stared at me.

I said, "I own seven thousand shares personally, and Mesa owns seventeen percent of Hugoton. It looks like I've got a lot more confidence in Hugoton than you do."

Bierwirth slammed his chair against the beautiful walnut table and stomped out of the room.

I couldn't have planned things better.

Wales and I were excused from the meeting to await the board's decision. I caught Alley's eye as I left the room and detected a smile of approval.

The receptionist said, "You know, not everybody here dislikes you, Mr. Pickens."

I smiled.

She added, "You may not realize this, but some of the directors are on your side."

About ten minutes later, Nicolais and McMillan emerged from the boardroom. Nicolais said he wanted me to meet with McMillan and see if we could work something out. I was disappointed, but I told them that we were going back to the hotel and could meet there.

When McMillan arrived an hour later, Wales and I were already packing our bags.

"I'll tell you what I'm going to do," he said. "I've talked to the directors, and we're willing to buy you out."

"That's not what we're looking for," I said.

He ignored me. "We'll pay you over three years."

"You've got to be kidding!"

He continued, "We all know you made a bad deal with your exchange offer. We're going to help you out, but you'll have to agree never to buy Hugoton stock again. And you won't have a seat on the board of directors. That goes without saying."

"Oh, hell, John," I said. "That's the stupidest offer I ever heard in my life."

"That's the best I can do," he said.

"Good-bye, John," I replied as I ushered him to the door.

Looking back, the board meeting was the turning point. Despite Bierwirth's hostility, the meeting had given all of us our first chance to size each other up. I think the board members realized that I wasn't as wet behind the ears as they had thought. I left thinking that they didn't have the heart for much more fighting. If we just hung in a little longer, maybe they would break down. This turned out to be one of the better reads of my career.

Wales and I returned to Amarillo and decided to strengthen our hand by acquiring more stock. Since our exchange offer was still open, we needed to get more stock tendered.

In today's takeover attempts, large blocks of stock are often tendered by "arbs" — arbitrageurs — who buy the stock and then tender into the offer. Back in 1968, arbs weren't so common, so we created our own. Randal McDonald got a call from someone in Washington who wanted to know if there was any way he could get a piece of the Hugoton action. Sure, said McDonald, just buy the Hugoton stock and tender it. By the time the exchange offer ended, Mesa owned 28 percent of Hugoton.

We were very close to killing the Hugoton-Reserve merger. It was time to stick our necks out one more time. We would borrow enough to bring our ownership up to the 34 percent level; then we could play taps for their deal. But there was a downside. We would now have $7 million invested, and we couldn't afford to carry the debt for very long. I was gambling that the Hugoton board would fold when they realized we were willing to keep fighting and even buy more stock.

By early January 1969, everybody knew we were there to stay. I played a hunch and placed a call to Nicolais late in the day; I reached him at home.

"Mike," I said, "I think we should try to work something out."

"What's on your mind?" He sounded bored.

"We're going to open up the exchange offer again."

There was a long silence at the other end of the line. "I wish you wouldn't do that," he said. After a pause he added, "Let me think about this."

As soon as I hung up, I went into Lawton's office.

"You watch," I said. "He's going to call back before we go home tonight."

Sure enough, an hour later Nicolais was on the phone. "Come to New York," he said. "We're ready to talk terms."

We had forced them into a good deal. Nicolais got us to raise the offer — from 1.8 shares of Mesa common to 1.875. We traded a little and got the dividend lowered from $2.50 to $2.20. Finally, they wanted two seats on a Mesa board of seven.

On April 7, 1969, the stockholders of both companies voted overwhelmingly for the merger. Hugoton Production Company and Mesa Petroleum Co. had merged, and Mesa was the survivor.

The Hugoton acquisition is still the most important deal we ever made. In 1969, it was terribly important for us to make that giant step forward. Hugoton's assets gave us the leverage we needed to expand our business and play in a bigger league. We were very confident with this great victory under our belt. Debt had never frightened me, and now we had both the experience and the balance sheet to expand. We were on our way.

· 7 ·

# Breakup

Just before the Hugoton deal, I turned forty. After years of struggle, I finally had a substantial net worth. Professionally things were fine, but it was also a time of personal loss.

In the fall of 1966, tragedy had struck. Lawton was living in Calgary, running the Canadian operation, and he and his wife, Sally, were on vacation in British Columbia. One afternoon I received a call from the Calgary office. They hadn't heard from Lawton and were wondering if I had. A radio report had said that a woman had drowned while fishing in British Columbia. I called Lawton at the number he had left, and he answered in a subdued voice.

"Is anything wrong?" I asked.

"I've been trying to reach you," he said. Then, after a long pause: "Sally's gone."

"Who's with you?" I asked.

"No one."

I said I would be there as soon as possible.

The Clarks had been fishing in the Seymour Narrows, a picturesque spot just north of the town of Campbell River. The Narrows generates powerful whirlpools, and their boat had headed toward one. No one, including the guide, saw it until it was too late. The whirlpool got control of the boat, and as it swung around the violently swirling water, everyone was thrown overboard. Lawton was pulled very far underwater by the whirlpool and nearly drowned. He told me later that he came to the surface just as he was going to give up. Sally fell directly into the vortex. She never had a chance.

I remember how helpless I felt, thousands of miles away, as Lawton sat in a motel room after losing his wife. I called the Calgary office and broke the news. Then I called Lynn and told her we were headed for Calgary on the next flight. We got there late that night and conveyed what comfort we could. All of us took the loss very hard. Sally was a good friend and we were all a team.

Lawton had moved to Canada when I really needed someone there I could trust. Al Whitehead, our Canadian manager, had resigned to start his own company, and we didn't have the confidence in our exploration manager to turn the operation over to him. This had happened just when we had decided to step up our efforts in Canada. We had experienced some success, but we were still hungry. We were confident we would find substantial natural gas reserves on some of the prospects we had accumulated.

Canada was very important to us, and I had no intention of turning over the operation to somebody I didn't trust. I couldn't go because I was up to my armpits taking Mesa public. That left only Lawton. When I first broached the idea of his moving to Calgary, he groaned. We talked about it for a few weeks, and he made it clear he didn't want to go. Finally, as we were waiting at the airport to make one of our frequent trips to Calgary, he said, "Aw, hell, Pickens. I know there's no one else to do it. I'll go."

Now it was three years later, and Lawton had done everything I could have asked of him. By 1966, we were drilling more wells in Canada than in the United States and were finding more oil and gas there than at home. We were preparing to drill twenty development wells in the Hoosier field, which we had discovered in 1963. The program was a huge success — sixteen oil wells, one gas well, and only three dry holes — and nearly doubled our oil reserves.

But now Lawton's family was more important than the company's business. He had two daughters, Peggy, nine years old, and

Anne, only six months old. By early 1967, it was obvious that we needed to take some pressure off Lawton and bring him home to Amarillo.

Canada was our hot spot and it was my turn in the barrel. Lawton replaced me in Amarillo, where things had become less hectic. He and I were so close that we didn't bother buying homes in our respective new cities — we temporarily swapped houses and furniture.

We lived part of two years in Calgary. It was an opportunity to make new friends, and I liked the challenge both socially and professionally. I prefer living in a smaller city, where life is simpler and the social pressures are fewer.

Calgary was different; it was Alberta's second largest city. It was an oil town, though a very cold one in winter. The pace was slower than that of a big city like Toronto, but not as slow as Amarillo's. The people were open and friendly, much like the people in Texas.

I had made some friends in Calgary over the years. One of them, whom I first met in 1957, was Harley Hotchkiss. A former Michigan State hockey player, he was a ruggedly handsome geologist who had gone from bank officer to successful independent oilman. He later became a close adviser and a member of the Mesa board.

During our stay in Calgary, I felt both physically and mentally distant from Mesa's Amarillo headquarters. It was a little like a retreat for me. Lawton once said that "it was the only time in history that the CEO was transferred to the division office."

What I remember most about living in Calgary was spending more time with my family. It's odd that it worked out that way. I was traveling as much as ever — more, in fact. Besides making regular trips to Amarillo, I was going to New York and Toronto frequently. Mesa was doing well; it wasn't a frantic struggle just to stay alive. Everything moved at a slower pace, and I didn't go back to the office after dinner.

Canada was a family adventure for all of us. Deborah and Pam were teenagers and interested in all the things that teenagers do. Mike and Tom were adventuresome and couldn't wait for the ski season. (All four children were good skiers, having learned during our many ski vacations in New Mexico and Colorado.) Our Canadian experiences broadened the children, whose world had consisted of the twenty blocks on either side of our home in Amarillo. Living in a foreign country, even in a place as close to the United States as Calgary, gave them a much deeper appreciation of their heritage.

I felt it myself. On rare occasions I would be the target of someone's anti-American feelings, something most Americans living in another country have to face sooner or later. There's nothing quite like living outside the good ol' U.S.A. to raise your level of patriotism a few notches.

And instead of my working on Saturdays, we took weekend trips. We skied in the winter and traveled around the countryside in the summer, going to Banff, Lake Louise, and Jasper. Our first winter, I made reservations at a ski lodge months in advance for every weekend in February. The people at the office thought I was nuts. Once February arrived and we headed for the slopes, I understood why: it was bitter cold, with temperatures well below zero. One weekend the Pickenses were the only guests at the lodge. But since we had come, we put on our face masks and skied and had a great time.

Much to my surprise, our time in Calgary, with its feeling of togetherness that affected the children, also affected Lynn and me for a while. We were getting along better than we had in a long time; we were talking more and enjoying each other's company. In 1965, we had come very close to getting a divorce. But we had decided against it and vowed to give our marriage another try. For the first time in years, I wondered if maybe it was going to work. But after the novelty wore off, we lapsed back into our old ways.

Once again I thought seriously about divorce and even discussed it with a lawyer in Calgary. He was blunt. I would do well to get the divorce in Canada, he told me, because Canadian law would allow me to keep the bulk of my assets. I didn't take his advice.

In 1968, the year we left Canada, Lynn and I had been married for nearly twenty years. In addition to raising four children, a full-time job in itself, Lynn had never failed to help me with the business associates who had visited in our home. I knew that when the day came for divorce, we would divide the assets right down the middle.

By 1971, I finally had some money. As Mesa prospered and the stock price went up, so did my own net worth. After years of cutting it thin and struggling, I had become a millionaire several times over. Money changes people, but I'd like to think it changed me less than most.

Then the inevitable happened: Lynn and I decided we had come to the end of the trail. Deborah was married. Pamela was eighteen and in college. Mike and Tom, seventeen and fourteen respectively, were still at home. Like so much else in our marriage, the divorce was initially neither friendly nor unfriendly, simply a matter of fact. There was no final fight or argument.

On a Saturday afternoon in late July while Lynn was shopping, I sadly packed my things. We had spent twenty-two years together and had raised four children we both loved immensely. Whatever problems our marriage had, we had shared a lot over the years.

Another loss at about that time was Lawton's leaving Mesa. After our acquisition of Hugoton, he could see that we were a different company, bigger and probably not as free-wheeling. He felt the family atmosphere that had been part of building PEI, Altair, and then Mesa would be gone. The feeling of having your back to the wall, which had driven us all at the outset, wasn't going to be as powerful a force — or so we all thought.

There were other departures as well: Doc Marsalis and John O'Brien and some of the other directors would go off the board to make room for the Hugoton directors.

I tried to get Lawton to stay. I emphasized that he was still important to the company and to me personally. But his mind was made up. He said he wanted the chance to run his own company — and no one understood that feeling better than I. Lawton had done well financially and was ready to give it a try.

He was right about one thing. Mesa would be different. We were bigger and more structured, as he recognized, but the biggest difference was that Lawton Clark wasn't there anymore.

*Three*

# A NEW ERA

# · 8 ·

# *Long Cattle*

Deals almost always begin with a phone call, whether it's a farmout of acreage in Hutchinson County, Texas, or a major acquisition. And over time you get to know a lot of people, those who can make deals and those who just talk about making deals.

Our venture into the cattle business began with a phone call in the spring of 1969, when the ink was barely dry on the Hugoton acquisition. The caller wanted to sell his cattle feeding operation.

Cattle feeding had become the hot new industry in the Panhandle of Texas. There had always been some cattle feeding on a small scale. But what we were seeing now was a major relocation of an industry, from the corn belt of the Midwest to the high plains of Texas. Traditionally, midwestern farmers had bought 600-pound steers from Texas ranchers, fattened them with home-grown corn to 1,100 pounds or so, and sold them to nearby packing plants. The high plains of Texas provided similar feed for the cattle, along with a much better climate. And the packers were now moving into the area.

If you lived in the Texas Panhandle, you couldn't help but notice all this activity. Americans were still in love with steak, and the supply of fed cattle could barely keep up with the demand. For a stretch of five or six years, it was hard to lose money in this booming business. A few entrepreneurs had introduced a profitable new wrinkle to the cattle feeding business. They were building "custom feedlots" capable of feeding from 10,000 to 50,000 head of cattle. They owned some of the cattle themselves, but mostly they fattened customers' cattle for a fee. As the packers closed their antiquated plants in the Midwest and moved to the Panhandle, the stage was set for the cattle feeding industry to boom.

Realizing there was money to be made, I naturally wanted to participate; I knew that before getting the phone call. Plenty of businessmen, especially in Texas, are drawn to cattle and land for sentimental reasons — they're a way to capture a bit of the state's mythic past — but I was never among them. I had bought a small ranch in the northern Panhandle a few years before, but that was primarily for quail hunting. It had been a long time since a ranch was bought with the expectation of making money.

I wanted to get into the cattle business in order to make money, and the feedyards were producing substantial cash flows. Mesa had developed quite an appetite for capital: it was the key to our doing bigger and hopefully more profitable deals. I was optimistic and thought we could put an unlimited amount of money to work in the Gulf of Mexico searching for oil and gas.

It was June 1969 when Mesa bought the Swisher County Cattle Company and the Harmon and Toles Grain Company, about 45 miles south of Amarillo.

Swisher County had a capacity of 25,000 head — a medium-size feedyard. Soon afterward we bought the Randall County Feedyard as well. Its 50,000 head capacity brought us up to 75,000 total. Randall County was better staffed, or so it seemed, and we needed experienced management to run a new $10 million operation.

Next, we increased the capacity of both feedyards and opened two smaller ones. In three years, Mesa became the second largest cattle feeder in the United States, with a capacity of 160,000 head. The feedyards generated profits almost as easily as mounds of manure.

We all got a kick out of going to the feedyards. It was exciting to see almost 100,000 steers being fattened in pens that covered only 320 acres. I was at a party one evening when the Randall County Feedyard was packed with cattle. The prevailing wind swept the strong odor right into Amarillo. A half-drunk fellow came up to me and said that our feedyard smelled like shit. "It may smell like shit to you," I replied, "but it smells like money to me."

Nobody laughed. I got the message.

Being in the cattle business seemed "authentic" to me. It was typified, I guess, by the man in charge, Tom Herrick. Tall and handsome, invariably dressed in boots and khakis, Herrick looked like the Marlboro Man. Of course, the cattle business had as much to do with cowboys as with computers. One of the recent innovations was the limited partnership. We raised money from investors, bought cattle for their account, fattened them in our feedyard, then shared the profits or losses when we sold the cattle to the packing plants.

We quickly developed a following in New York, and on our trips east we sometimes took Herrick along. He impressed people as the real thing — a walking, talking cowboy — and didn't bother too much with the subtle financial points, which only bolstered his image.

In 1969, during a temporary downturn in the cattle market, Herrick resigned himself to the loss. "Nothing you can do," he explained with a shrug, "except sit tight until things turn around." He then left on a two-week vacation.

I didn't yet know enough about the cattle business to argue with him. But I thought that when things were going bad you moved in on the problem, and with any luck you'd be able to come up with a solution, or at least shorten the length of time you were going to be uncomfortable.

The business bounced back, but I now had a preview of what was to come.

In the spring of 1973, we had 185,000 head of steers, which was 25,000 more than Mesa's feedyard capacity. This caused us to feed cattle in our competitors' feedyards. Herrick shrugged it off.

*

When an entrepreneur comes up with a winner, it isn't long before the field is crowded with others doing the same thing. So it was in the cattle feeding business. By the early 1970s, there were custom feedyards all over the Panhandle. With all the competition, it became exceedingly difficult to keep the feedyards full.

As the competition got tougher, we made our partnership proposal more attractive. If our investors lost money, they would pay the first $20 per head of the loss. Mesa would stand anything more.

So long as the market was good for fed cattle, this worked great. Our feedyards stayed full, and the profits rolled in. Cattle are a commodity, and, like all commodities, the price is a moving target. For the better part of a decade, cattle prices had been trending upward.

In the days when we fed mostly customers' cattle, a slump in the price didn't hurt us too badly. But now Mesa and its limited partnerships owned 90 percent of the cattle. Our exposure was tremendous. A drop of 5 cents a pound in the price of fed cattle could cost us as much as $8 million. It was that potential loss that held my attention. So our day at Mesa started with an early meeting on the cattle operation.

The first people to become concerned were the Wall Street analysts. Instead of being impressed by our success in the oil business, they were distracted by our exposure to markets in the cattle business, and their perception of that exposure was depressing the price of our stock. At first I was inclined to shrug off their concern. But the more I focused on the potential problem, I saw they were right. We really did have our necks stuck out.

Early in the summer of 1973, I decided it was time to cut our risk. There is nothing I can point to that led me to this conclusion, no sign that the boom times were about to end. It was based on instinct — and I had learned long before to trust my instincts.

I called a meeting and voiced my concerns. It was time to hedge our cattle. I was ready to lock in a nice profit and take no further risk in a market that was making me uneasy. So hedge it was, which meant that we would sell enough live cattle contracts on the Chicago Mercantile Exchange to cover our inventory of cattle. We were selling our cattle for future delivery.

When Herrick heard what I was up to, he was upset. "That's gambling!" he said.

In fact, it was the opposite. Herrick didn't consider the futures market a part of the cattle business. To him, the cattle business was buying them, fattening them, shoveling their manure, and shipping them to the packer. But the era of full feedyards and easy profits was over.

Mesa was probably the first big cattle company to hedge its inventory, and it took several meetings with the Mercantile Exchange to convince them that we were hedgers. Speculators are limited in the number of contracts they can hold, but a hedger is unlimited because he has the commodity to deliver. There were times when Mesa, with only 1 percent of the cattle on feed in the nation, owned 10 percent of the outstanding futures contracts, and in some distant months we would own as much as half.

On this particular hedge we locked in a $7 million profit. You very seldom pick a market at the top or the bottom, and that was the case here. After we hedged, the price of cattle kept rising.

When you've hedged a commodity and the price doesn't go in the direction you anticipate, you get "margin calls," which means that you have to maintain a required amount of equity in your account. By the end of the summer, we had paid $9 million in margin calls. Because we were hedged, we would get the money back in the fall when we sold our cattle or if the market came back down.

Herrick wanted to pull the hedge. "We look stupid," he said. "People are laughing at us."

Then consumer groups triggered the famous meat boycott of 1973. People were upset because the price of beef had been rising, and consumers were urged to stop buying until the price could be broken. There was panic as the price of beef collapsed. Cattlemen realized that they were going to be lucky to get out with the shirts on their backs, and they started dumping cattle.

Mesa owned 150,000 head of cattle, but there was no panic.

Our hedge had saved the day. It didn't take long when the market dropped to get our $9 million back from the margin calls. Our profit of $7 million was in fact because of the hedge. Had we not hedged, we would have lost $10 million.

I was quickly losing interest in the cattle business; it was too volatile and took too much time.

Our problems were compounding by February 1974. The price for fed cattle was starting to weaken, and so was my sporting blood. While shaving one morning, I had a premonition that the roof was about to fall in. I went to the office, intending to hedge our cattle one more time. We were already down $20 a head — a loss of $2 million. We could handle a loss of that size with no strain.

Unfortunately, I got talked out of the hedge. Before we could catch our breath, the bottom had dropped out of the market. When we finally hedged our cattle, the damage had already been done, and we lost $10 million.

We put the cattle division up for sale that spring. Our investment banker was trying to get $30 million. If I had decided to sell just six months earlier, I would have been a genius. We got an offer for $25 million and made a counteroffer of $27.5 million. We never heard from the prospective buyer again. Everybody knew by then that the cattle industry was a wreck.

The only thing left was for us to take our losses. I brought our key people together and told them we were getting out of the cattle business. It was not a pleasant meeting.

"How much is this going to cost us?" one person asked.

"About $18 million," another responded.

As the meeting drew to a close, I looked at the staff and said, "We all feel lousy, but this experience is going to be good for us someday. We'll remember this the next time we're tempted to diversify." It was an expensive lesson, and a humbling one, but one that saved us money in the long run.

I went to Wall Street to face the music. I knew I could make a good case for us as a net winner, in spite of the big loss at the end. Cattle had given us five years of good earnings. And the cash flow from the division had helped us get into offshore exploration.

We invited a group of analysts to hear the sad story, and we told them we weren't going to meet our projections for the year. I hate to fail, but when it's time to take a bath, I get in the tub. As my father used to say, "It's like murder, son. Don't try to explain it."

· 9 ·

# 2B

I was now leading a bachelor's life and enjoying it. I saw my children fairly often, though not as much as I would have liked, but they had their friends and activities. I worked my usual schedule and sometimes played golf, had dinner at the club, and played cards until late in the evening. I had some dates, but I soon learned that entertaining girlfriends can be a full-time operation, and I didn't have that much spare time.

In the fall of 1971, I was playing in a golf tournament in Canada when I got a call from Oklahoma City about an upcoming meeting with Cities Service Gas Company. It gave me an excuse to call Beatrice Carr Stuart, a very attractive woman I had known since college days who was now divorced and lived in Oklahoma City. I was forty-three years old and had been married since I was twenty, and I probably wasn't the smoothest bachelor around. It was a long time since I had been single.

Bea and I first met in 1952 at Oklahoma University, where I was visiting a friend. We saw each other occasionally over the years, usually at parties. Bea struck me as a beautiful, exciting, and very confident woman. I really couldn't have told you much more about her at the time. Oh, yes, I had seen her at a couple of pigeon shoots in the late 1950s. She was a good wing shot.

I called Bea, told her I was coming to Oklahoma City, and invited her to dinner. I expected her to tell me she already had a date, but she just laughed and said, "Well, I'm free that night and the night before and the night after — a divorcée thirty-nine years old with four teenagers doesn't have a full calendar. Sure I'll have dinner."

Well, I thought, she's just as honest as I remember her.

I returned to Amarillo, then flew to Oklahoma City in Mesa's Cessna. I was so nervous that I almost forgot to take my bag off the plane. Bea met me at the airport in her Mercury station wagon. We hadn't seen each other for about five years.

I found her in the parking lot and nervously said hello.

Bea said, "You're really surprised, aren't you?"

"What do you mean?" I asked.

She laughed. "I can tell from the expression on your face that you've never seen me with gray hair."

Well, she was exactly right. I was surprised. The last time I had seen her she had beautiful black hair and now she had beautiful gray hair.

We had dinner and brought each other up to date — just two friends talking. When she took me back to the hotel, I said, "I hate for you to have to drive home alone."

"Boone," she said, "I'm used to driving home alone."

I thought about her all the next day in the Cities Service meeting.

Two weeks later I called Bea for another date, inventing an excuse to go back to Oklahoma City. On that second date she casually said she never intended to get married again. I could tell that Bea was sad; you could see it in her eyes. I knew that if I ever hurt her, that's where it would show.

Bea could talk to anybody; she would have made a hell of a politician or politician's wife. An outdoorswoman, she read a great deal, claimed she couldn't cook but was one of the best, and was just plain interesting and fun to be with.

We had both grown up in southeastern Oklahoma. Bea had lived on a ranch near Atoka with her parents, two brothers, and three sisters and had spent her last twenty years in Oklahoma City. Her former husband had inherited an insurance company along with a ranch. While I had been trying to stay alive and build a business, they had been prominent in Oklahoma City society.

As our romance heated up, it took on its own rhythm. I would go to Oklahoma City late on Friday afternoon. Bea had a lot of attractive friends who loved to entertain, so the weekend would be great fun, with plenty of partying. It would start with a late affair on Friday. On Saturday there would be a couple of parties: one before and during the football game and another in the evening. On Sunday there would be a brunch, which could easily run into the pro football game and on into the evening. But I was on my way back to Amarillo after brunch, which led to Bea's friends' accusing me of not liking Oklahoma City.

"It's not Oklahoma City," I replied. "It's the parties. I can't stand the pace."

Over the winter of 1971 we enjoyed being together. Bea began coming to Amarillo more, where there was less social life than in Oklahoma City. Typically, she would come in Friday for a dinner party, stay with friends like Walter and Mumzy Kellogg or Wales and Abbie Madden, and then we would go to the ranch on Saturday to hunt quail.

The ranch was not the usual Texas hunting spot. I would pick Bea up early in the morning and drive to Pampa. We would get my trailer and a couple of bird dogs and then stop at the grocery store for cheese, crackers, and a six-pack of Big Orange. There was no house at the ranch, so we had to take everything with us.

On the first hunting trip, she fell in love with my scrubby 3,000 acres. (It may have been the reason she married me.) I had never used the place for anything but hunting, and that was obvious. On that first hunt she said, "You don't have a fence that would hold a sick cow or a road that you could drive a bulldozer on." But she did see the potential of the place. Bea sees a lot of things that I miss.

It was only 90 miles to the ranch, so we could be hunting before midmorning. We would hunt until late afternoon, then hurry back to Amarillo so she could catch the six-thirty Frontier flight to Oklahoma City. People in the Amarillo terminal were surprised to see Bea Stuart, the Oklahoma City socialite, wearing khakis and carrying a sack of quail — but not as surprised as those in the Oklahoma City terminal!

As our attraction for each other grew, marriage became a real possibility, though neither of us was in a hurry. I wasn't sure that Bea was ready to give up Oklahoma City for the much different life I had to offer. On New Year's Eve of 1971 Bea told me, "If our romance is going to amount to anything, I am going to have to quit smoking." (I intensely dislike smoking.)

She was a heavy smoker, having started when she was sixteen. I thought that she would sign up for one of the usual courses, but instead she went cold turkey. It was a tough experience; to occupy herself she did needlepoint almost full time, finishing an entire piano bench cover in two weeks.

I have never smoked, so I didn't fully appreciate how tough it was to quit. But I was supportive and developed a tremendous respect for her. I have seen other people try to quit, and I don't believe one out of a hundred serious smokers can do it cold turkey. I was seeing a woman with great depth and courage, and realized she must love me to take that step. I had fallen in love with a rare person.

When I voiced my concerns about Amarillo and what I could provide, she said it was exactly what she had been searching for. In April 1972 we were married.

I had assumed that Bea would go back to Oklahoma City regularly, to see friends or shop or maybe go to a few parties, but I was wrong. The day we left Oklahoma City for good, Bea said, "I'm dropping my anchor in Amarillo." I'll always remember that.

In our new life together, Bea quickly assumed the role of confidante, adviser, and sounding board. It is a role she has played ever since, combining a definite stylishness with a genuine warmth. It has been a great fifteen years. That doesn't mean we haven't disagreed; we've had some hot arguments. But neither of us pouts, and we have never had the verbal exchanges that leave lasting scars. We are a great deal alike in many ways; and I have moved in Bea's direction, and she has moved in mine.

We got married about the time everything was coming together at Mesa; this new life gave me a sense of stability and comfort that had been lacking before, and it must have done the same for Bea, also.

Bea devoted a lot of her time and energy to improving the ranch, which I had never named. Now it was a natural: it would be the 2B, for Bea and Boone.

We started a cattle operation that soon became profitable and a wildlife program that has grown every year. We spent a lot of weekends at the ranch. Bea has four beautiful daughters, Terry, Laura, Lisa, and Liz, and they and some of my children loved being there. We hunted, fished, rode, and watched the wildlife that steadily grew in number. Now we have eight grandchildren, and I hope that some of them will grow up with happy memories of days spent at the 2B.

As a girl, Bea was determined to do anything to get off the family ranch and go to the city, never to return. One day at the 2B she said, "I can't believe what I'm about to say, but if you told me we were moving to the ranch to live I would be tickled to death."

We later added 10,000 acres to the ranch, which gives us a total of 8 miles on the Canadian River. It also includes a beautiful wooded area where giant cottonwoods throw a deep shade and the view takes in the big mesas to the north. Bea named it SenTosa, which means "peace and tranquillity" in Mandarin Chinese. She has planted hundreds of trees there, developing the water and using parts of the area as a nursery, and has worked hard to raise trees that are not supposed to grow in that country — dogwood, hawthorne, redbud, red oak, live oak, magnolia. Through the years she has planted ten thousand trees all over the ranch.

We also planted alfalfa, rye, milo, and corn for the animals and plowed around the plum thickets so that weeds would grow, providing seeds for quail and other birds. Our wild turkey flock grew from a dozen to four hundred. We put more than a hundred feeders over the ranch, and the deer blinds are used more for observing deer and other animals than for shooting them.

*

I will never forget one day when Doc Marsalis dropped in for a visit. He said that he wanted to talk about the best deal we'd ever made. It was fairly common for Doc to reminisce about our deals because he had been an important part of Mesa.

"Boone," he said, "what do you think our best deal was?"

"Hugoton," I replied.

Doc shook his head.

"Pubco?" I asked.

He shook his head again.

"I give up, Doc. What was our best deal?"

He replied, "The day we got Bea."

## · 10 ·

# *The Sky's the Limit*

Even at the height of our deal-making, Mesa always had drilling rigs working and exploration projects in the mill. No matter what else we had going, we never lost sight of our main objective as an oil company: we had to replace our reserves.

Reserve replacement is like a treadmill. It just keeps coming around, year after year. The bigger the company gets and the more oil and gas it produces, the more oil and gas it must replace. Every year, when we set our budget, we made sure we provided enough not only to replace but also to increase the reserve base. And we have done it for twenty-two straight years.

The biggest single addition to our reserves came when we acquired Hugoton. It was great to have 1.7 trillion cubic feet of gas. But by the beginning of 1970 we needed a new reserve replacement strategy. Our budget had to expand dramatically, and I had to build a team capable of carrying out large exploration and production operations.

Our increased cash flow from Hugoton allowed us to hire the best people. I had looked forward to the day when we could have people who were better than I.

One of the first men I recruited was Jack Larsen, a big, friendly guy who was head of exploration at Southern Natural Gas Company. He had received his early training with Shell, where he spent more than twenty years. At last we had a well-trained, seasoned geologist who had seen it all. He was in charge of our expanding exploration group, a position he held until he retired in 1984.

With Larsen and his team ready to go, we increased our exploration budget substantially. Larsen wanted to concentrate on the Texas Gulf Coast and South Louisiana, the two areas with which he was most familiar.

His first deal was with a farmout 50 miles north of Corpus Christi. Coincidentally, it was close to where I had worked for Phillips in 1952. I didn't have a very high regard for the area, believing that it had been picked over, and what Jack found on his first well was small and noncommercial.

The next try was South Louisiana, where we got an expensive dry hole. After several more dry holes, I decided Jack was proving my theory: finding oil and gas onshore was tough and expensive. Jack was well trained and experienced, but he had a geologist's tendency to be too optimistic. I decided that we had to get into an area that was not picked over if we were going to do any good.

About this time, Jack and I were in San Francisco on business. We were going back to the Fairmont Hotel when I suggested we stop for a drink.

"Jack," I said, "there's something you need to know. I don't like to spend a lot of money confirming old theories."

He sagged a little.

"We've spent $5 million, and we haven't come up with anything," I went on. "I think your areas are in as bad a shape as the ones I've been working on."

He reminded me of the great prospects we still had to drill, but I cut him off.

"We're through in South Louisiana. It's not working, and we're not going to spend any more money there."

Jack knew me well enough by then not to argue. He took a couple of sips of his drink in silence. "When you hired me," he said, "you talked about wanting the company to grow. If we don't continue exploring, how are we ever going to grow?"

"We're going to the outer continental shelf," I replied. "We're going offshore."

Now Jack thought I was a dreamer. Although offshore exploration had once meant drilling in the shallow waters off the coast of Texas and Louisiana, it now meant exploring in much deeper water, a vastly different exercise in terms of expense. It was generally thought that the cost was prohibitive for anyone but the majors and a handful of the largest independents.

"We can't possibly compete!" he said. "The acreage is too expensive."

"We don't have any choice. We're not getting anywhere onshore. We either have to find some oil and gas or get out of the business."

I was dead serious. It seemed to me that if we couldn't do any better than we had been doing, we might as well distribute the cash flow to the stockholders and let them spend it.

The federal government holds the mineral rights to the outer continental shelf. An oil company leases tracts by making the high bid at a public sale. There was no way we were going to bid at those sales by ourselves, so in the 1970 sale we went in with Pennzoil, and Mobil joined us on a couple of bids. We leased five tracts. In the two most expensive tracts, East Cameron 270 and Eugene Island 330, Mesa owned only a 5 percent interest. In the three less expensive ones, our interest averaged about 40 percent. In all, we invested $10 million.

Our analysis of the tracts was about as good as you can get in this business. With the first well, we discovered gas on East Cameron 270. After it was developed, the proved reserves were about 700 billion cubic feet of gas, which classified it as a major gas field. Not bad for the first shot.

We were also exploring the second tract, Eugene Island 330, and hit another big one: when fully developed it had 100 million barrels of oil and 500 billion cubic feet of gas. When we found gas on the third tract, I could hardly believe it. Of the five tracts we leased, only one was a bust.

I had expected us to do well, but nothing like this. The first two tracts contained more than half as much natural gas as we had acquired in the Hugoton deal. If there was any disappointment, it was that we only owned 5 percent of those two big ones. But that just whetted our appetite. If this was typical of the results we were going to get offshore, well, in the next lease sale we were sure going to spend a lot more than $10 million and own a lot more than 5 percent interest in the tracts.

At about this same time, I began thinking about another acquisition. What we had accomplished in the Hugoton deal could be repeated, or so I thought. The corporate world did not lack for poor managements and undervalued companies, so acquisitions would become a key part of our growth strategy.

By January 1970, eight months after the Hugoton merger, we were in the middle of another deal. Our target was Southland Royalty Company, based in Fort Worth. It was also an undervalued situation. Its president, Bob Cain, was a geologist who was very conservative, and the company did practically no exploration. He had diversified — into the candy business — and had picked up the nickname of Candy. To be called Candy Cain at the Fort Worth Petroleum Club was downright humiliating.

Southland's CEO, on the other hand, was a hardheaded sort of guy. G. McFaddin Weaver had inherited his job because his family was a large stockholder, and he was proving to be a formidable opponent for a different foe, Gulf Oil.

Back in 1925, Gulf had bought a fifty-year term lease on the Waddell Ranch in West Texas; a majority of its mineral rights was owned by Southland. The fifty-year lease was a classic mistake by Gulf. Most oil companies would have taken a lease that would hold the property for as long as their wells produced. But in the 1920s — as well as in the 1980s and many of the years in between — Gulf's management had been lackadaisical.

The Waddell Ranch was a major oil field. By the early 1970s, there were still 100 million barrels of recoverable oil in the field. But, under the terms of its lease, Gulf was about to lose the remaining reserves to Southland.

Like most corporate bureaucracies, Gulf had platoons of lawyers without enough to do. So instead of being a big boy and abiding by the terms of the lease, it put one of those platoons to work developing a legal theory that would allow Gulf to extend the lease. A legal theory can be developed for almost any situation, and so it was. The big guy was going to steamroll the little guy. At the same time Gulf had other problems; in fact, it had a scandal brewing. For years the company had been making payoffs in the various countries in which it did business. This was at the time of Watergate, and with the American people in no mood to overlook such a situation, Gulf officials wanted to keep a low profile. Still, the company was applying intense pressure on Southland to come to terms.

Weaver dug in and refused to be run over. He was fighting very hard, and with good reason. He had a strong legal position, and a victory for Southland would transform it from a small company into one of the largest independents in the industry. There was little doubt that Southland would win if there was any justice in the courts. A key point in our analysis of Southland was that it was a good deal even if it lost to Gulf.

But we needed a large block of stock to get our foot in the door. We thought we had found the block we were looking for. A prominent Fort Worth family, the Moncriefs, had tried to take over Southland several years earlier. (The family patriarch, Monty Moncrief, was one of the great old wildcatters.) The Moncriefs' takeover attempt had culminated in a proxy fight, which Southland had won.

What interested me was that the Moncriefs had 12 percent of Southland's stock. With some difficulty, I got an appointment to see Monty's son, Tex, who was about as smooth as a stucco bathtub. Tex wasn't interested in who I was or what I was up to, though he did tell me that the family had recently sold their Southland stock to Gulf.

I did a little digging and discovered that the Gulf purchase had taken place on the very day that Gulf had filed suit against Southland. Now, I may have been born at night, but it wasn't last night. Gulf was sending a nasty message that if Southland wasn't going to negotiate, then Gulf would take it over. It was bold and heavy-handed — and could hurt Gulf in the long run.

My next stop was to see Del Brockett, the CEO of Gulf. It

turned out that Gulf had changed its mind since buying the stock. Seeing that Southland would not be intimidated and realizing that holding the stock might prejudice its lawsuit, Gulf had decided to sell. But if the stock was sold on the open market, it would take forever to get rid of it.

I offered to buy the block. Brockett didn't hug me when I left, but I wouldn't have been surprised if he had tried. Once we had Gulf's 12 percent — bought on credit, I might add; that's how anxious Gulf was to unload the stock — it was time to launch our offer. We filed with the SEC the day after Christmas of 1969, offering a share of Mesa preferred stock for each share of Southland common stock. It was an exchange offer, similar to the Hugoton deal.

When our bid was announced, I had no idea how good the opposition was: it was led by Joe Flom, a lawyer we would hear more about later, and by Jon Brumley, a bright young economist at Southland, later to succeed Weaver as CEO. We made two major mistakes. First, we ignored the large percentage of stock controlled by insiders at Southland. When they filed with the SEC after our offer, it was clear that the board controlled more than 30 percent of the stock. We should have folded our tents right then and there.

Second, we had not yet seen how litigation can destroy an exchange offer. Flom opened up fast, filing a lawsuit that raised all kinds of problems for us. We were getting caught two steps behind at every turn.

After the lawsuit was filed, the lawyers started taking depositions. I'll never forget my first encounter with Flom, in a conference room in New York crowded with lawyers. I noticed a short, lean guy with horn-rimmed glasses and an intense look. Flom had a reputation for being tough and intelligent, and that is just how I sized him up.

Soon after the deposition got under way, Flom pulled out a cigar that was damn near as big as he was. I moved my chair back, but Flom kept blowing smoke in my direction along with his tough questions. I was new at being deposed and sometimes volunteered information when I shouldn't have. Flom worked me over pretty well. I spent most of the morning trying to convince him that a Southland-Mesa merger made a lot of sense while also trying to impress him with my honesty.

At the lunch break, my lawyer pulled me aside. "Boone," he said, "I'm not sure you understand the game. Flom is not the judge. He's being paid a lot of money to make you look bad. You'll never convince him you're a nice guy."

Flom beat us in the Delaware court and got our offering delayed with the SEC. Our strategy was out the window.

In April, four months after we had launched, we terminated our offer. We were able to sell our Southland stock in the market for $16 million, made a small profit, and retreated to Amarillo to lick our wounds.

In the end, the deal did some good — for Southland. Nobody knew much about the company until we came along. By the time we left, everybody knew not only about Southland but also about the Gulf lawsuit. Largely as a result, Southland's market value increased by $200 million. And Brumley's performance during the fight cinched his spot as the heir apparent to Weaver. "If it hadn't been for Boone," he has said since, "I might never have been CEO of Southland."

That, too, was good for Southland. The company won the suit with Gulf, and history has proven Brumley to be a good manager. Over the years he and I became friends. In 1976, Mesa made an offer for Aztec Oil and Gas, but Southland topped us and took it over. We should have been more aggressive on that one.

Not only did we lose Southland, we also lost the opportunity to profit from its subsequent price run-up when we sold our shares. The $16 million block of stock we bought from Gulf would be worth an astonishing $300 million ten years later.

In 1970, we bought a substantial interest in Pubco Petroleum, based in Albuquerque, from Pennzoil. At that time Pubco's chief, Frank D. Gorham, Jr., made it clear that he wasn't interested in a merger with Mesa. "What in the hell are you doing buying my stock?" was Gorham's memorable question when I met him for the first time. "My" stock — it had a funny sound to it. It was a question I was asked many times over the next sixteen years. But Pubco eventually received an offer from another company, and it had no choice but to ask us to make a competing offer. Within a matter of weeks, the company was ours.

Like all our deals, Pubco had its funny moments. The funniest was seeing Bob Stillwell at a meeting of the Pubco board, unable to find the letter of intent he had hurriedly drafted. He opened his briefcase to search for it, only to have his underwear fall out.

Several weeks later, the deal was concluded on a sour note. Pubco had a luncheon — at our expense — for its employees. We had been very fair and had offered jobs to a number of its people. Although many people from its division offices had accepted, only one from Pubco's Albuquerque headquarters had signed on with Mesa. After dessert, the head of Pubco singled out that person and had him come to the front of the room. The president made a few stupid remarks and then gave him a nicely wrapped package — a good-bye gesture, he said. With everyone watching, he opened it. Inside was a box filled with cow manure.

The personnel and undeveloped acreage we acquired from Pubco became the backbone of our Rocky Mountain and Permian Basin divisions. And that deal, along with our Gulf Coast, Hugoton, and Canadian operations, plus new prospects in the British North Sea, had all combined to make us a much larger and more attractive company. And it had all happened in less than four years.

When I look back at our 1972 annual report, even I am a little startled by our growth. In 1968, Mesa had been a profitable little oil company, with nearly $6 million in revenues, $1.4 million in profits, and $15 million in assets. But by 1972 we had $92 million in revenues, $15 million in profits, and $189 million in assets. We had finally made that quantum leap.

· 11 ·

# The Beatrice Field

The discovery of oil in the North Sea in 1965 caught the world by surprise. It seemed that huge reserves lay beneath the deep, turbulent water; drilling was expensive and the weather unpredictable and sometimes dangerous, but the potential for profits was enormous.

British Petroleum had made the discovery, and soon other big oil companies moved in. Within five years the Forties, a major oil field, was being developed 250 miles north of Scotland.

The North Sea finds dwarfed anything being found in the Gulf of Mexico, where Mesa was working. I couldn't help thinking about the great possibilities across the Atlantic, especially when I learned that the 50,000-acre tracts were given free to companies willing to explore them. To oilmen used to paying millions just for the privilege of drilling, that was a real incentive.

The tug of the North Sea got stronger. We were always on the lookout for good prospects, and if we could find a big field in the North Sea it would help.

Jack Larsen started looking at prospects, almost casually at first, then seriously. A broker from Dallas brought us several prospects; two of them were interesting. One was 250 miles out, in the area where oil had already been found and rather close to British Petroleum's Forties field. It was a class B prospect, and if we hit, the development costs would be astronomical. The other one was just 14 miles offshore. It had been passed over by the majors as an unlikely spot, but the more we studied the seismic data, the more excited we became.

The North Sea was one big sedimentary basin. We were looking for the Jurassic sands, which were the best oil producers. Other companies, including the majors, questioned whether these sands extended that close to shore. But we saw seismic indications in the shallower part of the basin similar to those we saw 250 miles out; maybe they did extend that far "up-dip."

Larsen was convinced that he had a class A prospect, but I wasn't. The British government was peddling its culls, and this prospect looked like a cull to me. A well drilled in this area, even though it was in shallow water, would be a real wildcat. On the other hand, exploration and development would cost a lot less. Larsen, the eternal optimist, prevailed, and we flew to London to make arrangements with the United Kingdom's Department of Energy to drill both prospects. Mesa took 25 percent of the deal and found three other companies to take the rest; We were the operating partner, which meant that we would be in charge. We moved our vice president of Canadian operations, Peter Clarke, to London.

The weather in the North Sea could be terrifying. Gales, huge waves, and powerful currents were natural deterrents to both sailors and pilots. Servicing the operation was a major undertaking because of the elements and the distance. The rigs were equipped with a rec room for the crew and most of the amenities found on land, including movies every day, but in the North Sea everything was king size, including the cost. Workers were brought out by helicopter from Aberdeen to the "jack-up" drilling rig, where they worked twelve hours a day for three weeks straight, then were off for two weeks. Many of them were Texans who had naturally followed the discovery of oil.

The cost of development, already high, was increased further by government regulations. The U.K. was going to profit from our taking the risks but was bearing none of the expense, so it had little incentive to hold the cost down. We were a small company in a very expensive game, and we were spending more than we had anticipated.

After two years we had drilled two wells, one on each prospect. The well 250 miles out was a dry hole. But we did get oil shows from our drilling samples on the other well. When we reached total depth and ran our electric logs we were sure we had a discovery.

We wouldn't know how big it was until we tested — a more difficult procedure in the offshore. The production casing had to be cemented in place before we could start the completion. After a couple of weeks, I got the call I had been expecting. We were ready to test the well and they wanted to know if I was coming over to see if our investment had paid off. I decided to go, and Bea said she would like to go, also.

One of our vice presidents said, "You can't take your wife on that rig. The crew will raise hell." Women are supposed to be unlucky on oil rigs, a superstition that is still strongly held. "Tell her she can't go."

"You tell her she can't go," I said.

Bea and I boarded Mesa's Lear 35 in Amarillo with very little luggage and a cooler of food. This was Bea's first well test, and I thought what an exciting well it would be for her first test. I was sure she would bring us good luck.

It was the Friday before Labor Day, 1976, and everything looked fresh as we streaked northeast, toward the unknown. We had a pit stop in Gander, Newfoundland. The Russians were testing missiles, so all flying into the North Atlantic was prohibited for a few hours. We napped in the plane, and after several hours they cleared us to Aberdeen.

Because of the North Sea activity, Aberdeen had become the closest thing to a boom town you could find in 1976. We went to a hotel and freshened up, and I took a quick nap. Bea went shopping and bought a cap to wear on the drilling rig. Peter Clarke had checked with the superintendent to see if the crew would allow Bea on the rig — we didn't want a strike on our hands — but they voted unanimously in favor of her coming on board.

The men had worked hard to get everything cleaned up for

Bea's arrival. There was even a welcoming committee, and they presented her with a bottle of perfume. Seeing the Texans on the rig reminded me of how small the Oil Patch is: they would have been at home on a jack-up in the Gulf of Mexico, in the Persian Gulf, or on a rig in the Panhandle. They had gone to the North Sea because they knew the drilling business — I even knew a couple of the guys from my days in the field.

They had fixed up a stateroom for us, with bunk beds and our own bathroom, a real luxury. We ate dinner with the crew — great food, and all you could eat. The test was supposed to take place at daybreak, but this was a typical oil field effort, so there were delays.

The next day there were more delays. While we waited, Bea toured the rig; it didn't take her long to know almost everybody. Once I was talking to half a dozen men in the operations room, overlooking the rig floor, and I looked down and saw Bea talking to the crane operator. She climbed on the basket they used to hoist men and supplies onto the supply boat 60 feet below. The basket was covered with heavy netting and was connected by a cable to the crane. Bea looked up expectantly.

"Do you want the operator to pick her up?" the superintendent asked me, not believing I would say yes.

I said, "If he can operate the crane, she can hold on." The operator, a Dane who wore an earring, picked her up and swung the basket over the side and out of sight, down to the supply boat. In a few minutes the basket and Bea reappeared and swung back onto the rig floor.

"Gosh," said the superintendent. "I wouldn't let my wife do that."

When the basket was unloaded it rose again, Bea still hanging on, and dropped out of sight.

"Doesn't that bother you?" asked the superintendent.

"You have to wear her out during the day so she'll sleep at night," I said.

During a fire drill, Bea got into a flotation capsule with three German cooks. Everybody wore life preservers, and the men couldn't speak English and thought the drill was for real. They knew that if anybody got saved, it would be the American woman. All of them, including Bea, thought it was great fun.

I was getting tired of the delays, and the following night I sat upright in bed and said, "Goddamn it, I'm getting tired of entertaining you." Then I fell back, never having awakened. Bea never let me forget my sleeptalking.

Finally the drill-stem test was set to go. A hose attached to the tubing was placed in a bucket of water so that we could monitor what came out of the well. Everyone gathered around the bucket. Bea expected to see oil come out of the hose immediately, but the tubing was loaded with water, and all we saw was bubbles as the water was forced up.

Then the superintendent said, "Something's coming in."

We waited for several hours. Then the water started shooting out. We all but knew we had a discovery, justification for the millions we had spent, but you're never sure until you actually see it.

Someone finally shouted, "It's oil!"

The bucket filled up quickly, and Bea surprised everybody by dipping her hand in it. We looked at each other and laughed.

The pressure started to rise. Suddenly the oil surged up at full force and was flowing to the vent line. Someone hit the ignition switch, so that the oil would burn instead of spilling in the ocean, and a 100-foot flame roared out over the water. Bea and I stood close together, watching the proof of our success, feeling the heat of a flame so hot it blistered the paint off the side of the rig.

We let it burn for a while to be sure about the well's capability. It had been worth the risk: it was flowing at a rate of 6,000 barrels a day! Three years later, we had reserves of about 200 million barrels, a significant but not a giant North Sea find, but it was the largest oil field we ever found. It seemed appropriate to name the discovery for Bea and so it was — the Beatrice field — the only oil field in the North Sea named for a woman.

I was anxious to get back to Amarillo. The helicopter picked us up to take us back to Aberdeen, and I asked the pilot if he could give us a quick tour of Scotland.

We followed the coastline, circling over castle after castle with an eagle's-eye view. The shore was an incredible green and the water a deep blue, and the castles looked like something out of a fairy tale. As we got close to Balmoral, the most beautiful of all, the pilot said, "I think the queen's there now. If she is, they'll run us off."

He was sort of a hot dog and went in low, hovering just above the castle. The guards ran out, waving their arms. We didn't get to meet the queen, but I'm sure she knew we were there.

Finding the field had been one thing; developing and producing it turned out to be something else.

While we had been exploring in the North Sea, Britain had changed governments. The new Labour government had created its own oil company, the British National Oil Company (BNOC), and was aggressively trying to get its hands on North Sea reserves. When the Kuwaitis and the Libyans wanted to get control of their natural resources, they nationalized everything and threw the foreign oil companies out. The British Labour government was a little more subtle but did almost the same thing.

It wasn't long after we made our discovery that the rules changed. The Department of Energy told us we had to negotiate with BNOC, which wanted a "participation." I complained that we had a signed agreement, but the BNOC officials just shrugged. If I didn't like the terms, I was told, they could make things a lot worse for us.

"You guys are like Jesse James," I said, but they just looked at one another. They didn't get it, and I didn't bother to explain.

We had a series of sham negotiations, long and arduous. Finally a DOE official told me confidentially, "You might as well give up. This has all been decided."

BNOC wanted a big piece of our oil field, period: the final agreement gave BNOC a 20 percent interest in the Beatrice field. It was an unusual collaboration, since our new "partner" had no financial risk but veto power on everything, including our expenditures. The original partners would continue to share all the risks and the costs of developing the field — this was the British idea of "participation."

BNOC was not content to leave us alone and let us develop the field. Its representatives came to all the operations meetings, and we quickly learned that they were going to use their veto. To put it bluntly, they would decide how to spend our money. That's when the costs really started climbing.

One of the most inventive, and expensive, twists concerned the loading of our oil into tankers once we came on production. The method we chose had been used all over the world. We would pump the oil to a specially constructed buoy near the producing platform, one that automatically shuts off if anything goes wrong, preventing any spill. The oil would thus flow through the buoy and into the tankers. It was the safest method and by far the cheapest. BNOC wanted us to pump the oil to shore, some 30 miles away, store it in tanks, and then pump it back out to the tankers!

We had long-drawn-out fights over that one. First they claimed that their method was environmentally safer; we pointed out the worldwide use of the buoy. The fact that it would cost $300 million more didn't bother BNOC. Guess who won?

When we were running the test on the Beatrice wildcat, an engineer asked me how much it would cost to develop a similar oil field off the coast of Louisiana. "Probably $400 million," I told him.

"I bet it will cost you twice as much here," he replied.

I am told the final tally for developing the Beatrice field was $1.2 billion.

Watching the Brits in action, I understood the decline of England. Its economy punishes risk and strips away the incentives that promote growth. But growth provides real, lasting jobs in a way that a government-directed economy cannot. The entrepreneurial spirit, which flourishes so freely in America, is rooted in the desire to make money. But the bureaucrats and other like-minded people seemed to consider it undignified somehow. A London *Times* reporter wrote that I had done something vulgar:

I had not only named an oil field for my wife but had "given" it to her. I think he really believed it.

This point was brought home quite vividly during a dinner party in Houston in 1978. I was sitting next to a representative from the Department of Energy and complaining about the way BNOC had been treating us. "The U.K. is not sticking to the original deal," I said. "You are making us waste money and at the same time increasing our taxes, so there isn't going to be much profit for either of us. You're about to run us off."

The Briton smiled knowingly. "Oh, you'll stay," he replied. "We've studied people like you."

"What do you mean, studied us?"

"You're an entrepreneur. You have to keep risking your money because that's the way you are."

I nearly fell off my chair: this guy believed that finding an oil field was reward enough.

"I think you're confused," I said. "If there's no profit, an entrepreneur isn't going to be interested very long. At least not this one."

That night I decided to get out of the North Sea. Larsen, of course, disagreed. But I had made up my mind, and he knew it.

I went to London to see Lord Kearton, a gaunt, gangly old codger who ran BNOC. Kearton, who was in his seventies, had been the head of a large British company and came out of retirement to be BNOC's first chairman. He was crusty and sometimes amusing, but I had the feeling that he would screw you to the wall if he got the chance. Kearton was, to use a phrase from "Li'l Abner," "an inside guy at the skunk works." He looked like a lot of guys in corporate America and had his "short-boys" to do his dirty jobs.

BNOC had forced us to grant them an option to buy our production if we ever decided to sell. When I approached Kearton about selling, he said they needed a detailed study of the Beatrice field.

"You've got a current study. You have everything we have," I said, adding, "Did you forget, you're our partner?"

I knew that, just like the Phillips bureaucracy years before, the British government wouldn't do anything quickly. Having decided to sell out, the last thing I wanted was another round of lengthy negotiations. So I made Kearton what I thought was an offer he couldn't refuse. I told him we would sell our interest in the Beatrice field for our costs in the project plus a dollar a barrel for our share of the reserves.

"I don't know," he said. "That seems awfully high."

"It's a dollar a barrel and that's it," I repeated, then left for Amarillo.

A few weeks later Kearton called and asked me to come back to London. There he gave me his counteroffer: 28 cents a barrel. Kearton had read me well. I wanted out, and he had decided he would test my patience. But this was not the best time for Kearton to play hardball. The Labour party had a tough election coming up in a few months, and they didn't know what I might do. I had already made a casual comment to the effect that I expected to be treated fairly and that, if I wasn't, I had some experience drawing a crowd, meaning the London press. Kearton didn't need to be embarrassed.

Before I left, I told Kearton a story. When I was a young lease trader, I said, I once tried to buy an oil and gas lease from a Panhandle rancher, a Mr. Buzzard, in Ochiltree County, Texas. His asking price was $50 an acre.

"All I've got is $25," I told him.

"Son," he said, "I'm not interested. If you come up with $50 an acre, then come back and see me."

I went back a week later. Mr. Buzzard was in the barn, working. "Sir," I began, "I've got $35 an acre now."

"Young man," he said, "I don't know whether you're hard of hearing or I don't speak up, but I told you $50 an acre. If you don't have it, you're wasting my time, and time is money. Now get the hell out of here."

When I finished the story, I sat back and looked Lord Kearton straight in the eye. "My price is still a dollar a barrel."

"We will have to look at it again," he responded.

"In that case," I said, "I'm going to Amarillo."

In about two weeks, he called and asked me to come back to London. Bea and I packed for a short stay; I knew we were going to make a deal this time. Bea really didn't care about going but went along to keep me company. We never seemed to run out of things to talk about. In the middle of all the chaos, I wondered how I had ever gotten along without her.

As the Concorde took off from JFK Airport, Bea said, "How can a boy from Holdenville and a girl from Atoka be on their way to make a deal with the British government?"

Only in America, I thought.

This time, Kearton offered 68 cents a barrel.

"Do you want me to tell you that story about Mr. Buzzard again?" I asked.

"Surely you have some flexibility on price," Kearton said.

"Yes, but only if you want to pay us more. Our board has only given me the authority to trade down as low as $1 per barrel."

There was no smile from Kearton. He said, "Mr. Pickens, our information is that you have the authority to change the price to whatever you want to."

"You have the wrong information." I didn't show any more expression than he had.

He had a peculiar look on his face. It was the same reaction you sometimes see when you get to a big bet in a poker game. Was he going to call my bluff, or was he going to pay the dollar a barrel?

"No," he said and slowly smiled. "Don't tell me the Buzzard story again. We'll pay you the dollar a barrel."

"Plus our sunk costs," I said, and he agreed.

It took months to get the deal signed, but they stuck to it. That was the advantage of dealing with the boss instead of the short-boy.

Mesa came out with a $31.2 million profit. It sounds good, but we had just sold our interest in the biggest oil field we had ever found at a wholesale price.

We had a lavish dinner in Houston just before the final signing. The dinner was BNOC's idea, but we had to pay for it. The bureaucrats — and there must have been twenty of them — wanted a trip to the United States.

At the dinner, Bea was given a silver platter to commemorate the discovery of the Beatrice field, and there were a half-dozen laudatory toasts to Bea and me. What bullshit! They didn't like us and wanted us out of the North Sea. I had to be polite because I wanted them to keep the name of Beatrice for the field, and Kearton had promised Bea that he wouldn't change it.

When it was my turn, I said, "I want you to know that I feel about our oil field the same way the guy felt about buying a motorboat. He had two exciting times with the boat — the day he got it and the day he got rid of it. I've had two exciting times with the Beatrice field — the day we found it and the day we sold it."

When we got in the car, Bea said, "Not one of your better speeches."

The sour memories faded and the good ones got stronger. Every now and then, out of the blue, Bea would say, "Goddamn it, I'm getting tired of entertaining you." Then it would all come back: the long flight to Scotland on the Lear, the steel-gray water of the North Sea, and a pretty woman dipping her fingers into a bucket of newfound oil.

· 12 ·

# Good Ol' Boys

There is a club in America that has no name. Most of its members would barely acknowledge it, but its influence extends from coast to coast and is indirectly felt by most people in the nation. The club is a loose network of executives who run large, publicly owned corporations. It has no bylaws or official headquarters, and no official recruitment, but you can be sure that the members keep their eye out for rising businessmen who might qualify because of wealth, power, or, in a few cases, innovative leadership.

While I was in my late thirties, I was invited to join other CEOs, from much larger corporations, at social and sporting events. They were taking a look at me, and I was flattered to be included. I had been curious and even awed by some of these guys, and assumed they were a bunch of rugged individualists. After all, they had fought their way to the top of big companies and controlled billions of dollars.

I had a vision in the beginning of ideal CEOs — smart and independent. I soon learned that they came in all shapes and sizes. Some sounded like university professors and some like drill sergeants; some were unassuming and others pompous stuffed shirts. While a few were genuinely good guys, most of them seemed cut off from the real world.

My first invitation was to an annual two-day trip with a group of executives who fished in Yellowstone Lake. The affair was evenly divided among major oil people, independents, and executives from the oil service companies, with a politician or two thrown in.

I was the youngest one there and eager to get to know everybody. One of the first people I met was Jimmy Lee, the number two man at Gulf. He didn't appear to be the hard-driving guy I was accustomed to dealing with among the independent oilmen. Lee was friendly but, oddly enough, seemed a little slow. The first evening I could see he wasn't much of a card player. I was surprised at how he agonized over each discard. I couldn't help but wonder if he made decisions at Gulf with the same painful deliberation.

Our first night at the Lake Lodge we sang "God Bless America" before dinner, then again at breakfast the next morning. A group of Japanese tourists at the other end of the dining hall didn't know what to make of it.

You get to know people well in an informal setting like a hunting or fishing camp, usually better than when you're negotiating a deal with them. In such a relaxed atmosphere, personalities come out, especially after a few drinks. I knew independents who longed for the chance to rub elbows with the men who ran the major oil companies, and I remember thinking as I played cards one evening, "These guys really aren't that smart."

It wasn't long before I was invited to hunt at places owned or leased by different companies. More accurately, they were owned by the stockholders — for the exclusive use of the executives.

I'm a hunter, so I didn't pass up many hunting invitations and thus got to know a lot more of these captains of industry. A typical hunt would include from four to six of us. It didn't take long to check egos and observe who claimed kills they hadn't hit and who showed off their expensive foreign guns. I started thinking of them as Good Ol' Boys, willing to sound off about anything. They assumed that you thought the way they did or you wouldn't be there. I didn't say much, just listened. It would be a few years until I talked (and then probably too much). When these executives brought vice presidents along, they acted like butlers or valets ("Where's his coat? Where's his gun?"). The CEOs really didn't like the VPs and the feeling was mutual; it was a relationship based on fear.

Often the Good Ol' Boys didn't let the facts get in the way of their opinions. More than once I suggested that they might be wrong, but inevitably they were "hard of listening." For instance, few of the major oil company chiefs knew much about exploration, which surprised me. I realized later that it suited them, because they could stay above it all. They were almost all engineers, and they considered geologists and geophysicists to be impractical and "artistic," dreamers. This was ironic, since they were all totally dependent on the success of exploration for the growth of their companies.

Sometimes there were luncheon speeches at the lodge. One day we were treated to a talk by Dave Roderick, the CEO of U.S. Steel. He delivered a dandy. "Fellows," he began, "I just got in from Washington this morning, and it stacks up like this . . ." In his best "we're all in this together" manner, he talked about how the politicians didn't understand that cheap imported steel undermined the nation's smokestack industries, and that the Japanese were dumping, making it impossible to compete. Clearly, we needed quotas and import tariffs to protect ourselves. Almost everybody nodded in agreement. They could relate to this problem because the following week they might be on their way to Washington to get protection themselves.

I asked myself, "Is this free enterprise?"

I eventually was invited to one of the great private hunting clubs, Rolling Rock, near Pittsburgh, where the guests shoot pen-raised birds. I'm not big on shooting pen-raised birds, but I wanted to see Rolling Rock.

The first day, they want to see if you know how to handle a gun, so we shot a few rounds of clay targets. The next day we were to shoot ducks. They fed the ducks salty grain and gave them little if any water. When the shooters were ready, the keepers released the ducks from an elevated platform. The first thing the ducks saw was the lake down below, and they went straight for it, their tongues hanging out. The gunners were between the lake and the platform, and they poured the lead to the ducks as they flew over. Some of the ducks that had survived a similar experience got down on the ground and walked to the lake.

I enjoyed being outdoors and at the same time meeting prominent men from the corporate world, but that hunt seemed a little unfair to the ducks. A hunted animal ought to have a chance. I realized that these guys wanted to be sure of the outcome before the game started.

This scene reminded me of what my friend Ross Perot said about the auto industry and its continual complaint about the Japanese. The industry is always saying it needs a "level playing field." Perot remarked, "The 'level playing field' means a field where you own the bats, the balls, both teams, the dugouts, the stadium, and the lights. It's hard to lose that way."

I got a close look at the men who had made it to the top of some big companies. They had a lot in common; most of them had also spent their entire working lives in one organization. I could see at first hand why the entrepreneurs in those companies had become frustrated and gone on to something else.

After getting to know the Good Ol' Boys, I realized that only a few had ever made any money on their own. In fact, most of them hadn't made much money for their stockholders, either; they just weren't moneymakers. They were bureaucrats, caretakers. They had learned to move up through the bureaucracy with a minimum of personal risk. It was a special talent, and not one I wanted.

By the time these men reached the top, they weren't interested in opinions other than their own. They were out of touch with reality. As I gained experience and confidence, I was amused by their self-serving arguments. I was reminded of the story about the annual meeting at which the outgoing CEO introduced his successor. One employee turned to the fellow next to him and said, "He's heard the truth for the last time."

Hunting lodges aren't the only places the Good Ol' Boys club met. They all made good salaries, had plenty of time to entertain themselves, and had jets at their command. They seemed to prefer being together even though they don't particularly like each other. Even though all of them are well-off, they envy one another, constantly comparing the size of their companies and their executive perks. I remember one day when Fred Hartley of Unocal asked me very seriously if I knew how much John Swearingen of Amoco had paid for his house at Eldorado.

You can usually find their corporate planes on the tarmac at the U.S. Open, the Super Bowl, the Masters, and the Kentucky Derby. The clubhouse is movable, and it moves a lot. Often it's afloat. You can see the corporate yachts moored from Nantucket to South Florida, depending on the time of year, as well as in Southern California and Vancouver.

Gradually I became aware of the excesses of CEOs that I had either observed or heard about. One executive committed suicide when his board started investigating where the company airplane had been. His wife had used it on jaunts around the country. Another executive's wife used a company plane to take her dog to the veterinarian.

These aren't isolated cases. One CEO told me, after I had raised the subject, that hunting camps and airplanes didn't cost that much, compared to other corporate needs, and that CEOs should be free to come and go as they wanted.

"What does it do to the personnel?" I said. "What do the blue-collar workers think when they're working in the plant, hotter than hell, with a big fan on them, and up drives the CEO at ten-thirty in the morning in a limo?"

A CEO shouldn't leave until quitting time, just like everybody else. If he makes the biggest bucks, he ought to put in the longest hours.

As for limousines and corporate planes, I've got nothing against them as long as they are used as tools, not rewards. I use the company airplane. It's fast and efficient, and there have been times when it has made the difference between my making a deal and not making it.

The biggest hurdle in American corporations is the CEO's ego. Nowadays we talk about restructuring and "downsizing" companies, but what we really need is a way to downsize the egos.

Boards of directors don't stop mergers or block offers for companies. The CEOs do. Not one out of fifty boards will stand up to a CEO. In most cases, the CEO knows the board is beholden to him because he put them there in the first place. Nine times out of ten, board members should be chosen because of stock ownership, not because they are friends. A CEO should welcome a big owner on the board: their interests should be consistent.

Another problem, maybe the biggest of all, is the CEOs' lack of ownership. That absence of financial risk is inconsistent with the free enterprise system. Although most CEOs own a few thousand shares of stock, their value as an incentive is insignificant compared to that of the four P's: pay, perks, power, and prestige.

Today, the managements of America's two hundred largest corporations own less than one tenth of 1 percent of their companies' stock but receive salaries in excess of $1 million. Believe it or not, 9 percent of the CEOs from the *Fortune* 500 don't own a single share of stock in the companies they run. I thought you had to own at least one share to get a copy of the annual report.

I think CEOs should have at least 75 percent of their net worth in the company stock. Then management would have as much interest in the stock price as the shareholder. The only reason anyone buys stock in the first place is with the expectation that the price will go up, and the sooner, the better. That's not greed, that's common sense, and the CEOs ought to see that it happens.

Another place I ran into the Good Ol' Boys was at the Bohemian Grove, in northern California. Reporters often describe the Grove as a smoke-filled room, and I didn't know exactly what to expect on my first visit. I had received a lot of publicity from Mesa's activities, and I was asked to talk at one of the camps. I told the group, "What some managements are doing to the stockholders is unconscionable. They're getting ripped off. Does this bother anybody?"

I found more agreement than not. The men who agreed asked questions; the others were usually silent. I think it was the first time anyone had talked about shareholders at the Grove.

You have to walk a mile at the Grove to get to a telephone, and if you want to dodge phone calls for days, it's easy to do. I didn't get the idea that big business was plotting anything at the Grove. There was no Trilateral Commission stuff, no price-fixing discussions. It's just a few days of relaxing and talking about everything but business. A little bit of this goes a long way for me.

I came to realize, though, that there really is a smoke-filled room in America. It's not the Bohemian Grove but an association called the Business Roundtable. Several times a year, two hundred of the largest and most powerful companies in the country send their CEOs and chief operating officers (COOs) — no one lower than COO is included — to a meeting in Washington, D.C.

Corporate America today — the regimentation, the stifling of the entrepreneurial spirit, the disregard for stockholders, and the obsession with perquisites and power — is symbolized by the Business Roundtable. Andrew Sigler, the CEO of Champion International and a leading spokesman for the Roundtable, has said that stockholders do not own companies, "society" does. "Things that affect free enterprise," Sigler told the New York Financial Writers, "affect the whole society. So that the underlying issue is not the shareholder of the business. It is the society."

I asked myself, "Does this guy understand what the free enterprise system is? Does he think people would buy stock in a company owned by 'society'?"

Although they love to talk about the good of "society," the Roundtable prefers to do things quietly, behind closed doors, and to use political influence in Washington to shape the laws to serve their interests. For years, the Business Roundtable wanted Congress to keep hands off all takeovers because the big companies were gobbling up the little ones. That was all just good fun. But now that some of the big ones have been brought down, the Business Roundtable wants Congress to step in and protect them.

Their plan is to outlaw "hostile" offers but to let all the "friendly" acquisitions go on without interference. I can't believe that Congress, the stockholders, and the people of this country will fall for this stupid argument, perpetrated by the most financially powerful people in America.

At one time, the managements of the really large companies believed they were out of reach because of their size. But the takeover game changed dramatically when the capital became available for the little guys to go after the big ones.

The many devices managements have come up with to protect themselves border on grand theft, pure and simple. And they get away with it. Some poor guy who steals food to feed his family can be put in jail for years, but these corporate leaders can literally give themselves millions of dollars at the expense of the stockholders and they don't even send a thank-you note. The ownership of public corporations is so fragmented that nobody blows the whistle and managements know they're safe.

If I had needed more instruction in the difference between an owner — i.e., a shareholder — and an employee, I got it one day when I ran into a retired major oil company executive at Augusta National. He had been a member in good standing of the Good Ol' Boys club, but now he was out of the game. "Boone," he said, "is there any chance for our company?"

I thought I knew what he was talking about, but I said, "I don't understand."

"Do you think what happened to Gulf could happen to us?"

I get letters from stockholders all the time asking similar questions, but it was unusual to hear it coming from a former CEO. "Would you like that?" I asked.

He said he sure would. He'd like to see his stock go up.

"When did you first start feeling this way?" I asked.

"Oh, about thirty days after I retired."

It's not that all CEOs are bad or even self-indulgent. I was impressed with John Opel, the retired CEO of IBM. John was over sixty years old and looked forty. When he played golf he played to win, and he talked business the same way. He had all the attributes of a leader, and I just wish there were more like him.

Carl Reistle, Jr., the retired chairman of Humble Oil and Refining Company (now Exxon USA), was another outstanding executive who didn't believe the company belonged to him. Reistle was a good fisherman, card player, and storyteller. You name it,

Carl could do it. Carl's independence set him apart from most executives.

There was a time when it looked as though I might become a Good Ol' Boy. I was well acquainted with John McKinley, the head of Texaco and a charter member of the club. He had inherited the biggest bureaucracy outside the federal government.

McKinley took a keen interest in me, and Bea and I were invited to Texaco's hunting lodge near Sheridan, Wyoming. Though I considered McKinley a good guy, the Sheridan affairs were no different from any of the other hunting weekends I'd attended. There was hunting during the day and a cocktail hour, when ties and jackets were required, followed by dinner. There wasn't a phone on the premises. Here were people in charge of major companies with worldwide operations, yet the nearest phone was 15 miles away, at a Texaco production camp. I could only assume they didn't want to know what was going on.

I explained to McKinley that I had to check in with my office by phone at least twice a day. He assigned a man to drive me to the production camp, where I was given a private office to make my calls. I spent a few minutes visiting with the Texaco employees and felt that I might just as well have been back in the Amarillo office of Phillips Petroleum in 1954.

McKinley and I got to know each other well and talked about Texaco's acquiring Mesa. I would become the president of Texaco USA and on a track to the CEO's position.

When McKinley invited Bea and me to an important affair in New York, she said, "This is your audition for the job."

John and I had a lengthy talk in the fall of 1978 at Texaco's hunting camp near Port Arthur, Texas. I wasn't enthusiastic about what I was hearing. Not that I didn't want to run a major company; for a long time I'd wanted to do just that.

"John," I said, "why would I want to give up running Mesa to be part of Texaco?"

"Don't you understand?"

"I guess not," I said.

"You may be" — his eyes lit up — "the head of Texaco!"

"Being the head of Texaco isn't all that interesting unless there's more to it."

"Like what?" he said.

"How do you make it work? How do you make money for the stockholders? How do you make money for yourself?"

"Look, Texaco is the third largest oil company in America. Do I need to say any more?"

Texaco and Mesa signed a joint exploration agreement in 1980. I bumped into Ray Burke, a vice president of Unocal, who was convinced that the exploration agreement was a prelude to my becoming CEO at Texaco. "Goddamn," he exclaimed. "You'll have so much power you won't believe it."

"Power to do what?"

Burke didn't answer.

Since I had spent time with the Good Ol' Boys, I knew how they thought, the value they put on perks and prestige. I also had gotten a look at their ballroom-size egos and saw how little they knew about their own companies. I realized that we might have some success going after one of these behemoths. The companies all badly needed restructuring, which would greatly benefit the stockholders as well as the employees. It was just a matter of time until somebody would do it. In takeover battles, the big companies had money, size, and power on their side. Mesa's much smaller, younger, leaner group was faster moving, smarter, and far more imaginative. I decided that we could outthink, outwork, and outfox the big boys, and that would beat all the money in the world.

# · 13 ·

# *Energy Crisis?*

The oil booms of my father's time — the real booms, the ones that transformed the landscape of the American Southwest in the 1920s and 1930s — were created by the discovery of the great oil fields. But fifty years later there were no more great oil fields to be found in the United States, and damned few small ones.

Nevertheless, we had a boom in the 1970s and early 1980s — or was it a boom? It was driven not by new discoveries but by higher prices and, more than that, by the expectation that prices would go even higher. The most dramatic change brought about by this boom was not the physical transformation of the landscape but the psychological transformation of the oilman. For almost ten crazy years, an entire industry lived in a dream world.

It began with the Arab oil embargo in the winter of 1973, when members of the Organization of Petroleum Exporting Countries (OPEC) agreed to production quotas. By 1979, the momentum was building when the second shock hit. Americans remember long lines at gas stations, the soaring cost of home heating oil, and pleas from Washington to conserve energy and keep thermostats at 68 degrees. They also remember the feelings of frustration and even fear that a handful of small countries, most of them halfway around the world, could disrupt the lives and economy of the most powerful nation on earth. It was called "the moral equivalent of war."

There was a lot of talk about the "shortage" of oil when in fact there was no shortage; it was simply being withheld from the market. At the time, oilmen seemed to share the national outrage, but they were crying with a ham on their shoulder. We all thought we were rich, for the price of oil had been steadily moving up since the first embargo.

Just as the rest of the country headed into a recession fed by the high cost of energy, the oil industry was moving straight up. There was a widespread perception that we had become dangerously dependent on foreign oil, and a consensus developed that the domestic industry needed to intensify the search for oil and gas.

With the "energy crisis" of 1979, brought on by the fall of the shah of Iran, the domestic industry took off. Iranian production dropped from 5 million barrels a day to almost nothing overnight, and the world oil price rose from $13 to $30 a barrel almost as fast.

The industry wanted the government to decontrol oil and gas immediately and let oil prices rise to the world level, for government regulation had kept prices artificially low. Decontrol would make exploration profitable again. It would also cause conservation, but nobody was focusing on that possibility.

The decontrol of oil came in 1980, and in December 1981 prices reached their peak. Oil had topped $40 a barrel, and newly discovered natural gas had skyrocketed to more than $10 per thousand cubic feet.

The perception of an eternal short supply caused euphoria in the oil patch. If you didn't believe it, all you had to do was ask the experts, who were all predicting prices of $50, $60, or even $100 a barrel. There seemed to be no limit to how high they could go, based on the myth of the "shortage."

Many of the experts distinguished themselves by the absurdity of their predictions about the future of energy, as probably epitomized by James R. Schlesinger, secretary of energy. He said, "What we face in the middle 1980s is a national and worldwide shortage of about five million barrels of oil a day." *Business Week* announced, "The price of oil now seems firmly locked into a steep upward spiral for the foreseeable future." The Central Intelligence Agency agreed: "The oil supply problem is likely to get worse later in the 1980s." Clifton Garvin, Jr., the chairman of Exxon, which was making money hand over fist, soberly announced, "We're going to be on the ragged edge for years." Whatever that meant.

As I write, in 1986, oil is selling at about $15 a barrel and has been as low as $10 this year. There were limits, after all. In the past four years, banks, service companies, drilling companies — hundreds of businesses in the Southwest that bet that the boom would never end — have gone under. Before the shakeout ends, hundreds more will join them. As the industry struggles to cope with its most severe slump ever, it's no wonder that oilmen look back on the energy crisis with nostalgia.

It was quite a ride — from $3 to $40 a barrel. For better or worse, I was on board for a lot of the journey. My own theories about the energy crisis went against those of most oilmen. I have never been all that concerned about America's so-called dependence on foreign oil. As long as OPEC is willing to sell cheap, it seems we should buy. It makes much more sense for us to deplete foreign oil reserves at a cheap price instead of our own. After all, there is no safer place for oil and gas than in the ground. On the other hand, the domestic industry should be free to drill anytime we want. I'm not suggesting that U.S. exploration be shut down.

I don't think the oil boom is anything to get misty-eyed over. Admittedly, I'm using the wisdom of hindsight here. We did get carried away at Mesa, although we came to our senses sooner than most. But it's clear that the boom was never much more than a mirage. It was fueled by dreams — that prices would keep going up, that more oil would be found — rather than by facts. It was a boom devoid of reality. Some oilmen don't understand, and some don't want to understand, the great damage that was done.

High prices can cover up a lot of sins. The domestic oil business had become a mature industry, like the smokestack industries of the Northeast. And, despite increased exploration, the industry was not making the discoveries to justify the expenditure.

In 1970, the domestic oil industry failed to replace its annual production with new reserves for the first time. By 1980, the larger companies were lucky to be replacing 50 to 60 percent of their reserves. That led to the harshest truth of all: throughout the boom, most oil companies were actually in a state of liquidation, because they were producing more oil than they were finding. Indeed, the production of many companies actually declined. But with higher prices leading to record profits and cash flow, it was easy to overlook these unpleasant facts.

The boom served to sharpen the distinction between the Good Ol' Boy philosophy of management and my own. Through no action of their own, almost all the oil companies were swimming in money; certainly the large ones were up to their armpits in cash. In many cases, profits and cash flow doubled and tripled in the space of a year. America's oil executives now had to decide what to do with this windfall. They also found it a little difficult to explain.

Giving the Good Ol' Boys excess cash flow is like handing a rabbit a head of lettuce for safekeeping. Some of the worst deals in the history of corporate America were made during this period. Exxon spent $1.24 billion on Reliance Electric. Not to be outdone, Mobil paid $1.86 billion for Montgomery Ward. After the initial investment and operating losses, they both lost over $2 billion. In 1984, *Fortune* magazine published a story about the seven worst mergers of the decade: four of them involved big oil companies.

The boom made the oil company CEOs more full of themselves than ever. From their lofty view, if their companies were earning record profits, then, by God, management must deserve the credit. The real reason for the record earnings — the OPEC price increases — was conveniently overlooked. It was a classic case of self-delusion. The major oil company managements had become legends in their own minds, the business world's newest "rocket scientists."

Perk mania swept through the industry. Once oil reached $35 a barrel, every executive in the industry became obsessed with keeping up with the other CEOs. One man insisted that I come aboard his company's new jet so that he could show off a bathroom so spacious it had a changing closet.

I'm convinced that without OPEC's help, the industry would have had to face its problems much earlier, like ten years earlier. Many of the things going on now — the restructuring, the spinoffs of properties to stockholders, the stock buybacks, and so on — would have taken place in the 1970s. There would have been a lot less pain had it happened over a longer period and not just after a boom that wasn't paid for.

Coincident with the energy crisis, the majors were getting kicked out of some foreign countries. After World War II, the big oil companies had spent most of their time in foreign exploration. Foreign oil was much cheaper to find than domestic: finding costs in Saudi Arabia were as low as a nickel a barrel, whereas the average finding cost in the United States in the early 1980s had risen to more than $10 a barrel. An average oil well in Saudi Arabia produces about 12,000 barrels a day — yes, 12,000 — compared to 14 barrels a day for domestic wells.

And for Big Oil, foreign governments were so much easier to deal with. Both the governments and companies were large, unwieldy organizations. The big companies flocked to the Persian Gulf and elsewhere, ending up with giant stakes in all the OPEC countries and gaining control of much of the world's oil — but only temporarily.

What they couldn't control was the resentment generated by their presence as nationalism grew. Thus it was inevitable that after the oil embargo, most OPEC members took steps to nationalize their natural resources. For instance, Gulf Oil, which "virtually owned the country of Kuwait," as one writer put it, was thrown out of Kuwait in 1975. Suddenly, the majors had no place else to turn but back to the United States.

The majors were not used to a steady diet of stiff competition, and that's exactly what they got from the independents. They weren't used to scrambling to acquire acreage or hustling to find good deals. They were used to big departments and nearly unlimited budgets. So back in America, Big Oil's way of competing was simply to outspend everyone else.

It wasn't long before the majors had bid up the price of everything — from acreage to drilling costs — far beyond its true economic value. In the process, they helped create the false economy that characterized the boom. To stay in the game, the independents had to pay the same outlandish prices, even though they didn't have the money to cover their mistakes. But as long as the price of oil was going up, it didn't seem to matter. Everybody — doctors, lawyers, and tennis pros — wanted to own a piece of an oil well or a drilling rig. There were investors on every corner.

The American consumer was getting worked over, and when the price for oil neared $40 a barrel, the Saudis attempted to moderate the price by selling their oil for $35. But Aramco, the Big Oil consortium that bought the Saudis' oil, was so greedy that instead of passing on the savings to the consumer, it just kept reporting bigger earnings. The Aramco partners took the Saudis to the cleaners by buying their oil cheap, selling gasoline high. Seeing this class act, the Saudis gave up and charged the full price.

All of this is a lot clearer to me now. Like everyone else, I was concerned with getting out there and making money. I continued to be uneasy about the economics of domestic exploration. It was clear that the price for crude hung by a thread, and that thread was Saudi Arabia. If the Saudis wanted to hold the price up, they could continue to curtail their production.

If they decided to really open the spigot, the price of oil would go through the floor.

Between 1973 and 1981, Mesa had really taken off, becoming one of the largest independents in the nation, with assets of more than $2 billion. We did it in part through shrewd trading and innovative deal-making, but we also did it by exploration. We found a lot of oil and gas in that period. We made some mistakes, too, but the high prices that oil and gas were bringing made them a lot less painful.

Mesa's activities were scattered around the world: some were profitable, and some were questionable. The price of oil was not going to go up forever, and we were too strung out. It was time for us to start consolidating before the bubble burst.

In Canada, fifteen years of hard work had paid off. We had accumulated extensive land holdings over the years — more than 3 million acres. When Canadian natural gas was difficult to market, back in the 1960s, we had several shut-in fields, and our partners thought we would never find a purchaser. A decade later, those fields were on line, and we were selling all the gas we could produce.

Canada had come "into heat." This renewed interest dramatically increased the value of our acreage. We bid aggressively for more acreage and drilled some successful wildcats.

In 1979, we put all of Mesa's Canadian properties up for sale, and it was a seller's market. Dome Petroleum, the largest Canadian oil company, and a number of its pension fund partners bought us out. It had been twenty years since Lawton Clark and I began accumulating those interests with our original $35,000. When we sold out in 1979, they brought more than $500 million.

For all of us, the occasion held mixed emotions since Canada had been such a success. Mesa had accelerated all its stock options and stock purchase plans as well as the profit-sharing trust for the employees. Most of the people working for Mesa left with more money than they had ever seen in their lives.

We were also doing well in our U.S. operation. And we had sold out profitably in the U.K. and moved our people to Australia. Soon after arriving in Perth, we acquired several tracts and contracted for an offshore drilling rig. We made a three-year contract at the peak of demand — $66,000 a day for a deepwater jack-up rig, with an additional $31,000 a day for helicopters and boats. This was not unusual at the height of the worldwide demand for rigs. But I hated the deal.

Toward the end of the seventies I started talking about the high price of oil. I was outspoken about the big oil companies' wasteful ways and the problems they created for the independents. At the same time I plowed ahead, nervously looking over my shoulder, afraid that prices were peaking but still drilling our share of the wells.

It was getting progressively harder, and more expensive, to replace reserves. We wanted to grow, but there were fewer and fewer opportunities. We were stretching the balance sheet beyond where I wanted to take it.

In early 1979, I made a speech in New York to a group of analysts and money managers at Merrill Lynch. When I got to the part about the industry's failure to replace reserves, a new thought popped into my head: it was one of those moments when you don't know what you're going to say until all at once you've said it.

"Mesa is not going to hang around with a depleting reserve base. That would be unfair to the stockholders," I said. "If we fail to replace our reserves two years in a row, we'll either figure out something else to do or we'll get out of the business. I consider two years a trend, and I promise you we won't be around for the third year."

But on the way back to Amarillo, I could tell that my comments had shaken up others besides the analysts. My people pressed me to explain the implications of my statement.

I told them I didn't know what the "something else" was. "But," I added, "if we can't replace our reserves two years in a row, we really shouldn't be in the oil business, should we?"

Mesa was a big operation by 1979, with a budget approaching $400 million. Reserve replacement was costing us hundreds of millions of dollars every year, and the expenditures could only rise as we brought more platforms on production in the Gulf. I could see that by 1985, with our replacement philosophy, we would need an annual exploration and development budget of $1 billion. I did need to come up with "something else."

It was in March 1979 that I woke up suddenly one morning at three o'clock. I sat up in bed and said to myself, "You could solve your problem by making Mesa smaller." I went into the study. I thought, Why not spin off some of the reserves to the stockholders?

The next morning I couldn't wait to talk with some of my men.

They saw the advantages immediately and shared my enthusiasm. Cutting back the empire may have been abhorrent to some executives, but I felt that size was meaningless. Results were what mattered.

The idea needed a name: we decided to call it a royalty trust. Like most good ideas, its appeal lay in its simplicity. We would take about half of our gas reserves and distribute them to the stockholders.

In November 1979, Mesa distributed trust units, which traded on the New York Stock Exchange, equal to the number of shares each stockholder held in the company's common stock. It was almost the opposite of the roll-up we had done back in 1964, when drilling interests were converted to stock. Now the stockholders would receive 90 percent of the profits directly, in quarterly cash distributions. Mesa retained the "working interests," which allowed us to manage the properties and didn't require any reduction in personnel.

The royalty trust spinoff alleviated our reserve replacement problem. Our reserve base — those properties that Mesa retained — had become smaller, so replacement was easier. At this same time, we were bringing several platforms on production in the Gulf of Mexico, so we didn't suffer a reduction in revenue or cash flow.

The timing could not have been better. Analysts were giving us credit for long-term planning, which included our purchase of offshore tracts throughout the 1970s. Realizing that the increased cash flow from our discoveries would be consistent with the spinoff was brilliant, they said. I never bothered to tell them that I was just luckier than hell.

The restructuring did wonders for the stock price. When we announced the royalty trust in June 1979, the price was $54 a share, and by October when the stockholders approved the trust it was $86. By early 1980, Mesa and the Mesa Royalty Trust combined were selling for $112.

If the big oil companies had followed our examples, they would be smaller, healthier, and better able to compete today. Their executives would be hailed for having delivered for the stockholders rather than having to explain huge write-offs. They really could have been "rocket scientists."

Instead of realizing the merits of the trust, they ran to Washington and killed the concept, wiping it out in the Tax Reform Act of 1984.

It was like a selling or buying climax on the stock market. The buying climax for the oil industry was Mukluk. The North Slope of Alaska was thought to have the greatest potential for giant U.S. reserves. This was fostered by the development of the huge Prudhoe Bay oil field in the late 1970s. Another big structure on the North Slope also had great potential, and it was tagged Mukluk. It was not as large as Prudhoe but looked very impressive on the seismic surveys. When the leases came up for sale the prices were also impressive, and several billion dollars were spent by the oil companies. Sohio and Texaco, the high bidders, bought most of the Mukluk structure. They quickly drilled a wildcat, and their results in 1982 were similar to mine in 1959 with the Cowden well. They got a deep, very expensive dry hole: the final tab was $2.1 billion, including the cost of the acreage. This was the climax: the engineer CEOs running most of the major companies were brought face to face with reality whether their companies owned part of Mukluk or not. The best prospect in North America had struck out, and the cost was over $2 billion.

By 1983 the party was over. The boom had been exposed as a bummer; oil prices were coming down, and the rig count was collapsing. We were all getting ready to pay for our mistakes. When we looked over our list of problems, the Australian venture loomed like an outhouse in the fog. Then we got lucky: we made three small oil discoveries off the west coast. I hoped this was our chance to unload, and I told Larsen to put all our Australian holdings up for sale. The rig we had under contract was getting heavy as lead. Our partners were asking about cutting the rate from $66,000 a day. We were the only ones on the contract, and we now had restless partners and twenty-five months of uncommitted time; we were staring a $50 million loss right in the face. The first offer we got was $12 million; the second was $44 million and they wanted the rig. I couldn't believe it. We had turned a potential $50 million loss into a $27 million gain. We couldn't have come close to making the same deal three months later.

In the meantime, we hadn't been doing so well in the Gulf of Mexico. Offshore exploration can play tricks on you because it takes so long to evaluate the results. By the time we made the discoveries on the tracts we'd acquired in 1970, we were already lining up our strategy for the 1972 sale. By the time we began enjoying the revenues from those original finds, we were into the 1973 sale. By the time we realized that the 1972 results were poor, we had a couple of discoveries on our 1973 tracts, which inspired us to pay up at the 1977 sale. Often the discoveries seemed more significant than they really were, and the initial excitement affected our judgment.

We weren't alone. Rampant optimism was the order of the day. Indeed, watching our industry partners get enthused and seeing billions of dollars bid gave us a lot of starch.

The gas transmission companies were getting carried away. They gave interest-free financing for a call on any gas that we found. The big companies shied away from it, but we stepped up and borrowed about $100 million.

Showmanship and salesmanship were the order of the day at partnership meetings. I'll never forget a technical session with two other companies in New Orleans. Mesa's exploration manager, after an emotional discourse on the merits and potential of Eugene Island 333, put both hands on the large wall map, covering the tract. With tears in his eyes, he said, "Gentlemen, you can't drill a dry hole on this tract." In fact, we drilled several dry holes but did find enough oil and gas to set two platforms. In the final analysis we paid too much for the tract.

As early as the mid-1970s, I was doubting the potential of the Gulf of Mexico. Unfortunately, I stayed in the game, waiting for the big one that would bail us out.

A common misconception is that the industry had a windfall on federal acreage in the Outer Continental Shelf (OCS). With more money than could be spent effectively, the industry paid several billion dollars of excessive lease bonuses. In fact, only a handful of companies made modest profits from offshore exploration. The OCS was a great deal for the government and a disaster for the industry.

At one time Mesa had more jack-up rigs operating in the Gulf than any other company except Arco. We were obsessed with reserve replacement at almost any cost. By 1980, though, there was no getting around it: the Gulf was bleeding us dry. We had spent almost $300 million buying tracts and three times that much exploring for and developing our reserves. We had not found the big one that would cover the dry holes, and I doubted we ever would.

In September of 1980, several Texaco people met with their counterparts at Mesa in our Houston office. They had geophysical data on certain tracts in the Gulf of Mexico called the Brazos area. Texaco had had a disaster there back in 1968. They spent an enormous sum and came up almost empty-handed.

Most of Texaco's current explorationists hadn't been around for the Brazos fiasco, but they knew the story, so they were reluctant to approach management about bidding in that area. They thought that if they could get Mesa interested, then we might take the lead in selling the idea to their management. It may seem weird, but bureaucracies do screwy things.

Texaco's data on two of the tracts, Brazos A-7 and A-39, were very impressive. Larsen was convinced that both would be major gas discoveries, and I was desperate. It looked as though it was time to ignore the blind mule and load the wagon.

We joined Texaco and bid $169 million for A-39 and $81 million for A-7. There were nine bids on A-39 — from $21 million to $169 million, all strong bids — but the runner-up was $78 million. Texaco and Mesa left $91 million on the table. There were eight bids for A-7, and we left $34 million on the table with our $81 million bid.

In a state of shock, Texaco sold part of its interest in each tract to Bechtel, making the ownership Mesa 50 percent, Texaco 40 percent, and Bechtel 10 percent.

From there, things went downhill rapidly. Texaco didn't have any rigs, so we moved two of ours in and began drilling on both

Brazos tracts. We had a lot of problems. Our drilling department underestimated the severity of the area, and the service companies and the drilling contractors were stretched for good people because of the boom times. We finally got the two wells drilled and completed for $75 million, three times the amount we had budgeted. We made two discoveries, but the thickness of the pay zones was a disappointment, and our total Gulf operation was costing over $500,000 a day — a colossal amount of money for a company our size.

We might have made some money if the price of gas had kept going up, to $12 or $15 per thousand cubic feet, but it didn't. It was now the fall of 1981, and the boom would peak in a few months. The price of oil slowly went down, eventually to $10 per barrel, with natural gas doing the same, eventually dropping to almost $1 per thousand cubic feet by the summer of 1986.

This caused some pain for the majors, but it was a tolerable pain, cushioned by billions of dollars in cash flow. For the independents, it was a disaster.

Our failure to make a big find at Brazos, with so much riding on the results, sobered me up. Our finding costs were climbing every quarter, and we weren't making the discoveries that would justify our exploration expenditures. We had fallen into the trap: Mesa was now totally dependent on continued OPEC price hikes in order to stay active and to amortize our debt. We were in the same boat with most of the other independents, but I wasn't really interested in what they were doing. Mesa's problems had my full attention.

Like everyone else, we were overstaffed; we had nearly doubled our number of employees and added nine vice presidents (from three to twelve; today we're getting along fine with four vice presidents).

In 1981 we peaked, with fifty-one rigs working. The service companies were making more money than they could count. The oil field contractors were catching them faster than they could string them; they were literally jumping in the boat! But it couldn't continue, because there was no payoff for those spending the money.

Mesa's finding costs were unacceptable. I saw the results and I hated myself. I had recently gone on the Hughes Tool Company board and we had a meeting in Denver. The Hughes executives were optimistic and were chomping at the bit to continue their very aggressive expansion program. As I listened, I wondered whether the new guy on the block should be the one to speak up. It took me a few minutes to explain Mesa's finding costs and how we related to other companies. I concluded, "Mesa isn't the best oil finder and we aren't the worst, but I can promise you that if we're the average for the industry, then everybody is in trouble." (I was naturally against further expansion, and my good friend Ned Broun, who had made the pitch for expansion, wanted to kill me.)

A study by Arthur Andersen and Cambridge Energy Research Associates stated: "We estimate that in 1980-81 alone, on the order of half a trillion dollars was invested around the world on the assumption that oil prices would continue to rise throughout the rest of the century."

We all should have been monitoring our results more closely. We shouldn't have gotten so carried away with the cash flow our older production was generating. We were actually kidding ourselves, for it wasn't a boom, it was a disaster.

But there's usually more than one way to solve a problem. When you're in trouble, you look at your pluses, stay cool, and ask yourself how you can get your cart out of the ditch. Since 1979 we had been carrying an investment in Cities Service, a large, integrated company. Although not on the same scale as the Seven Sisters, it was twenty times larger than Mesa. Maybe, just maybe, Cities Service was the answer.

*Above:* With my mother, 1932. *Below, left:* Practicing for the Holdenville Wolverines, 1943. *Below, right:* With my father at the time of my initiation into Sigma Alpha Epsilon fraternity at Oklahoma State, 1949

My children in 1961: from left, Tom, Deborah, Pam, and Mike

At PEI with (from left) John O'Brien, Lawton Clark, and Wales Madden, 1959

In Scottsdale, Arizona, with (from left) Terry, Bea, and Liz, 1974

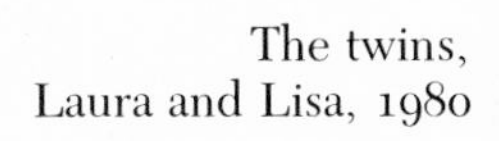

The twins,
Laura and Lisa, 1980

Four generations of Pickens men, 1981; Mike holds Michael

With Bea and Char at the 2B Ranch, 1983

Jimmy Lee, the CEO of Gulf, looking confident at the stockholders' meeting, December 1983

With President Reagan in Dallas, 1986

My father at T. Boone Pickens Day in Holdenville, 1986

Conferring at Mesa, 1986: from left, Tex Corley, Sidney Tassin, Paul Cain, Drew Craig, and David Batchelder

With Michael on a visit to the ranch, 1984

*Four*

# THE BIG CAT WALKS

# · 14 ·

# *Cities Service*

## High Noon

I have often been asked when I first became interested in Cities Service. After the deal was over, Bea answered the question for me: "Boone's been talking about Cities Service for as long as we've been married, and that was 1972."

Sometime before then I decided that the undervalued assets of oil companies offered a great opportunity. That insight led me to Hugoton, the Southland Royalty and Aztec merger attempts, and our successful acquisition of Pubco.

Even at the height of our exploration activity offshore, I was trying to find a way to capitalize on these undervalued situations. In 1976 I flew to four cities in one day and made formal offers to four companies. I talked to all four CEOs. They listened and said they'd get back to me. In each case, our offer was at least 50 percent more than the market price of their stock. It must have been a record for friendly offers in one day. Two wrote brief letters turning me down; I am still waiting to hear from the other two.

By the late 1970s, Mesa often took sizable stock positions in other oil companies. We would sometimes suggest to management that certain actions might increase the value of the stock. The response was generally cool, to put it mildly. The standard reply was, in effect, If you don't like the way we run the company, then sell your stock. That's like saying, If you don't like the way the gardener mows your lawn, sell your house.

Cities Service was a case study in what was wrong with Big Oil's management. Based in Tulsa, Oklahoma, Cities was a large company. By 1982, it ranked thirty-eighth on the *Fortune* 500 and was the nineteenth largest oil company in the country. It was unusually sluggish, even by the less-than-demanding standards of the oil industry, and had been for fifty years. Its refineries and chemical plants were losers, and although it had 307 million barrels of oil and 3.1 trillion cubic feet of gas reserves, it had been depleting its reserves for at least ten years. While it had leases on 10 million acres, it was finding practically no new oil and gas. Cities' problems were hidden by its cash flow, which continued in tandem with OPEC price increases. The stock, however, reflecting management's record, sold at about a third of the value of its underlying assets. The management didn't understand the problem or didn't care; either condition is terminal.

No matter how much I thought about it, and I knew the company well, I couldn't come up with a plan for taking over Cities. They were just too damn big: Cities' assets were $6 billion, six times Mesa's. We had successfully gone after a larger company when we got Hugoton, but times had changed. It was unlikely that an exchange offer would be successful in an unfriendly deal now, nor could we count on winning a proxy fight.

Our old investment bankers were Donaldson, Lufkin and Jenrette, and we added Merrill Lynch, too. Periodically, I met with DLJ's and Merrill Lynch's merger and acquisition people to discuss the possibility of a Cities Service takeover.

They paid it lip service, which they charged us for, but they couldn't stretch their imaginations enough to come up with a creative strategy. Over two years and several meetings they advised us to forget it, or at best file it away. That wasn't the advice I was looking for. We cut our overhead and dropped Merrill Lynch.

In early 1981 we came up with a plan. If we were too small to do the job by ourselves, why not get partners? We developed a list of prospects and ranked them according to guts, first, and money, second. Our goal was to go after Cities. We had accumulated approximately 4 million shares of their stock in a two-year period. This was slightly under 5 percent, hardly an overpowering percentage.

Our average price was $44 a share, but now they were down to only $36. If Mesa hadn't been involved, Cities probably wouldn't have been $25 a share: our presence was supporting their price.

We were down about $33 million, with little chance for recovery unless there were big changes at Cities. As the largest stockholder, we should have joined forces with their management and worked on the problem. Unfortunately, their management didn't understand the predicament that we were both in.

As we searched for partners, rumors of our making an offer became rampant, and my "no comment" didn't slow down the speculation. Business writers and analysts were intrigued that we would consider anything so wild. As soon as Cities' management perceived their jobs might be threatened, they came alive. They hired not one but two investment banking firms, Lehman Brothers Kuhn Loeb and First Boston; both had been successful in protecting entrenched managements. They had done it many times, and it brought in big fees. Investment bankers are like a good bird dog: they will hunt with anybody who has a gun.

Cities' new CEO was Charles J. Waidelich, a relatively unknown company veteran. He began making public statements, which nobody at Cities had ever done, and he tried to deflect speculation that Cities was ripe for a takeover by saying that the company was not for sale, and that potential suitors should "buzz off." He was coming off as a real novice.

Waidelich had been with Cities for thirty-one years and was earning about $500,000 a year. He owned only 39,000 shares of stock. One member of the board represented a family that owned 2 million shares, but the rest of the board had practically no ownership: one director had 392 shares, another 450, and another 300. A recent arrival had a whopping 60 shares. No wonder they couldn't relate to the stockholders.

Early in my search for partners, I met with James E. Lee, the

CEO of Gulf Oil, who had expressed an interest in participating in a deal with Mesa. "We would like to look at anything you think would make sense and make us money," Lee had told me at an American Petroleum Institute (API) meeting. Gulf had lots of money, but there was some doubt about their intestinal fortitude. I called Lee and explained that we had something worth considering but that it would probably be hostile.

"Oh, we can live with that," Lee said.

Mesa's chief financial officer, Gaines Godfrey, and I went to Pittsburgh to see Lee on a cold February day in 1981. It took two hours to present our idea to him and his chief financial officer, Harold Hammer. Lee had a small pad, and as I talked, he kept saying "Just a minute, just a minute," while scribbling down information as fast as he could write. Hammer sat steely-eyed and said very little. I thought to myself, This guy must piss ice water.

After allowing us to show them everything, including our strategy, Lee dropped a bombshell. "Boone," he said, "I'm sorry, but we can't be in a hostile deal."

"Jim, I thought we cleared that hurdle yesterday on the phone."

"Well, I got a call just before our meeting from one of my directors, and he said we shouldn't be involved in deals of this kind."

When we got on the elevator, Gaines was furious. "Do you realize what those bastards did?" he said. "They got all our information."

I agreed. "But I'm not sure those two birds know what to do with it," I added.

A call to Tulsa was probably made while we were on our way to the Pittsburgh airport.

Another prospective partner was Marathon Oil, based in Findlay, Ohio, a company about the size of Cities. Marathon's CEO, Harold Hoopman, was also eager to talk to us. I had met "Hoop" at the Yellowstone outings. He had started as a young engineer and worked up to the top in the conventional corporate way — in other words, he had outlasted his peers. Even as CEO he looked like a district production superintendent, always with the brim of his hat turned up.

We arrived in Findlay on a hot Saturday morning. Once we were seated in the conference room, the Marathon executives began filing in. Each was a portly five foot ten inches or so and weighed about 225 pounds. They all wore golf shirts with a pocket full of "freebie" cigars. The procession reminded me of U.S. Cavalry horses that walked through a hole in a wall to ensure uniform height and width.

Hoopman began, "You should be running this company." I wasn't prepared for that one. He paused to let it sink in. "That's what Kurt Wulff said," he went on, "that you could do a better job with our assets than I can." Kurt Wulff was a respected oil and gas industry analyst with DLJ. I knew if they were reading Kurt's stuff in Findlay, Ohio, then all of Big Oil's CEOs knew what Kurt was saying.

I laughed and said, "That isn't what we are here to talk about." We presented our deal in detail, but I wasn't convinced they grasped all of it. Then came lunch — sixteen-ounce sirloin steaks, mashed potatoes with gravy, rolls and butter, and a big slice of apple pie with ice cream. While his boys dozed, Hoop called me over to the side and told me that Marathon was interested. There was only one problem: they were afraid of hurting Marathon's image. I didn't think their image could get any worse, but I didn't say so.

About ten days later, Hoopman called and said that they wouldn't be able to join us. Ironically, at the same time Hoopman was turning us down, Marathon itself was a sitting duck for a takeover and was being stalked from all sides. Mobil jumped in first, but ultimately Marathon was taken over by U.S. Steel (now USX). If they had gone along with us, their fate might have been different.

By the summer of 1981, after months of searching for partners, we were close to signing two large independent oil companies, Louisiana Land and Freeport McMoRan. But Cities learned who our partners were and showed unusual speed in reacting. Lehman Brothers called the CEOs of both companies and gave them a little advice: if they didn't back away from Mesa pronto, Cities would make an offer for their companies. Our prospective partners dropped out.

We took a few months off to rethink our strategy. By the spring of 1982 our enthusiasm had returned; and we were still down more than $30 million on our stock position. By May we were getting close to putting together another partnership. This time it was a mixed bag: a silver mining company, a New York investment firm, a small independent oil company, and Southland Corporation, our largest partner, owner of the 7-Eleven convenience store chain. The first three would put up $500 million jointly, with Southland also providing $500 million.

Gaines and I met in Houston with a group of bankers to explain how the partners' $1 billion and the Cities stock already owned by Mesa would be the collateral for an additional $1.3 billion loan. The $2.3 billion would allow us to make an offer for 51 percent of Cities.

Tender offers, in which stockholders are asked to sell — "tender" — their stock for a premium price, had become the takeover strategy of the 1980s. The $2.3 billion would allow us to make an offer of $45 a share, a healthy $10 higher than the price of their stock.

Even with the premium, Cities' assets would be cheap. We would be getting its oil reserves for less than $5 a barrel. We wanted to make our offer on June 4, so with the offer date close, it was necessary to get the financing in place.

The bank meeting was to be confidential, but we should have known it wouldn't be. (It's never smart to trust a room full of bankers.) A week later, Cities knew everything except the names of our partners, the one detail we had withheld. We eventually learned that one of the bankers had given Cities our briefing book. With that kind of warning, its investment bankers had plenty of time to prepare a counterattack — or an attack.

Just days before our tender offer was to be launched, Cities struck. On May 28, it announced that it was planning to make an offer for Mesa.

In some respects, the offer was a joke. Mesa was selling for $16.75 a share, and Cities' offer was only $17. Nobody considered it a serious bid, just a warning shot across our bow. Coincident with the announcement, one of Lehman's short-boys called the CEO of Southland Corporation, Johnny Thompson, and threatened him with a tender offer if he joined Mesa.

The fact that an offer for Mesa was announced gave Cities a real advantage on timing. In a tender offer, the bidder has to wait twenty business days before paying for the stock that has been tendered. In this case, Cities would be able to buy our stock on June 28. Even if we could have begun our offer the next day — which was impossible since we didn't have our financing — we wouldn't be able to buy its stock before June 29. They could buy us before we could buy them.

Cities announced its offer on the Friday before Memorial Day. We spent the weekend scrambling to keep our fragile partnership alive, and strategizing to counteract its offer. There were long meetings at Baker & Botts with investment bankers and lawyers trying to figure out what we could do. I was taking a shower on Memorial Day when I thought, Why don't we try a bear hug? I got out of the shower and called Stillwell.

A bear hug is a ploy that puts pressure on a target company's directors. It is a "friendly" offer, made to the company's board rather than to the stockholders, and it is contingent on board approval. The difference here was that we couldn't just walk away if the Cities board turned us down; we would have to come up with something else — quick!

Given Cities' actions, the chances of being turned down were high. But a bear hug would generate press coverage, alert the company's stockholders that we were making an offer of sorts, and give us a little more time to get our tender offer under way. It was important to let everybody know we weren't taking a dive at the first sign of trouble. We had to proceed because of our ownership in Cities; we were down $30 million; and if we dropped our plan, it would be at least a $60 million loss.

I went directly to Baker & Botts's offices. "Is there any reason we can't do a bear hug?" I asked.

No one could come up with anything better, so we decided to give it a try. I placed the call to Waidelich of Cities.

"Chuck," I said, "our offer for Cities is $50 a share —"

He cut me off: "We're not interested, and it's not a formal offer anyway. It's not in writing."

"Hell," I said, "we'll have an offer to you in three hours."

"I don't want it."

"We've got to bring it to you now. The stockholders of both our companies need to know that we've made you an offer." And I added, "We'll make a public announcement, and I suppose you'll have to call your directors."

"I have no intention of calling them," Waidelich insisted. "We're not interested."

It didn't matter. My phone call had accomplished its purpose: an offer was on the table, and we would make it public.

We drafted a press release, giving the details of our offer. On the plane to New York, I called a handful of reporters to give them the news in time for their next editions. Now that the ball was rolling, New York was the place to be.

A football team's preparation for the Super Bowl must be a lot like the excitement of a hotly contested tender offer. A small group of people come together for brief, intense, nonstop activity, all of it directed toward a common goal.

Whatever is going on in the rest of the world seems insignificant compared with what happens in your battle, and a natural camaraderie develops. In this case I got very close to my five or six trusted advisers; I already knew their strengths and weaknesses, and they knew mine. We used a suite on the thirty-ninth floor of the Waldorf-Astoria Towers, with an uninspiring view. But no one had time to look out the window, anyway.

The pressure we'd felt in Houston over the previous three days increased dramatically on Tuesday morning, when I got a call from Johnny Thompson at Southland saying they had decided not to join us. The other three partners held firm, but the opposition had knocked out Southland, the key partner. There went $500 million.

Stillwell and I weren't surprised, but we were disappointed. Lehman's guy had made a "slam dunk" on us, and now we were in real trouble. The Cities tender offer had started that morning. All we had going was a bear hug, and they were going to turn it down. Even if by some miracle we did find new financing, Cities was ahead of us with its offer. That day was the low point in the deal; I felt helpless.

Then I thought of someone who might be able to help and called Joe Flom. I'd learned a few things in the Southland Royalty deal, and one was to have Joe on your side. Mesa had put him on retainer several years back.

We got to his office early Wednesday morning. Joe seemed glad to see us and a bit amused; he seemed to be saying "What took you so long?" As we explained our problem, he smoked his pipe. Finally he said, "Why don't you make a Dome-Conoco offer?"

It was a million-dollar suggestion, and that's about what he billed us. We wanted to kick ourselves for not having thought of such an obvious solution. The DuPont-Conoco merger had begun with a partial tender offer for Conoco by Dome Petroleum. Dome didn't want to acquire Conoco. It just wanted enough stock to trade it for Conoco's Canadian interests, so its tender offer was for 20 percent. It figured that if it got 20 percent, that would provide the leverage to make the trade.

I remembered the day Dome announced the results of its tender offer. I was playing golf with John McKinley of Texaco. I got a call from one of my people and was told that Dome had more than 50 percent of Conoco's stock, and it was still counting. So all Dome needed was enough money to pay for 51 percent of the stock, and it would have control of Conoco. I was surprised at how easy it was for Dome to get into such an advantageous position.

Flom had been heavily involved in the DuPont-Conoco deal. He had been working for Conoco, which may explain why he saw the broader implications of a partial tender offer.

Flom asked, "How much money can Mesa borrow?"

"About $600 million."

Our original plan had been to pay $50 a share if the offer was friendly, somewhat less if it was unfriendly. We decided to make a $45 offer. With our $600 million, we could buy an additional 15 percent, which would bring our ownership to 20 percent. It was safe to assume that the stockholders would tender much more than 15 percent to our offer. Then we could use the lure of the additional stock to attract partners.

It was a gutsy play — and our only prospect.

We needed to find partners who would put up the additional $2 billion for the controlling interest when it was tendered. Another hitch was that the partners had to commit to us even though Cities had a tender offer for Mesa, a complicating factor. They would naturally be hesitant, not knowing if we would even be around to finish the deal. I left the meeting with Flom thinking, for the first time in a week, that we were back on track again. Our launch date was Monday, June 7, only five days away.

Godfrey and David Batchelder, Mesa's controller, began pulling the consortium of banks together that would make us the $600 million loan. Stillwell and his team of lawyers — now from three different law firms — were working around the clock to get the tender offer documents ready for the Securities and Exchange Commission before the market opened on Monday. Lawyers and investment bankers like working for us because our people work right beside them. Our financial people and the investment bankers massaged the numbers and prepared the data to show prospective partners.

I held strategy sessions that ran deep into the night. Cities wasn't willing to talk to the press, but we were, and we were pleased when the press billed us as the underdogs. We saw ourselves as David out to slay Goliath, and the press more or less agreed. A couple of enterprising reporters took the time to compare our record with Cities', which was the best publicity possible.

I also used the interviews to deflect some of the fears aroused by Cities' management. The term "corporate raider" hadn't been used extensively, but there was a lot of talk from anonymous sources on the Cities side suggesting that if we won this battle, we would wipe out the company and do great harm to the Tulsa economy. I countered those remarks by promising that if Mesa took over Cities, Bea and I would move to Tulsa and keep Cities there. But an entrenched management fearing for their own jobs will do damn near anything. They use scare tactics on the employees and citizenry, and the smaller the town, the more effective they are.

After a weekend of near all-nighters with the lawyers, we launched our bid on Monday morning, then waited to see the market's reaction. If "the Street" is enthusiastic about an offer, it will be reflected in the stock price.

In our case, the volume of trading in Cities stock was very light. The price didn't respond because it already reflected some run-up caused by our bear hug. Despite our $10-a-share premium, the Street didn't believe we could pull it off. A few phone calls confirmed what we already suspected: the Cities tender in front of the Mesa offer gave the Street some problems.

I got a call from a *Wall Street Journal* reporter, who asked me if we had the bank financing lined up for our tender offer.

"Sure," I said.

"There are some who think you're bluffing," he said.

"Well, we didn't come to town on a load of watermelons," I told him.

"I don't understand."

I laughed and said, "I may not be from Wall Street, but I know what I'm doing."

I like to go into tough deals with smart, young, experienced players. Some of my men had had no previous playing time, but that wasn't totally necessary as long as there were a few veterans around. I have compared some of our young people to an eighteen-year-old on a battlefield: if he lasts thirty days, he's a veteran. We had some great ones at Mesa, led by David Batchelder, Sidney Tassin, and Drew Craig. The veteran support came from Bob Stillwell, Steve Massad, Joe Poff, and Joe Cialone, all of them with Baker & Botts. Their age spread was from twenty-five to thirty-eight (if you took out Stillwell, who was in his forties). It wasn't too many years back when Stillwell and I were the inexperienced ones.

In a high-stakes deal like this one, decisions must be made quickly, where in the normal course they might take days or weeks. There are always impending deadlines. You sleep and eat when you can. The room service charges are staggering; even with no liquor on the bill, they can run to $500 a day. The pressure to analyze and re-analyze never ends. When there's nothing to do but wait for the reaction to the latest strategy, some people play racquetball or jog or do something else physical to stay clearheaded.

Finally Cities called a press conference and Waidelich announced that his board had unanimously turned down our bear hug. I thought the board would at least meet with us — it was clearly in the best interest of their stockholders. If they ran us off, their stock would drop like a rock. But I still had some things to learn about what entrenched managements and boards will do to protect themselves.

Waidelich used the press conference to take some shots at me. He told the reporters that when the deal was over, and Cities owned Mesa, he hoped I would stay on. "I think Mr. Pickens could make a contribution," he said, and several of the reporters laughed. I wondered, if I would make a contribution after they acquired us, why I wouldn't make one now.

One reporter, Bob Cole of the *New York Times*, called to get my response. I said, "I suppose if Cities took over Mesa, then Chuck would offer me a job as the Southwest Kansas district geologist based out of Ulysses."

We had been in New York for nearly a week and a half; there was no doubt we were doing some good. By scrambling and improvising, we had kept ourselves in the game. We had initiated a partial tender offer for a company twenty times our size, and the press was starting to understand the deal.

But on two major points we were still behind the eight ball. The clock was ticking on the Cities offer. The way things stood, they would be able to buy our stock on June 28; we would have to wait until July 2 to buy their stock — if we were still around.

On June 8 we had a big change but not a big surprise: we had been expecting Cities to raise its offer and it did — from the anemic $17 offer to a coercive $21 offer for half of Mesa's stock. The second half would be merged out for Cities' securities, worth about $10 a share. Thus the average of this two-tier offer was only $15 per share, $2 less than the current price of the stock. This is about as coercive as you can get. This was unfair to Mesa's stockholders, and it had a particularly vindictive twist. The Mesa officers and directors would not be able to tender into the first step, leaving only the inferior second step.

Institutions owned a majority of Mesa's stock, and some of the savviest analysts in the world knew we were doing a good job. But no matter how much a pension fund manager liked me, he would have to tender to Cities' two-tier offer. If we couldn't slow them down, they would control Mesa before we had a chance to do anything.

The real scrambling began on the afternoon that Waidelich held his press conference. We had to come up with a way to sidetrack Cities' offer. And we did. It was a move that had never been done before, or even tried, but that didn't bother us.

We realized that if a new player came on the scene and made a competing tender offer, then ten days had to be added to Cities' original offer. Ordinarily, this regulation applies to a situation involving two or three companies with competing bids, as in the Mobil/Seagrams/DuPont battle for Conoco. But a tender offer didn't have to be for a controlling interest. Why couldn't it be for 10 percent of Mesa?

The more we talked about it, the more we liked it. If we could find a friendly company willing to make a tender offer for 10 percent of our stock, Cities' offer would be automatically extended an additional ten days. Our offer then would be in front of theirs, and the time advantage would be ours. The question was, Who could we find to make a partial tender for us?

When you've been in business for thirty years, you make some good friends. Most of them play by the same rules you do. You know you can trust them, and they know they can trust you.

I called on one such friend, an oilman, Tom Brown, founder of Tom Brown, Inc., in Midland, and explained our situation. This was no small thing I was asking Tom to do. A 10 percent tender would cost about $125 million, a substantial amount of money for a company the size of Tom Brown, Inc. There was every likelihood that Brown would make some money — that would have to be his reason for going along — but there was no way I could promise him anything.

If for some reason the deal got hung up in litigation or if Cities got us, there was no telling what would happen to Tom. When I talked to him, I explained the risks. I told him if he couldn't do it, I would understand. Brown never batted an eye. "When do we get started?" he asked.

Having lined up Tom Brown — now identified as Buffalo Bill (only in part for security reasons) — I turned to my other problem, finding a $2 billion partner or partners. It seemed I had spent most of my working life looking for money and partners. But I didn't have much experience looking for a couple of billion!

If we didn't put it together quickly, we would let our stockholders down, and they would be stuck with a coercive two-tier offer.

It was like a scene from *High Noon.* We were starting to count the hours until the showdown. I was on the phone until late at night and all the next day. I called friends, like Hugh Liedtke at Pennzoil and Sid Bass from Fort Worth, as well as more casual acquaintances like John Harbert from Birmingham. I called big oil companies, independents, and companies that had nothing to do with oil. I was desperate to find a partner.

My pitch was this: partners would be buying oil in the ground at less than $5 a barrel. With oil above $30, and industry-wide "finding costs" at $15 a barrel, it was a great deal. They wouldn't have to put up a dime until they knew that the Cities stock was tendered, ready to be bought. They wouldn't have to worry about Cities' money-losing divisions or the complications of trying to integrate Cities into their own operation. They were buying a part of the reserves and none of the problems.

Interest was high, but it was hard to tell the serious players from the tire-kickers. We had to get a second suite at the Waldorf to show the deal to two groups at once. At least 75 percent of those invited showed up — Allied, Sohio, you name it. I know some of them just wanted to see what we were up to. We were doing some unusual things, and it was natural for them to be inquisitive.

By the weekend, we had a handful of serious players. The best prospect was Occidental Petroleum. Its CEO, Dr. Armand Hammer, was approached by Donaldson, Lufkin and Jenrette, and the doctor checked us out with his friend Joe Flom. We were invited to L.A. for a meeting and arrived on Monday, June 14, at about midnight. We were tired — it was three o'clock in the morning, Eastern time — but we went directly to Occidental's headquarters. We were shepherded into the executive suite and a conference room overflowing with people. For a minute I thought I was back in Britain, getting ready to negotiate with BNOC.

At the head of the table was Dr. Hammer, looking as tired as I felt. I wanted to get right down to business while I still had some adrenaline flowing. The people in the room had heard the basics from DLJ, so I opened with a few remarks on our strategy and how the partnership would be structured. I said, "We need to decide tonight whether we're going to get together or not."

Occidental's number two man, Bob Abboud, stood up. All the others had their coats off and ties loosened, but Abboud wore a pin-stripe, double-breasted suit that didn't have a wrinkle in it. He talked for about twenty minutes, explaining in detail the weaknesses of our offer. All around the room, eyes were fixed on the ceiling or the floor. There was one set of eyes that was not directed at anything, however — the doctor's. His were closed; he had been asleep for twenty minutes.

When Abboud concluded, I said, "Bob, our time is short — we can't change the structure. We've made our offer, and we're going to get over fifty percent of their stock. We need a partner to help us. Are you interested?"

Abboud started to lecture again.

"Look," I said, cutting him off, "if the deal is that bad, why don't we just go to bed like Dr. Hammer." I turned toward Hammer, who had started snoring. "I'm tired, he's tired, everybody's tired. Let's just forget the whole thing."

"Oh, no," Abboud said. "I think we can live with it."

After an hour of constructive discussion, I was pretty sure we had our partner about lined up. For the first time since this battle had begun, we were looking pretty good.

On the way back to New York I stopped in Houston, to serve as emcee at a big fund-raiser for Governor Bill Clements. I was the state campaign chairman for the governor's reelection bid, and this dinner had been scheduled for some time. President Reagan and President Ford were there to help. I had had about four hours' sleep in the last twenty-four and was more than a little weary. I had gotten so wrapped up in my own deal that I thought the rest of the world had been following it as intently as I had. When I made a couple of remarks about the Cities deal, one got a few laughs, the other a few groans.

The next morning we were on our way to New York, and suddenly, it seemed, the Cities deal was over. Or so we thought.

We didn't need partners anymore, and we didn't need Buffalo Bill, either, because on Thursday, June 17, Gulf Oil announced a $63-a-share cash offer for 100 percent of Cities. I guess it had taken Gulf's bureaucracy that long to evaluate the information Godfrey and I had given them more than a year earlier. The announcement also said that Cities' board had agreed to accept the offer. It was an unbelievable offer.

That made Gulf the so-called white knight. In the jargon of Wall Street, that was a company solicited by the management under attack to top the hostile offer. I couldn't imagine Gulf's ever being called a white knight, given its record. White knights are supposedly friendlier, but usually there isn't much difference. However, they sometimes cut special deals with the management and give some therapeutic help to their egos.

This white knight had an ulterior motive. Gulf was a bloated bureaucracy in a declining industry, and the management knew they were going to have to cut 20,000 employees. It was a coincidence that Cities had 20,000 employees; it wasn't a coincidence that Gulf's management saw a solution to their overstaffing. Gulf's bureaucracy would be safe for a while.

Critics said that I had "driven" Cities into a merger that was a poor deal for its employees. We were trying to take Cities over, and, had we succeeded, we would have moved to Tulsa. (It wouldn't have been feasible to move Cities to Amarillo.) Mesa had only 900 employees, so there would have been a minimum of discomfort for the Cities people.

Cities ran into the arms of Gulf because it was probably tipped off about Buffalo Bill. And it knew we were close to getting a partner. It decided to run for help. Its management never understood what was going on and made little effort to learn. They just followed the instructions given by their investment bankers and outside legal counsel. Their bankers had structured a fee arrangement that made a white knight the most profitable outcome for themselves. Cities had been set up for a sale by its own investment bankers.

The stockholders of Cities would do well. The Gulf offer was almost $20 a share more than ours, and it was triple what the stock would have been if Cities had fended us off.

Even if we had had the money to compete, the offer was too much. It was time for us to throw our hand in and look for another game. We had lost and we were unhappy about it, but it wasn't a total loss. We were going to make some money on the 5 percent of Cities we owned. I was proud of my team, and it was a good experience for all of us.

By late Thursday afternoon we had called Tom Brown. The only thing to be decided was whether we would negotiate with Cities to sell our block or tender it to Gulf. We all assumed that this detail could be wrapped up the next day, and we'd be back in Amarillo in time for dinner. We thought the deal was over.

I woke up the next morning with a hangover. Bea and I had gone to "21" with some of our group, then Stillwell and I had stayed up until three in the morning, rehashing the deal. I had presumed the day would consist of a little mopping up, but before it was over, Mesa came very close to being acquired.

As we started packing to leave I got a call. I discovered that Cities' investment bankers, primarily First Boston, had encouraged the company to stick with its tender offer for Mesa. That way, Cities could take over Mesa while Gulf was taking over Cities. My source, who was close to the Cities board, had learned that First Boston's oil analyst had flown in from Denver the night before and was giving an analysis on Mesa to the Cities board that morning.

Their investment bankers wanted Cities to take over Mesa because it would mean an additional fee for very little additional work. And it would be one for the record books — the first "double takeover" in history. It would be dubbed a "cluster shot" by Wall Street.

Somebody must have been a helluva salesman to get the Cities board to go along with such a plan. Waidelich must have realized that if Cities didn't drop its tender offer, we would do anything to break up the Gulf-Cities merger, tying it up in litigation. Why would they take a chance on messing up a $5 billion deal?

There could be only one reason — revenge. "First Boston," my source told me, "is trying to exploit the human emotion of people like Waidelich, who want to stick it to Boone Pickens."

I couldn't believe they were serious; it was inconceivable to me that the Cities board would go along. They were weak, but not that weak — or were they?

"I can believe it," said Flom. "After all, there's something in this for First Boston, and they're selling hard."

By late morning, things had gotten pretty tense. It looked as though Cities might have the last laugh. I counted fourteen people in our suite, including Bea, Stillwell, Godfrey, Batchelder, and Tassin. Nobody said much; matters were no longer in our hands.

I said, "You know they can picture this little scene over here, and they're loving it."

Flom suggested calling Tom Brown. If Cities did decide to continue its tender offer, Brown was our best prospect for sidetracking it. But if Brown came in at this point, there would be no upside for him, since the ten-day reprieve his offer would give us didn't mean we would get Cities. Cities was going to Gulf.

I called Brown. He was out, but would call back shortly. As I sat there in the crowded suite, I mentally removed myself from my surroundings and started thinking. What if Gulf had made this generous offer just to scuttle the Tom Brown strategy? Even if Tom came in now to help, all he could do was give us a few days.

But wasn't Gulf going to zap Cities? Well, maybe, and maybe not. Gulf had been devious when we met with them in February 1981. Did they call Waidelich then and start setting the stage for this bizarre conclusion? Were they that smart? Was the grand plan to shut Boone Pickens up, maybe for good, after Gulf saw itself as possibly being the next target? We had laid it out for them in Pittsburgh, after all; the plan would fit a dozen big oil companies, Gulf included.

I decided they weren't that smart. Cities may not have been surprised by the Buffalo Bill rumors and had a plan to take care of them. Gulf would make a generous offer; then, after evaluating the Cities assets, they would decide the offer was too generous. Gulf could then back out, but only after Boone Pickens had been buried.

I had an idea. "Why don't I call Jimmy Lee?"

If I could get Lee on the phone, I thought, I might be able to convince him that Cities' plan to pursue its tender offer for Mesa could be dangerous for his deal. Everyone thought it was worth a try. This time, there were no watermelon jokes — in fact, no jokes at all — as I placed the call.

Lee wasn't in.

It was creeping toward noon. The phone rang and I grabbed the receiver. It was Tom Brown. I explained our predicament and said, "We may need your help again."

Tom told me his banker was on his way to Europe and all his people had scattered. He had tried to help when it made sense, but he was out now. I didn't blame him.

The mood in the room went from grim to very grim. The stark reality of the situation became clear. If Cities really wanted Mesa, there was no way we could stop it. I tried Lee again, without success.

One of the investment bankers said, in a timid voice, "Maybe it's time to start thinking about a white knight."

"No!" I said angrily. "We're not going to do that unless we're really out of options, and we're not there yet. Hell, I haven't talked to Lee. Gulf is running this thing, aren't they?"

"It's their call," said Flom.

Just then, the phone rang. It was Marty Lipton, the outside counsel for Cities and a lawyer who had made a lucrative career out of defending entrenched managements. He wanted Flom, who went into the bedroom to talk. At last we were going to find out what Cities was up to.

Flom emerged a few minutes later with a proposal. To get Cities to drop its tender offer, we had to either sell our stock back to Cities at cost, thereby wiping out any profit, or else sell it on the open market for a profit and — here was the kicker — pay Cities $35 million for the privilege of doing so.

"Basically," said Flom, "it's a $35 million holdup. The silver lining is, they don't want you. They only want to embarrass you."

They were gambling that we wouldn't bet Mesa to save $35 million.

Flom added, "And you're betting they won't take a chance of screwing up their deal for $35 million."

Stillwell nodded in agreement. "It's down to a blinking contest."

The $35 million penalty was to teach me a lesson for trying to play in a league with the big boys. Waidelich wanted to say he had forced Boone Pickens to pay $35 million to keep Mesa independent. But there was no way I was going to pay Cities a damn thing. There would be no blinks from our side.

Ten minutes later the phone rang again; it was Jimmy Lee. The room got very quiet. "Jimmy," I began, "let me bring you up to date. Cities is asking us to give them $35 million just to get our tit out of the wringer. We're quite willing, as Cities' largest stockholder, to endorse your offer, but it looks like their $35 million demand may jeopardize your $5 billion deal."

It was clear from Lee's response that he didn't know what was going on, which was no surprise.

"You know that I'll fight if I have to," I continued. "So if the $35 million penalty stays, we're going to throw everything at you, including the kitchen sink. It's going to cost somebody a helluva lot more than $35 million." I added a final note: "What we have here are some real amateurs, Jimmy, and they are vindictive. What we need is a cool head like yours to say 'Let's get this damn thing over with.' "

I smiled as I hung up.

"Lee says they're stretching for this deal at $63," I told the group. "He isn't interested in Mesa. That's just a wild idea of First Boston's."

My hangover was starting to disappear.

A few minutes later we got another call and a new, much improved proposal. Lipton told Flom they would buy our Cities stock for $55 a share, with no mention of a $35 million fee.

I asked Batchelder to give me a quick estimate of our pre-tax net. He ran a few numbers and came up with $30 million.

"Better than a punch in the eye with a sharp stick," I said.

Things were starting to be fun again.

I couldn't totally discount the fact that the $55 offer was still $8 a share less than Gulf's $63 offer. But after talking with Lee, the Gulf offer didn't sound as firm as the press release indicated. I could imagine Gulf's pulling out of the deal, causing the Cities stock to go into the tank.

It didn't take long for us to make up our minds. Flom phoned Lipton and accepted the $55 offer.

It took from two in the afternoon until seven to draft the agreement. Stillwell, Godfrey, and Batchelder put everything in final form at Wachtell Lipton's offices.

This was Gaines Godfrey's last Mesa deal. A few months later, he resigned with a brief statement: "Boone, you told me ten years ago if I would leave the Continental Illinois Bank and come with Mesa and work hard that I would make a lot of money: I am leaving because I have made a lot of money, and I don't want to work that hard anymore."

I had seen it coming. Gaines had always been a good professional and had shown a lot of guts in the past by sticking with his analysis. He was worth a lot of money and was ready to slow down, and I didn't blame him. Batchelder was ready to move up to the starting team. When they are ready, you either get the young ones in the game or they'll leave you.

I waited at the Waldorf with Bea and a handful of others. Then the lawyers called to say it was over; it was time to go home, everything was signed.

Bea and I walked out of the Waldorf, and when we got to the limo that would take us to the airport I told everybody good-bye. We turned to get into the car, and then started to laugh.

In the back seat somebody had put a big watermelon.

Six weeks later, Gulf pulled out of the deal. Cities' stock took a real dive, to the low $30s — a $2 billion hickey for their stockholders. Gulf claimed that antitrust problems had proved too great an obstacle, but no one believed them; Gulf's management had proved again how weak they were.

A week later, on August 13, Cities announced that they were merging with another company — Dr. Hammer's Occidental Petroleum! Dr. Hammer had finally awakened. This time the price was $53 a share, making it a $4 billion deal.

I'm sure Gulf and Occidental had used at least a part of our evaluation of Cities. You would have thought somebody could have sent us a thank-you note.

# · 15 ·

# *Time Out*

Between the end of the Cities deal in June 1982 and the beginning of the Gulf investment in August 1983, we were busy at Mesa. It was a period of restructuring based on the fundamental changes we had predicted for the oil industry.

The major oil companies were still generating more cash than they could put to good use; the industry was "overcapitalized." Vast sums were being squandered on frontier exploration, refinery improvements, and disastrous diversifications. Thanks to OPEC, the money was still pouring in, covering up a lot of sins.

At Mesa we reduced our exploration spending, pared back our staff, and closed some of our field offices. We sold assets that were least likely to appreciate. Cities Service was a good learning experience, and we continued searching for undervalued situations. The industry was moving away from the technical people, toward the financial people, and I thought Mesa could profit from the change.

Many of our senior managers were asked to step aside to make way for the younger players, and most did so quite willingly. "We've had our turn," as one vice president said. "Now it's their turn." Thanks to our benefit plans, they all left with good net worths, in most cases more than $1 million.

The financial group was now led by David Batchelder, then thirty-three, and his younger associate Sidney Tassin, then twenty-seven, both accountants formerly with big accounting firms. They had ideas, initiative, and a lot of energy. In most corporations, people like Batchelder and Tassin are considered too young; they are seen as a threat to their superiors. Over the years, however, organizations lose their aggressiveness when they can't hold their best young people.

Mesa now had the entrepreneurial spirit I had hoped to encourage, as well as vision and confidence. We all had a lot invested in Mesa, and we were willing to tie our compensation to the results of our efforts.

When you are small and want to play the big boys, you better know how to block and tackle, and we were about to become the best at blocking and tackling in corporate America.

Then we decided to make an offer for General American Oil (GAO), a Dallas independent that was much older but about the same size as Mesa. The offer was a "no-brainer." GAO had good reserves, which we wanted. But if we got outbid, there was a consolation prize.

Mesa had owned 8 percent of GAO since 1976. Several years earlier, we had issued bonds that gave the holders the right to convert them into the GAO stock we owned if they wanted. We were obligated to hold the stock as long as the bondholders had that right. But the price of GAO had dropped as a result of the industry's decline, and it was unlikely to recover. When the bonds matured, Mesa would have to pay them off and would be left holding GAO stock that wouldn't be worth a fraction of what we had paid for it.

When I explained the situation to my people, I didn't have to suggest a solution. They had already been working on the problem. The only way to avoid a sure loss was to make an offer for GAO. It was incredible that GAO's management didn't see it coming. We put everything together on our own and waited until the week before we made our offer to tell our investment bankers, Morgan Stanley. They were delighted to get the business, for GAO was not part of the establishment that Morgan caters to.

In late December 1982, we offered $40 a share for GAO when it was in the low $30s. It was the same old story: GAO's executives owned practically no stock and weren't interested in this opportunity to do something for their stockholders. The company had no management or future; it was dead in the water. A GAO vice president told a *Wall Street Journal* reporter who called him for a comment that he didn't take such calls at home, and hung up on him. When I read this story, I knew we would have an edge with the press, even though this time we were not the underdog.

GAO hired First Boston and launched a self-tender. We were studying the self-tender when we heard rumors that somebody else was moving into the deal. Our group was working in a Morgan Stanley conference room when one of their guys came in and said, "They're friends of Boone's, and they won't surface with a better offer if you don't want them to." He knew who the bidder was but wouldn't say. (For what we were paying him, he should have told us, but the mystery company was also a client of Morgan's.)

I said, "Tell them that we want GAO, so if they're friendly, go away." When he was gone, I commented that the mystery company would become unfriendly in a couple of hours. I missed it by thirty minutes.

The second call revealed that it was Phillips Petroleum and that it was serious. I wanted to talk to its CEO, but he was shooting quail in Georgia and wouldn't be back at the lodge until evening. Bill Douce was an avid hunter. I knew he would get in to the lodge at about six o'clock, have a Scotch and water, talk about the kill for half an hour, take a shower, and have another drink; maybe then he would be ready to talk.

"We have time to go eat," I said. "It will take him two or three hours."

When Douce finally called, he said, "Boone, we've been pals for a long time, and I really hate to do this to you, but I have no choice."

"Sure you do. Don't do it."

"Phillips is a big company," he continued, "and we have to put some reserves on the books, bad."

"Bill, why don't you let us have this one and we will take you as a partner and go after a big one?"

He was interested, but wouldn't back off on GAO.

I tried to get him to take a jack-up rig off our hands. After all, it was Mesa that had teed up GAO for them. He turned me down, but agreed to pick up our expenses. When I told him they came to $15 million he screamed, saying we had paid too much to the investment bankers and lawyers. I couldn't have agreed more with him about the bankers. (In 1985, Phillips paid the same ones, as well as First Boston, more than $40 million to keep Mesa's offer away from their own stockholders.)

If he didn't agree to pay the $15 million expenses, I told him, we would top his offer, going from $45 to $47.50.

"Boone," he said, "are you going to try to outmoney Phillips Petroleum? We can blow your ass out of the tub. We'll raise your $47.50 to $50." Then he gave me a two-drink laugh.

"You're missing the point," I said. "If we force you to go to $50 a share, that will cost your stockholders over $100 million."

"What in the hell are you talking about?"

"Multiply GAO's twenty-four million shares by $5 per share and it comes out to $120 million."

There was a long pause. Finally he said, "You wouldn't do something chickenshit like that, would you?"

"Just try me."

Even Douce, an engineer, could see the merits of my argument and agreed to the $15 million. I had the distinct feeling that he and I just might cross paths again.

Wachtell Lipton was preparing a letter setting out the terms of what Douce and I had agreed to. We all sat around Morgan's office, waiting for it to arrive and speculating on whether Phillips would try to get us to agree to a standstill. If we agreed, it would mean that we could not make an offer for Phillips in the future.

The letter showed up and was read out loud: when it came to the standstill, there was no mention of Phillips. We couldn't believe it. One of our men said that they didn't have the guts to try it.

We were on the edge of several other deals — Mobil's attempt to take over Marathon Oil, a battle finally won by U.S. Steel; the

Texaco-Getty merger; and the fight for the control of Superior Oil, which was eventually acquired by Mobil — looking for a way to make some money. The transactions were immense, and that eliminated a lot of players. Our few hundred million was not much more than an ante in some of these games.

As the Mobil-Marathon battle got under way, Mobil was getting horrible press, as usual. If the combination of these two integrated giants could be worked out, they would surely face antitrust problems before it was over.

We devised a solution to these problems, and I called Alex Massad, Mobil's executive vice president, the number three man in the company. I found him in Austin, Texas, and said I had an idea that might move the Marathon deal off high center. He said he would be in Austin for only two hours, so we flew down and met in Mobil's plane, a big G-2.

Our plan was for Mobil to put up $4 billion for the part they wanted — Marathon's giant Yates field in West Texas. We would take a small piece of Yates, maybe 10 percent, and all the other assets, including the refinery and marketing operation. Mobil would sidestep the antitrust problem. The clincher was for Mobil to step back and let us make the offer, for the deal had a lot better chance with us out front.

You'd have thought I'd tossed a polecat into his big airplane. It took Alex a few minutes to regain his composure. "That's pretty interesting," he said. You could tell it was inconceivable for Mobil to let Mesa front the deal. He promised to get back in touch.

The next day Mobil announced that it was taking a partner. I called Massad. "I see you liked our idea," I said.

"Oh, no," he replied. "Our partner is Amerada Hess." Their deal looked an awful lot like the structure I had shown him in Austin, but he denied it. "We've been working on this a long time," he said.

Even with Amerada as its new partner, Mobil couldn't bring itself to take a back seat. "Alex," I said at the end of the conversation, "you're never going to make a deal because of Mobil's image."

He didn't like hearing it. And in the end, U.S. Steel bagged Marathon and the giant Yates field.

With Superior Oil, we were just an investor looking for a place to make a buck. The pressure for change was being applied from within instead of from the outside — a nice difference. What got my attention was Willametta Keck Day, a dissident Superior shareholder, threatening to wage a proxy fight. She was unhappy with Superior's board and wanted a plan that would make a change of control easier to accomplish.

Mrs. Day was the daughter of Superior's founder and owned a big piece of the company, so this was no idle threat. She was also the sister of Howard Keck, who had recently stepped down as CEO after many years but was still on the board. All of this made things pretty messy — and, in an odd way, more appealing. Family feuds over how companies are run usually lead to a decision to sell the company.

We took a position in Superior, buying 4 percent of its stock for $135 million, an average of $34 a share.

Once we announced our support, I got calls from large stockholders asking for advice, and we probably influenced several million shares to go along with Mrs. Day. Our involvement annoyed our investment banker, Morgan Stanley, which was also Superior's banker. Morgan's people called and asked me not to vote with Mrs. Day. "She doesn't know what she's doing, and she's going to lose," they said.

Over several weeks, Morgan decided we were the swing vote. To get me to change our vote the day of the stockholders' meeting, I was offered a plum: I could meet and have lunch with Howard Keck! With our help Mrs. Day won her proxy fight.

Mrs. Day's lawyer, Jerry Carlton, called and asked if I would meet with her in Santa Barbara, California. Mrs. Day turned out to be a charming lady — except when she got on the subject of her brother, Howard. At the mention of his name, her blood pressure went straight up. After a few minutes, she ushered Bea and me through her home and out to the pool house because, she said, Howard had bugged her house. We talked about different ways the management might add value to the Superior stock, but it clearly was not the topic closest to her heart.

She talked about her feud with Howard. Jokingly, I had told Bea earlier that it probably went back to their childhood; maybe Howard had strangled her pet cat. That proved to be close to the truth. The animal turned out to be a pet ostrich, and he had strangled it by stretching its neck through a picket fence and putting an orange in its throat. This incident, Mrs. Day said, had taken place when she was four years old, and they had never gotten along since.

"Look, Mrs. Day," I said, "I don't hate Howard. I'm just trying to figure out how we can all make some money."

She smiled sweetly. "Don't worry, Mr. Pickens, I hate Howard enough for both of us."

Later I said to Bea, "We have to get out of this deal. All she cares about is revenge. She'll burn the barn down to get Howard."

I had two meetings with Superior's CEO, Fred Ackman, to talk about getting the company's stock price up, but my heart wasn't in it. So, when we got a call from Superior offering to buy back our shares for $42 — only if we sold by the next day — we took it. We made $30 million on the transaction. Afterward, Mrs. Day called me a Lear jet cowboy. That's what you get for jumping into a family fight.

Next came Getty. That deal didn't make us a penny because we never bought a share of Getty stock. By now I was well known as a critic of entrenched managements and a vocal advocate of the stockholders. Big Oil didn't like Boone Pickens. Doing business with Mesa was seen as a traitorous act among the Good Ol' Boys. But stockholders were another story. They loved me, particularly those who had stock in the companies we were involved with.

Gordon Getty was an unhappy and very large stockholder in a very large company. The son of J. Paul Getty, he was one of the wealthiest men in the world. The cornerstone of his fortune was a family trust that owned 40 percent of Getty Oil. Though he had not followed in his late father's footsteps — he was an accomplished musician and composer, not an oilman — he realized that Getty's management was among the poorest in the industry.

I met with Gordon at the Beverly Wilshire Hotel in Los Angeles, after calling to thank him for a nice remark that he had made about my looking out for stockholders. He seemed to share my feelings about professional managers in corporate America. We touched on a multitude of subjects, all related. I remember Gordon's asking me, "How can I get Sidney to go along?" Sidney Petersen was Getty's CEO.

I said, "Get his ownership up so that he thinks like a stockholder."

Our meeting ended on a friendly note, and we agreed to exchange ideas in the future. In April 1983, I called Gordon and asked to see him in San Francisco. He was agreeable. Bea and I and Michael, our eighteen-month-old grandson, went to San Francisco the evening before. I met early the following morning with our investment bankers, Morgan Stanley. The Mesa financial team had developed a plan to maximize values at Getty and I explained it to the bankers.

We went from the hotel to Gordon's home, overlooking the ocean. The Morgan people discussed the virtues of the royalty trust, how it would put tremendous value into the hands of the stockholders — the rightful owners of the company. It was interesting to see Morgan selling the royalty trust idea; a few months later, they did an about-face and said the royalty trust did not create value.

The idea being presented to Gordon Getty was a complicated plan involving the creation of a large royalty trust that would have been spun off through Mesa. On paper, Mesa would take over Getty Oil. I assured Gordon, however, that our management had no interest in staying on with the combined companies. We knew this would be necessary to get Getty's management to even listen to the idea.

Gordon didn't understand all the intricacies of the proposal, but he did understand the part about putting 50 points on the Getty stock. He asked me to take the idea to Sidney Petersen.

I called Petersen. He refused to see me unless Mesa and I signed a standstill agreement. We agreed not to buy any Getty stock for several years, thus eliminating ourselves as a potential acquirer. This was stupid, but it was the only way we could talk to Getty's management, so we reluctantly signed.

If somebody came to see me with a plan to put 50 points, even 5 points, on our stock, I would hug him. But these guys wanted only the standstill agreement. A secret meeting was set up in Los Angeles. It took our group about half an hour to go through the presentation. When we finished, I asked if there were any questions. I expected quite a few, since the deal was both innovative and complicated.

Petersen asked, "Has Gordon Getty seen this material?"

I could see the muscles in his jaw tense up when he heard my response.

"What is the date on Gordon's presentation manual?"

"May," I said, and that was it. Petersen's was dated June. Oh, his lawyers asked a few questions, but they weren't interested in our deal.

As David Batchelder, Bill Griffith, the tax expert with Baker & Botts, and I walked through the lobby of the Century Plaza Hotel and out into the bright June sunlight, I said, "That company won't be around very long."

If I hadn't signed the standstill agreement, I would have bought a carload of Getty stock. It was a cinch.

If you were ever looking for proof of the contempt in which managements hold stockholders, Getty would be Exhibit A. There could be no doubt that the management and the board saw their largest shareholder as a growing problem. During the last board meeting before hostilities broke out, someone called Gordon out of the meeting to take a phone call. While he was gone, the rest of the board voted to participate in a lawsuit filed to depose him as the trustee of the family trust. In other words, the management in cahoots with the board was taking over the company.

We took the same idea that we had taken to Getty to John

Swearingen, the CEO of Standard Oil of Indiana (now Amoco). It was the same presentation: large royalty trust spinoff; Mesa would be the surviving company on paper only; the Mesa team rides off into the sunset and leaves the management in place. The results would have added between 30 and 50 points to Amoco's stock.

There were two compelling reasons why I thought Swearingen would be interested. First, John, unlike other oil company CEOs, owned a lot of stock in his company — over 500,000 shares — more than any other major oil company CEO. Second, he was only a few months away from retirement, so this was his last chance to cash in. It seemed that this would give him a powerful incentive to do something for the shareholders.

No matter how many shares he owned, he couldn't make the mental switch from manager to stockholder. He cleared his throat, put down his pipe, and said, "Boone, we have a different situation here than you do at Mesa. Our stockholders are different from yours."

"I don't understand," I said.

"You see, we have some regular stockholders, which you also have. But then we have long-term stockholders. And we even have future stockholders whom we have to consider."

I was floored. "John, you're talking about people that haven't bought the stock yet?"

"Yes," he said, taking another puff from the pipe. "That's the difference in our companies. We have future stockholders to consider."

In fairness to Swearingen, who is a good friend, I will say that he kept the material for thirty days, then told me it wouldn't work because of Standard Oil's foreign tax credits.

As we walked out of the meeting, I told Batchelder, "We should call a hundred of his regular and long-term stockholders and ask them if they would prefer to have thirty to fifty points on their stock or to leave it for the future shareholders."

All these warm-ups had prepared us for the main event.

· 16 ·

# *Gulf I*

## The Seven Sisters . . .

It was a cold, wet day in December 1983, and I was hurrying from the parking lot to the Baker & Botts offices in One Shell Plaza in Houston. I had just arrived from New York with a couple of investment bankers. A man drove by with his window down and his arm stuck out, fist clinched, and yelled, "Go get 'em, Boone!" It was an old pal, Hunter Martin.

It was Gulf Oil he wanted me to get, the sixth largest oil company in America. One of the fabled Seven Sisters, it was founded at the turn of the century by the legendary Andrew Mellon. Gulf had $20 billion in assets and $30 billion in annual revenues plus 40,000 employees. A company of such size and stature was considered immune to outside pressure, yet it was running from something.

Gulf Oil was the biggest and most highly publicized deal of my life. It resulted in the largest corporate merger of all time — $13.2 billion — and 400,000 Gulf shareholders reaped profits of $6.5 billion. There had never been anything like it in the annals of Wall Street. Upstart Mesa changed the whole dynamics of mergers and became a landmark in the history of acquisitions. Why it began in Amarillo, Texas, instead of New York said volumes about the corporate system that Mesa shook up. Everyone else was looking to the past; the Wall Street firms had for years coveted their work with organizations like Gulf and were afraid of offending these old clients. Mesa appeared on the scene with new determination, an ability to devise its own financing, and an entrepreneur's view of how to restructure the lumbering hallowed giants.

The stakes for Mesa were very high. This is the moment I described at the outset of this book. Despite our profit in the Cities Service deal, we were deep in the hole in our Gulf of Mexico operation. We had to make $300 million — fast — or we were going to be a different company. But now we had a plan, and despite its boldness it was not as dangerous as it looked to some people.

There are two common misconceptions about the Gulf deal. The first is that because of Gulf's enormous size, the transaction presented an incalculable risk. In the press, the deal was perceived as the business equivalent of a high-wire act without a net. We were going against a company twenty times our size. Some people thought we were nuts, others, that we would be smashed against the wall. We knew we might be wasting our time, but our financial risk was slight since our investment was in Gulf stock, which we knew was selling at a fraction of its underlying value. We might take a small loss, but there was no way we were going to lose our whole stack.

The second misconception is that we were trying to acquire Gulf as we had Cities. They represented two entirely different situations. With Cities, we had gone after the company. With Gulf, the prospect of acquiring the giant was unthinkable; we were just trying to get the management to do something for the shareholders, namely, get the price up. We were better prepared after the experience with Cities and GAO. We had used the time to groom the team, rethink our objectives and methods, and come up with a better strategy. Our near-escape in the Cities deal had taught us to protect ourselves against a counter–tender offer.

Also — and this was a crucial point in assessing risk — Gulf was even more undervalued than Cities. Knowing we were buying at a discount gave us comfort and confidence. The odds of our making money on Gulf were a lot better than exploring for oil and gas at a time of plunging prices and excess supply.

For the first time, the world was about to see that size alone no longer protected an entrenched and stagnant management. With cleverness and tenacity, and a well-thought-out strategy, a small company could go after a big one and make something happen. Companies who were chronic underachievers would no longer be safe from so-called corporate raiders just because of their size. Tremors from the Gulf deal would run through every other industry.

The Gulf deal made me a controversial figure in corporate America, and clearly it changed my life. One oil company director told me not long afterward, "We spend more time talking about Boone Pickens at our board meetings than anything else."

My name became synonymous with "corporate takeover," which led to attacks from the Business Roundtable and an avalanche of favorable mail from stockholders. I became a lightning rod in the ensuing debate over the value of mergers, a role I was happy to assume.

But we didn't take a position in Gulf Oil because we wanted a landmark deal, or because I wanted to become a celebrity, or because we hoped to create a national debate about takeovers. The reason was more mundane. We did it because Gulf was an undervalued company in the public marketplace, and we needed to make some money.

We had made $20 million here, $40 million there. You don't flick off deals that generate that kind of profit. Believe me, we were happy to have the money from our previous transactions. But by the spring of 1983 it was becoming clear that we needed to do something bigger — much bigger. It was time for the big mamou. If we didn't pull something off and the industry continued to head south, we were going to be in trouble.

Our losses from the Gulf of Mexico and the failure to reduce our exploration budget fast enough were squeezing us. Twenty-million-dollar deals were not going to bail us out — we needed

$300 million. And we knew one place that offered that opportunity — the major oil companies, whose stocks sold at a fraction of their real value. They had been undervalued for fifty years in the marketplace, although the managements claimed otherwise.

The image that we would get for jumping on a major didn't bother me; the big oil companies had been trying to put the independents out of business forever. Maybe this was one time the fireplug would piss on the dog.

Our original plan never suggested that we would attempt to acquire Gulf. Instead, we were confident that the fundamental changes facing the industry would cause such companies to restructure, perhaps in the form of stock repurchases or the creation of royalty trusts or limited partnerships. This action would in turn create substantially higher values for all stockholders.

When we made our original filing with the SEC — as we were required to do when our ownership reached 5 percent — we listed our Gulf holdings as being "for investment purposes." This was true. But Gulf's management panicked. The wise thing would have been for them to invite us in to talk. It's too bad they didn't; we had some good ideas. Gulf's management had substantial stock options, and they should have listened to anything that would increase the stock price, but egos overpowered reason.

This is what the Business Roundtable calls raiding. The way I see it, when you invest $1 billion in a company's stock — as we did in Gulf's — you're not a raider, you're a very large stockholder. You should enjoy all the rights of ownership, including the right to an open dialogue with management about changes that could benefit all shareholders. We weren't asking for anything special. We just wanted to talk. But based on my experience, I was getting more realistic and didn't expect Big Oil to invite us in. If we'd learned anything, it was that managements hated to look at somebody else's ideas — the "not invented here" syndrome.

We realized early that, no matter what company we invested in, the chances were we would be identified as "hostile." It would require us to protect our investment with expensive tactics like a proxy fight or a tender offer. But if we were lucky we could make $200 million to $300 million without a scrap. That would depend on Gulf's cooperation in adopting some of our proposals. Jimmy Lee, Gulf's CEO, had a passive personality that worked against his and Gulf's interests. Instead of talking to me, he allowed himself to be controlled by lawyers, investment bankers, and others in his management group. Some of his advisers were convinced that I wanted to get on their board and that, once there, I would have a lot of questions — not very appealing for a company whose past was marred by political scandals, foreign bribes, and other questionable activities. I repeatedly said that I had no interest in going on the Gulf board.

Gulf's need for restructuring should have been self-evident. Oil companies were generating substantial cash flows, but the prospects for reinvestment were poor. The dramatic changes within the industry in 1985 and 1986 have caused many people to comment that our plan for Gulf was right, but that the rest of the world didn't know it until years later. That was the time to move, the time the oil companies should have been making fundamental changes. It was time to downsize by finding a way to distribute excess cash flow to shareholders. There were a number of ways a company could do this, but we favored large royalty trusts, in which the cash flow from a substantial part of the producing properties would be distributed to shareholders.

The royalty trust concept was now four years old. Over that period, several independents had spun off royalty trusts, and the results were spectacular. The market had rewarded the creation of value, even if Big Oil executives had not. Our young team at Mesa ran numbers on the large oil companies, estimating the impact of royalty trusts, and the results were always good for the stockholders.

At one point, we convinced Morgan Stanley's merger and acquisitions (M&A) group that royalty trusts could be used to create value for companies that were not replacing their reserves. This meant all of the majors with the exception of Shell Oil. The big companies were really no more than inefficient royalty trusts. A properly designed royalty trust takes natural resources that are depleting and distributes the cash flow to the owners without paying corporate taxes. On the other hand, a corporation producing oil and gas first has to pay taxes on its income and then can distribute a dividend to its shareholders. If you were liquidating your primary asset, you should at least do it as efficiently as possible. That way shareholders would get the maximum value from their oil and gas production.

Early in the summer of 1983, Bob Stillwell and I had a dinner meeting with the key people at Morgan Stanley to talk about oil industry restructuring. We discussed which managements might be least hostile and the tactics we might use to restructure one of the giants. The Morgan people were skeptical at first, but by the end of the evening they agreed that our theory was sound. It probably wasn't lost on them that this could mean big bucks for an investment banker. But an old firm like Morgan Stanley had some other considerations as well.

One of the oldest firms on Wall Street, it had a client roster full of the *Fortune* 500 companies, the largest companies in America. The Morgan people realized that advising us on what we were proposing, no matter which company we selected, would alienate some of their clients — the Good Ol' Boys in spades. They knew their clients better than anybody, and so I wasn't surprised when I got a call from Joe Fogg, Morgan Stanley's head of M&A. "We've got some problems," he began; he didn't have to say anything more.

In a way, I was glad to see them go. I had more confidence in David Batchelder and his group than I did in any investment banker. After that, we used bankers only in special situations, but we no longer relied on them to generate ideas. We were better on the analysis, and we knew what our objectives were. More than that, our people had their money and reputation at risk. And — not a small point — when you cut out the investment bankers, you usually cut out the leaks.

We then got down to the business of choosing the most likely company. Gulf was not the obvious choice because of its size. But as we screened a dozen others, we kept coming back to Gulf. It had what we were looking for: its stock traded at a huge discount and it had a strong cash flow (more than $3 billion), primarily domestic oil and gas reserves, and a history of poor management. Once a great American corporation, it was now considered the weakest of the Seven Sisters, in part because of the bribery and payoff scandals of the 1970s.

On Wall Street, Gulf's reputation was even worse. Between 1978 and 1982, its U.S. reserves had dropped by an astonishing 40 percent: 600 million barrels had been depleted and not replaced. The only thing saving Gulf was OPEC.

It was deeply involved in the uranium business and had a major price-fixing lawsuit. It also owned a uranium mine in New Mexico which had lost a billion dollars. It also had weak refining and marketing, a money-losing chemical operation, and so on. Although its underlying assets were worth more than $100 a share, the all-time high for the stock was $53 during the pseudo-boom of 1980–81 and was now anchored in the high $30s.

With Gulf's reserves in a steep decline, there was little chance the stock would ever go above $40. And now that oil prices had started to come down, Gulf was a dead duck. By the time prices rose again, the reserves would be depleted. In the middle of the Gulf deal, a financial magazine published a survey that ranked more than a thousand companies in terms of profitability, growth, and stock market performance; Gulf placed in the bottom third in all three categories. But management couldn't see beyond their cash flow of $3 billion a year.

One story sums up the company's ineptitude. Back in 1964, Gulf was sure it had found a huge natural gas field in the Gulf of Mexico. So sure was the company of its discovery that it actually negotiated a contract to sell the gas to Texas Eastern Transmission Company before a single well was completed for production. The contract called for Gulf to deliver 4 trillion cubic feet of natural gas over the next twenty-six years at 21 cents per thousand cubic feet. That was a good price at the time, but gas prices have skyrocketed since then. The original discovery was not nearly as large as Gulf had thought. It could have been saved but for its contract with Texas Eastern, so for years Gulf has had to buy expensive gas, or produce its own high-cost gas, to deliver to Texas Eastern at 21 cents. Gulf lost well over a billion on that deal — one of the biggest blunders in corporate history, and another reason it didn't want an outsider on the board, asking questions.

Gulf's image on Wall Street was terrible. When it backed out of the Cities deal in 1982, it cost the Wall Street professionals and institutions hundreds of millions of dollars. Having been burned once by Gulf, the investment community — whose impact was crucial in any deal — would probably side with us. Gulf's dividend actually made the carrying cost slightly positive for us, which meant that holding the position for an extended period would be no problem.

In the final analysis, my people had done their job, and it was up to me to evaluate Gulf's management. I knew Jimmy Lee and had a feel for how he would act in a tight situation. I could still remember him back at Yellowstone, agonizing over which card to throw in a gin game.

Lee was a reasonable man; that could work in our favor. I had the feeling that he wouldn't do something stupid and that he might even take positive steps without our prodding him. Another Gulf executive, Harold Hammer, concerned me. Abrasive and foul-mouthed, he was one of the most disliked men in corporate America. Hammer volunteered for the unpleasant jobs at Gulf and enjoyed carrying them out. But how much influence did he have on Lee? Only time would tell.

To his credit, Lee was the first Gulf CEO in decades to make some changes: he cut 20,000 people out of the company's bloated bureaucracy, sold some of the company's losers, and shored up the stock price by buying in more than 30 million shares. My instinct told me that when push came to shove, Lee would do the right thing for the shareholders. Also, he had a stock option for more than 200,000 shares at $34, which didn't hurt.

One evening, when I was sitting in the study after a long day of looking at the Gulf numbers, Bea asked me how things were going.

"We're very close," I said.

"Well," she said, "when are you going to do it?"

"If we wait thirty more days, we'll be overtrained."

By August we were ready to go. The first step was to start accumulating the Gulf stock. It was important to keep our buying a secret, in part to maintain the advantage that comes with surprise, in part to avoid a run-up in the price. Federal law requires anyone who buys 5 percent of a company to so inform the Securities and Exchange Commission within ten days. For the time being, we would stop our purchases at 4.9 percent. At that point, our investment would be about $350 million.

We devised an elaborate security system. Only a handful of people at Mesa were privy to our buying, and only two knew the details of the transactions. We drew down our entire credit line in advance, so that our banks would not detect a pattern of borrowing and buying. We established numbered bank accounts with restricted transfer procedures. Only one person at each bank knew that the accounts belonged to Mesa, and only Sidney Tassin knew all the account numbers and transfer authorizations. When it was time to pay, we would transfer cash from a Mesa account to one of the numbered accounts, then transfer it again to another numbered account at a different bank. The money was then transferred to Bear, Stearns & Company to pay for the stock.

We had to do everything we could to keep Gulf from getting suspicious. Market professionals watch for stocks that start trading above their normal volume, a tipoff that something is going on. To give us the best chance of succeeding, we contacted a real pro, Alan ("Ace") Greenberg, the chairman of Bear, Stearns. We knew Ace well from earlier dealings.

David and Sidney met with Ace in New York on August 11 and worked out the details. He had one last question: "Can I start this afternoon?"

"Sure," said David. There were about twenty minutes left until the market closed. Ace went to work, and a half hour later he called David and said, "I picked up 123,000 shares."

David said, "Wow! Ace is out of the silo."

Forty-eight days later, on September 28, we had bought 8.5 million shares of Gulf Oil, exactly 4.9 percent.

It was time to start the process of bringing in partners. For several months I had been considering who we would contact: the Belzberg brothers, Sam and Bill, who controlled one of the largest financial empires in Canada; John M. Harbert III, of Harbert International, a privately held construction firm in Alabama; Cyril Wagner and Jack Brown, who owned Wagner & Brown oil company in Midland, Texas; and Mike Boswell, the CEO of Sunshine Mining in Dallas.

A week later, on October 4, we met with our prospective partners at the Meridian Hotel in Houston. With millions, sometimes billions, of dollars at stake, interested companies and Wall Street professionals have had people tailed and have been known to place "spotters" at airports and other strategic locations. We kept everyone in the hotel; meals were brought to the meeting room, and our people didn't waste any time in the lobby.

The Mesa team had prepared a complete analysis of Gulf: assets and cash flow, charter and bylaw review, the royalty trust case, the carrying costs, the upside potential and the downside risk. It was a good presentation. Everybody saw the potential of the royalty trust. Harbert said, "If a big stockholder came to me with an idea like this, I'd sure sit down and listen to him."

Toward the end of the meeting, someone else asked, "How hard will it be to accumulate a position in Gulf?"

"We have a position," I told them. "You come in at our cost. In fact, we've got a $16 million profit today."

The Gulf stock had risen 2 points above our average cost of $38 a share. Our prospective partners would have a third of the gain and we would have two thirds — since we had two thirds of the partnership. The question was whether they wanted to be part of a deal that would attract a lot of publicity, and possibly a lot of heat, but also make a lot of money.

Late that afternoon the decision was made, and we signed an agreement forming the Gulf Investors Group (GIG). The agreement protected us in the event of Gulf's coming after Mesa. If Mesa were taken over, it wouldn't stop things, because the voting rights of the group's Gulf stock would shift to Harbert International.

Our partners gave us such financial strength that Gulf would never know for sure how much money we could come up with. For starters, GIG agreed to put up $550 million of equity, two thirds of it Mesa's. Since we could borrow an equal amount on margin financing, that gave us a $1.1 billion war chest. Now we were ready to start buying again. So we put Ace Greenberg back to work. That meant we had ten days of buying stock before we had to file.

On October 17, we filed with the SEC. GIG owned 14.5 million shares of Gulf — almost 9 percent — making us Gulf's largest stockholder, larger than even the Mellon family. We had spent $638 million.

Speculation had been rampant in those final ten days as Gulf's volume rose. When you're buying as much stock as we were — 6 million shares in ten days — it attracts a lot of attention. Soon after we began the latest round of buying, Gulf — the sleeping giant — started to rouse, and on October 11 made its first defensive move. Without knowing who their new, large stockholders were or their intentions, Gulf's board announced a special shareholders' meeting for early December. They wanted to change their state of incorporation from Pennsylvania to Delaware and to change their charter and bylaws to eliminate various shareholder rights, including cumulative voting.

I had seen some odd defenses in my time, but this one took the cake. It turned out to be the biggest break we got. We would much rather fight Gulf in Delaware than in Pennsylvania; they'd given up the home field advantage right off the bat. The board must have gotten that advice from their investment bankers and legal counsel, who had convinced them that the enemy would use cumulative voting to elect a member to their board — a major concern. For under Pennsylvania law, corporations are required to use cumulative voting, which allows shareholders to allocate their proxy votes among any or all candidates for seats on the board. For example, Gulf had thirteen directors, and the owner of one share could cast a single vote for all thirteen seats or 13 votes for one seat only. Under cumulative voting, we had enough shares to elect one person to the board.

If Gulf moved to Delaware, cumulative voting would no longer be in effect. Gulf's strategy was to cut us off at the pass. They wouldn't accept that I didn't want to go on the board. Why would I want to be in a situation where every vote would be 12 to 1 against me?

The two months before the special shareholders' meeting would give us valuable time to sell our plan, and talk to Gulf shareholders, primarily the large ones — the institutional money managers. It was a mistake on Gulf's part to let us have contact with the shareholders so early in the game. We got to talk about the royalty trust and what it would mean to the stockholders.

Gulf had been in liquidation for years, and we could point out the company's history of mismanagement. With all the media attention, we would have ample opportunity to tell our story to the public as well.

On October 24, we amended our SEC filing to show that GIG had approximately 11 percent of Gulf's stock. Two days later, Gulf mailed proxy material to the shareholders. Early on, Gulf must have thought they could stop this thing in an afternoon. The first comment to the press from their advisers was that they were strapping on their six-shooters and going after this guy (their largest stockholder!). At the same time, a Gulf vice president said, "Pickens doesn't know anything about integrated oil companies. He's never had any experience in marketing and refining." My response was that I had been smart enough never to get into marketing and refining, where Gulf was losing more than $100 million a year.

Harold Hammer made a few unprintable comments about me that ended up in print anyway, to our advantage. On October 31, we reluctantly announced that we would lead a proxy fight against reincorporation.

The battle was on.

· 17 ·

# *Gulf* II

## . . . and Then There Were Six

Proxy fights can get expensive real fast. You hire lawyers, bankers, printers, advertisers — and a proxy solicitor to get the votes. The goal is to communicate with the stockholders — in this case, 400,000 of them — and start rounding up the votes. (Whenever you print and mail something in 400,000-piece lots, it gets expensive.) The heat gets turned up as soon as the proxies are mailed.

The Gulf proxy fight cost us about $15 million. This exercise in "shareholder democracy" differs in significant ways from the kind of elections you and I know. For one, the ballots aren't confidential, so the management knows how all the stockholders are voting. For another, stockholders can change their votes as often as they want, right up to the deadline — for us it was December 2, the date of the special stockholders' meeting. You can even change your vote at the meeting.

The combination of these factors gave management plenty of time and incentive to twist the arms of the shareholders, especially the big ones. They bullied the institutional holders, and many of them broke under the pressure. Lee was quoted as saying that the banks "have given the corporate raider a hunting license. Without the loans, the raider couldn't raid."

There's no telling how much money Gulf spent. Once the proxy fight was in full swing, the board instituted a toll-free hot line for shareholders who wanted "advice" on how to vote. Gulf's Pittsburgh headquarters became one giant phone bank, at the stockholders' expense. Engineers, personnel administrators, financial people — they were all pressed into service to contact the stockholders. Some were called as many as eight times. Those who voted against the reincorporation were called in an effort to get them to switch their vote.

Don Carter, our proxy solicitor, estimated that the small stockholders would vote 6 to 1 for management — the traditional response. People who have owned stock in a company for a long time are reluctant to vote against management; many of them have the misguided view that to oppose management is to be disloyal. That attitude will change as the individual shareholders realize it's the company that owes them.

Like most proxy fights, this one centered on large institutional stockholders — the pension and mutual funds, the money management firms, and the trust departments of banks. One of the revolutionary trends over the past twenty years has been the growth of the institutional stockholder, a result of increased pension and retirement funds and the desire of individuals to have professionals manage their money. This was good as long as the institutions took their fiduciary responsibility seriously. The stock market had become increasingly complicated and fast-moving, and the institutions should have been able to keep up with it better than most individuals. So even a company as unattractive as Gulf could count on having about 40 percent of its stock in institutional portfolios in blocks that ran to millions of shares.

We didn't have the time or money to get in touch with each of Gulf's 400,000 stockholders; but in the month we had, we could hope to see most of the institutional holders. We counted on them to grasp the royalty trust concept; although it was not the direct issue in this proxy battle, it was likely to be at the annual meeting in the spring of 1984.

Institutions are so important in a proxy fight because, while an individual can vote on the basis of sentiment, loyalty, or even a whim, institutions don't have that option. They are legally obligated to the people who have entrusted them with their money. In theory, at least, sentiment and loyalty should have nothing to do with their decisions, but many don't measure up to that standard of fiduciary care.

We met with the proxy committees at the institutions, explaining that we saw no reason to eliminate shareholder rights through the reincorporation, particularly just when an activist shareholder had come on the scene. We also pushed the royalty trust as a way to share some of Gulf's huge cash flow with the stockholders. Gulf's management argued for the status quo, which was no surprise.

In the first few weeks of the proxy fight I heard one question over and over: What will you do if Gulf offers to buy back your stock for a substantial profit? In other words, are you working for all the shareholders or will you take greenmail?

Greenmail can occur when management has perceived a threat from a large stockholder and is willing to pay a premium to buy back the stock to remove the threat. When management makes such a payment, they squander the stockholders' money to keep their jobs — there is no other explanation for this act.

It was important that we put the greenmail question to rest. On November 10, we had a meeting at the Waldorf-Astoria to explain our position as Gulf's largest stockholder. Many people thought we were crazy, and an equal number thought we wanted greenmail. And a few believers said we shouldn't be counted out.

The day of the meeting an unrelenting rainstorm soaked New York City, and I thought few people would come. But when I arrived at the Waldorf, I learned that the meeting had been moved to the larger Empire Room to handle the overflow — about three hundred people, including stockholders, reporters, analysts, and arbs.

Looking over the sea of faces, I recognized at least half the people in the room. For twenty years I had been coming to New York and I had gotten to know a lot of people. Many of them were friends. It took nearly ten minutes to walk from the door to the podium, shaking hands.

At the beginning I introduced Bea. Many of the people in the room knew her, too. "Bea's here to catch any soft fruit that comes my way," I said, and the laughter that followed was warm. I was more nervous than I let on; I knew we were riding a tiger and that if we got off it would eat us.

I made a few remarks about why the Gulf Investors Group opposed the management's proposal and why a royalty trust made sense to consider. Then I said what everyone wanted to hear but none expected: we would not accept greenmail under any circumstance. "Our objective," I said, "is to participate in the enhancement of the value of Gulf shares on an equal basis with all Gulf shareholders. Accordingly, we will not sell our holdings back to Gulf."

Greenmail had become a common practice in corporate America, and many people had denounced it. But no one had ever before *renounced* it in the middle of a deal, thereby cutting off a profitable option. There were loud, sustained cheers.

Someone in the audience asked me how I was promoting the royalty trust. "Door to door," I said, "shaking hands." There was another round of laughter. Selling the idea wasn't much different from how we had done the roll-up in 1964; this one was just nationwide and much larger.

After the meeting, Batchelder got a call from an associate of Ivan Boesky. Boesky was then flying high, the most famous arb in the business. Later, of course, he would become infamous when he ran afoul of the SEC for insider trading. Still not convinced, Boesky wanted a letter obliging us not to accept greenmail. But we would write no letters or contracts; they could take us at our word. (Judging by how well Boesky came out in the Gulf deal — with a profit rumored to be $75 million — I guess he took us at our word.)

It wasn't unusual to start the day at a breakfast meeting in Boston, to move on to a luncheon in New York, a dinner meeting in Pittsburgh, and to end the day having a drink with a money manager in Chicago.

Early in this whirlwind I came face to face with Gulf's real weapon, which dwarfed even its size and money and its ability to call every stockholder eight times. That weapon was the Good Ol' Boy network. In the Cities and GAO deals, the Good Ol' Boys were content to sit on the sidelines because the deals didn't affect them. But our taking on Gulf was a threat to every Good Ol' Boy company in America.

Nothing could compare to the pressure that Gulf and its allies were applying to the institutions, and we spent all month fighting this pressure we had heard about but couldn't see. The institutions had a fiduciary duty that paled in comparison to the economic force the Good Ol' Boys used to make them vote with Gulf's management.

T. Rowe Price, the investment firm, had been a Mesa supporter and shareholder; it also owned 600,000 shares of Gulf. I had lunch with its proxy committee to explain the royalty trust concept and outline what it could do for the price of Gulf. They were so enthusiastic that several of them followed me out to the elevator and were almost cheering, as if I was back on the Amarillo High School basketball team. Those 600,000 shares were in the sack, but whose sack?

Three days later T. Rowe Price's proxy came in; they had voted with management. I couldn't believe it. I called one of the people who had supported me enthusiastically. At the last minute, he said, the proxy committee's recommendation had been overturned upstairs. They had succumbed to the pressure.

State Street Research & Management, in Boston, also felt the heat. The firm had 4 million shares of Gulf in many accounts. A 20-point rise — the minimum we were projecting if it spun off a royalty trust — would mean an $80 million profit. The firm should have loved me. Yet when I walked into the executive dining room, I was met with an apprehensive response.

State Street had made money as a Mesa stockholder over the years, yet almost every question they asked implied that I was the bad guy. I think if Bea hadn't been with me they would have had me for lunch. (I wonder how they would have treated me if they had known they were about to make over $100 million.)

Gulf was pulling out all the stops to win the fight. At times, its tactics went too far. One of our supporters was the New Jersey State Pension Fund, which had a large block of Gulf stock. A money manager who was a friend of mine had a visit from a Gulf representative. He told my friend that the only reason the New Jersey fund stuck with us was that I was having an affair with a woman who worked there. He said he knew of four clandestine meetings I had had with her. When Bea heard this story, she said, "If Boone's having an affair with somebody, she's not getting much time."

Gulf hired a private detective — several, in fact. One came to Amarillo from New York and hired a local man to sit in a car at the airport and watch Mesa's hangar. He reported our time of departure and the number of people on board — and billed Gulf $400 a day, even when he didn't show up for work. Hiring detectives, unfortunately, is a common practice by many big corporations. It's partly arrogance and partly a total disregard for fair play and the rights of others. "Put the heat on the son of a bitch," they say, "and run him off." I can honestly say that we have never spent a dime for a detective to follow anybody. Besides, I would be afraid of what I might learn about some of these guys.

One of Gulf's detectives called a former FBI agent in Amarillo and offered him a job digging up dirt on me. "I don't do that sort of thing," the man said, "and in any case it wouldn't do you any good. You're not going to find anything." But the management spent several hundred thousand dollars of the stockholders' money trying to stir something up. They spread the rumor that I was tipping off my friends to takeovers. They fed Dan Dorfman erroneous information that he reported on Cable News Network; he later had to retract it publicly. A CNN executive said, quoting high SEC officials, " 'There is nothing there . . .' " then went on, " 'Boone Pickens does not need inside information to make money, and he has no profit motive to give it.' "

Not since the Bendix–Martin Marietta takeover battle the year before had a story so dominated the business pages. Every day I had a stack of phone calls from reporters looking for a new angle.

The Gulf proxy fight had all the elements of a good news story, and a looming climax in the December 2 stockholders' meeting.

I tried to convince the media that they were overreacting to a rather straightforward situation. I told them that we were just a large stockholder that wanted to work with the management to develop a plan that would best serve all the stockholders. They would have no part of my "oversimplified" version of what was happening.

Both sides made plenty of remarks to the press that fanned the flames. Lee called me a shark and an opportunist. Hammer told reporters that I didn't have the experience to be on the board and added, "We're kicking them where it hurts." Every time Harold said something, it helped us. They were trying to kick us, but couldn't find a spot. I was accustomed to the bullying tactics of Big Oil and fought back in any way I could. I told my people not to get discouraged. "Because you have a down day doesn't mean you've lost," I said. I compared it to a boxing match between a good, young lightweight and an aging heavyweight. "We have to move in and out, jabbing and dancing. We can't relax. We're not going to knock this guy out, but we can wear him down." First we had to bloody his nose. Then we would concentrate on one of his eyes. Once it was closed, we would go for the other eye, then to the midsection.

In sports, you always want the other team to play your game. Gulf's management wasn't accustomed to all this; they behaved about how you would expect Big Oil to act — arrogant and very slow. They were doing their best to make me into a bad guy; I tried to see as many people as I could and convince them otherwise. More important, the larger issues were being raised and publicized, just as we had hoped.

We prepared a detailed analysis on the advantages of a royalty trust. within ten days, Gulf's investment bankers published a weak rebuttal that attempted to show the disadvantages. The *Wall Street Journal* and the *New York Times* were doing a fair job of analyzing both sets of data, but the royalty trust was new, different, and somewhat complex, so it was easily misunderstood.

The primary misconception was that we were proposing to liquidate the company. I pointed out that Gulf had been in liquidation for twelve years because it hadn't replaced its reserves since 1971. They never responded to this charge.

Gulf's investment bankers' first mission was to attack the royalty trust and create as much confusion as possible. The other Seven Sisters helped Gulf wherever they could, for obvious reasons — any one of them might be next. The good analysts dealt with the data on the merits. Kurt Wulff, of Donaldson, Lufkin and Jenrette, wrote in strong support of the royalty trust. So did Art Smith, then with Oppenheimer & Company and now the owner of John S. Herold, Inc., which specializes in oil company appraisals; and there were others as well who saw the merit of our proposal.

After having tried to sell our royalty trust idea to Gordon Getty, Morgan Stanley now wrote a scathing attack on royalty trusts. The company claimed that a "Chinese wall" existed between their research department and the investment bankers. We responded with a press release saying that less than a year earlier, when Morgan Stanley was working for us, it had prepared a detailed presentation demonstrating that a royalty trust would increase values for major oil companies by more than 50 percent. Morgan sent word back that it was "hurt" and "disappointed" that we would issue such a release.

When we got our twelve banks together, the New York banks — with one exception — wouldn't touch us. The exception was Citibank, which had no use for Gulf because of a nasty lawsuit some years back. Citibank executives blamed the bad relationship on Harold Hammer; it was probably well placed.

By the time the special stockholders' meeting rolled around, we had generated a lot of "talk time" on the royalty trust. It was easy to establish that Gulf had done very little for its shareholders — something that even Jim Lee conceded. And by announcing that we wouldn't take greenmail, we had clearly allied ourselves with all the Gulf shareholders.

Everybody was feeling pretty good about our progress, and as we were flying home from New York for the weekend, Sidney said, "I think we've got their nose bleeding."

In the heat of battle your mind and emotions do funny things. We went into the proxy fight expecting to lose. But after putting in twelve-hour days, six or seven days a week, for five straight weeks and spending close to $15 million, we had all but forgotten that we were supposed to lose.

Gulf's 400,000 shareholders made this the biggest proxy fight of all time. In a proxy fight, both sides get their votes and an independent third party does the count. The firm hired to count the votes had rented a shut down Delaware racetrack in order to handle the volume of material. It would take several weeks for them to make a final tally.

With no official count available, the special meeting was a chance for Goliath to joust with David or vice versa. I supposed the audience would be unfriendly, but I got some comfort from knowing I was on the right side of the issue. I was sure a lot of the attendees didn't like Gulf's management, even though they owned Gulf stock or worked for the company. I decided to address my remarks to them and to make a strong case for maximizing values.

It had rained earlier that day in New York, and in Pittsburgh it had turned to snow. At the hotel, before the meeting, I told Bea that I wasn't sure she should go: some people might be hostile and we might even be shoved around.

Bea said that she wouldn't miss it for anything.

In the car going over, with Sidney, Stillwell, and Don Carter, things were pretty quiet. I was thinking about what I would say. Things were about as tense as I had seen them for a long time. When we arrived at the David L. Lawrence Convention Center there was a huge crowd of people; they were not hostile but very interested. A lot of them smiled and spoke to us. I hadn't expected the close scrutiny I got in the Pittsburgh papers the next day: my clothes were described in detail — they said I was wearing a gray suit and a blue and red tie — and commented that I looked just like anybody else. Did they think I would wear chaps and carry a six-gun and come in shooting holes in the ceiling?

Jimmy Lee and one other Gulf executive, the secretary of the meeting, sat on a large elevated platform that could have easily supported forty people. They towered over the crowd in front of a huge Gulf logo on the wall. Bea leaned over and whispered, "My God, he looks like the Soviet premier with his short-boy."

The Gulf directors sat in the first row at the foot of the chairman, staring up at him, about to get cricks in their necks. They all wore navy blue suits.

"They look like pallbearers," I told Bea. I knew some of them, but they didn't look our way.

Although our 12 percent made the Gulf Investors Group the largest shareholder, there was no place for us on the platform. There weren't any seats among the "pallbearers." We were seated off to one side, at about the twenty-yard line. You would have thought the directors would speak to their largest stockholder; after all, we were paying a large part of their directors' fees.

Lee nervously called the meeting to order. He announced that he would make his remarks and that then Mr. Pickens would have an opportunity to speak, followed by a question-and-answer period.

Jimmy Lee had been prepped to deliver a scathing denunciation of GIG and me. As soon as he began, I realized that this was not the person I knew, a calm, almost timid guy. This new version was loud and belligerent. Throughout his ten-minute speech he waved his finger in the air, pointing at me from time to time. He repeated all the weak arguments he had used for the last month and threw in a few new ones. I had "a history of hit-and-run tactics." A royalty trust was a "get rich quick" scheme that would "cripple the company and severely penalize the majority of the stockholders," although he never explained how putting 30 points on the stock would penalize stockholders. He didn't mention that a royalty trust would pay shareholders twice as much as the common stock dividend, and he failed to tell the whole story. He said that if we won, the Gulf dividend would have to be scaled back dramatically, one of Gulf's favorite horror stories. That was a flat lie.

He talked about the constructive things Gulf had done in the last two years, such as the sale of its European refining and marketing operation, and on a particularly sensitive point he said that Gulf would replace as much as 60 percent of its reserves in the upcoming year. (It was actually about half that.) If Mesa had replaced only 60 percent of its reserves, we wouldn't be bragging about it!

He also used the Good Ol' Boys' favorite PR hype: national security. "The consequences for this country would be immense if major industries were dismantled in search of short-term profits!" he said. I had never thought of Gulf's maintaining the security of the United States. He failed to mention that Gulf owned only 1 percent of the world's oil. They knew we weren't going to dismantle Gulf, but the idea frightened people, and management was using it. Fear is probably their best defense. Scare hell out of everybody in sight.

Lee said that we had borrowed the money to buy the Gulf stock and that consequently we were not the real owners of the stock. He added, "The banks own the stock." That was an unusual statement (Did you borrow to buy your house?), and almost everybody in the room knew it. He was being directed by so many people, he didn't realize how foolish he sounded. But the more his lawyers and investment bankers could heighten the controversy, the bigger their fee. Poor Jimmy didn't have a chance.

Lee finished, and it was my turn. A microphone stood in the aisle, and I walked over to it, holding a couple of sheets on which I had written my remarks. An attendant handed me the microphone and then removed the stand, so I had to hold my papers in one hand and the microphone in the other. It seemed like a deliberate attempt to make me look awkward — as nervous as I was, they didn't have to help me. But, by putting me at floor level, Gulf had unwittingly given me an advantage. "I appreciate your giving me the chance to speak today from the same level as the Gulf employees and stockholders," I said. "Frankly, that's where I feel most comfortable." The applause was longer and louder than anybody expected.

During the Q&A session, I was surprised by the number of Gulf shareholders who were critical of management. Even in Pittsburgh, on Gulf's home turf, our message was getting through and we were providing starch for the stockholders. I took my share of hostile questions, however, and was glad when the three-hour meeting was over.

Now for the press conference; then we were headed for home. Gulf demanded to have its press conference first, which was fine with us. It was a one-hour wait, but well worth it — the more they talked, the better I liked it. Lee spent a good part of his time explaining that Gulf didn't hire the detectives that were following Pickens but that it may have been Gulf's law firm that was doing it. Big Oil was having a rough day.

At our press conference, I knew almost all of the fifty reporters by name; I had been practically living with them for the last month. I was elated with their questions and knew that the press was understanding things a lot better. What a great opportunity Gulf had given us to show the right side of such an important issue.

I felt pretty good about things in general. I knew we were still in the game, and said so at the press conference. We were already preparing for the next battle: while we were at the meeting, David Batchelder had been on the phone in the hotel room, buying 800,000 more shares of Gulf stock.

This was all the business we had in Pittsburgh — for that day. It snowed all the way out to the airport, and they were de-icing the plane when we got there. John Stone, one of Mesa's pilots, said we could take off; we were ready. Everybody was tired, but once we got off the ground the conversation picked up and ideas started to flow. By the time we got to Amarillo, we were ready to answer the bell for the next round.

We had developed a new strategy on the way home, and in the week that followed we worked on a Christmas package for Gulf's management. We talked to the other members of GIG; they were satisfied with the way things were going. We continued to buy stock until we had 21.7 million shares — about 13 percent.

Gulf was crowing about having won the proxy fight; they had whipped our ass — at least in their own minds. If that's what they thought, it was fine with us. We wanted the next round to be fought in Delaware, not Pennsylvania.

Lee's personality began working to our advantage. He was a decent guy and wouldn't do anything to damage Gulf, yet he was indecisive enough not to do anything smart, either, like restructuring the company. So he did nothing. We were afraid they would do an insignificant royalty trust. This would be the same as half-pulling a bad tooth.

In mid-December, Gulf held a "financial briefing" for oil analysts and large institutional investors. They wanted to give the appearance of business as usual. Nothing much happens at these affairs. The analysts enjoy the cocktails and food and laugh at their hosts. Few are convinced that they should buy the company's stock, but they have the meetings anyway.

We asked to be invited, as Gulf's largest stockholder, and consequently received an invitation. We wanted to stay current on Gulf, and if they were passing out information, we wanted to be there. Sidney attended, and as an afterthought he took Billy Pike to record the proceedings, not knowing how useful the notes would prove to be. The meeting was long and uneventful, but the wait was worth it.

The Gulf people were in great spirits. They were sure they had wiped out GIG, and had some unflattering things to say about us, even with Sidney there. Little did they realize that the lightweight boxer was starting to warm up again.

Near the end of the day, an analyst asked how Gulf was going to handle GIG. One of Gulf's executives grabbed the microphone and glibly replied, "We'll take care of them the same way we took care of the Mellons!"

There were gasps, then nervous laughter, then silence. It was a stunning statement — the arrogance of big business at its worst. The moderator said, "Well, that's the last question. Let's all go across the street for drinks and a nice dinner." We made sure that those remarks were in the hands of some of the Mellons within twenty-four hours.

We worked through the Christmas holidays, and on December 29, 1983, delivered a fifty-seven-page royalty trust proposal to each of Gulf's board members, describing the benefits to shareholders. We might as well have sent a roll of toilet paper. The proposal arrived on the day the results of the December 2 vote came out. Gulf had received 52 percent, a narrow margin that I thought would encourage management to now give our proposal serious consideration. I was wrong; they sent us a two-page letter dismissing the royalty trust.

"We are satisfied that the royalty trust concept," Lee wrote, "as it might be applied to Gulf Oil Corporation, has been thoroughly studied and thoroughly discredited and that your continuing public advocacy of it is a disservice to our shareholders."

Morgan Stanley had come out with a second report, this one saying that Gulf's stock, then trading at $45, was fully priced. This report was not taken any more seriously than the first one, and Morgan's analyst was fast losing credibility. It was the beginning of the end for its self-serving oil industry research group. On one of my trips to New York in January, I was invited to the River Club for a meeting with a large group of the Mellon heirs; they ranged in age from twenty to eighty-five. A Morgan Stanley analyst had been brought along to expose me for the rascal I supposedly was, but he got tongue-tied. I offered him four opportunities to comment on what I had to say, and he declined each one. I might not have won the older Mellons, but I know I picked up some of the younger ones.

Citibank was our lead bank, and Harold Hammer did us yet another favor by referring to Walter Wriston, the chairman of Citibank, as "a little fart" in a *Fortune* article. It offended even Gulf's friends. That was probably the remark that sunk Hammer, whom Lee referred to in the same article as his "field commander."

We began considering ways to buy more stock. Bill Belzberg,

one of our partners, suggested we should talk to Mike Milken, at Drexel. "Milken has an uncanny ability to raise money," Bill said. That was the understatement of the year.

The next morning, Bea and I went directly from Houston to Los Angeles and met with Mike Milken, Peter Ackerman, and Mike Brown in Drexel's office on Wilshire Boulevard. I told them we were looking at several options and one was to increase our position in Gulf. In fact, we might be talking about a substantial increase. Milken said, "You're talking about a lot of money." I agreed. It could be several billion dollars. I also told them that we were considering other possibilities. I didn't tell them that I thought Gulf's best option was to do a royalty trust, but I thought that was what they would eventually do.

We weren't there more than an hour, and we left with the understanding that Brown would come to Amarillo the next week and meet with Batchelder and his group. Brown said it would take him several days to get up to speed on the deal. Bea and I took a few days off and headed for Palm Springs.

It was from Palm Springs to New York, and on January 31, at the Helmsley Palace my secretary in Amarillo called. "Bob Anderson's looking for you," she said.

"There are a lot of Bob Andersons. Which one is it?"

"The one from Arco."

I called Anderson, who got right to the point. "Boone, would you be interested in selling your Gulf stock?" I asked on what basis. We talked for twenty or thirty minutes about several things, but what Bob wanted was for Arco to acquire Gulf. He had made two big deals at Arco in his career, the Richfield and Sinclair acquisitions, and he was warming up to do the hat trick. I listened but wasn't convinced that all the Gulf shareholders would get the same deal. We had a commitment to see that they received the same price we did. He seemed surprised that we felt that way.

We talked about price, and he allowed that Gulf might be worth $65 a share. I knew he was trading, but I told him that $65 wouldn't do the job. He didn't argue, so I was sure he would raise. I have always liked Bob. He's probably the only major oil company CEO I've ever met with entrepreneurial instincts.

We decided we had something worth spending at least an evening on, so we picked Denver for a rendezvous. Bob came in from Los Angeles with Arco's new CEO, Bill Kieschnick. Bea, David, Sidney, and I flew in from New York. While Bea went to bed, the rest of us had a late supper with Anderson and Kieschnick in their suite at the Fairmont Hotel. We discussed how the industry was moving, restructuring and all. At one point I said, "Let's be partners."

"No," said Anderson, who was doing all the talking for Arco. "I want to do a friendly deal with Jimmy."

Going back to the room, David said, "We have something working now. Anderson is probably going to make an offer to Lee." Sidney said, "They think acquiring Gulf will solve their problems. If they only knew."

The price of poker was going up. Texaco was in the process of acquiring Getty, establishing a value for a big oil company and making our evaluation of Gulf much more credible. Everything seemed to be falling into place, and it was starting to be fun. We had a secret: Arco is interested.

We flew out early the next morning — David back to New York, Bea to Amarillo, and Sidney and I to Milwaukee. We had to keep working on all fronts and not get overconfident. Milwaukee was our first stop on a marathon tour for potential backers. From there we flew to Chicago and then to Cincinnati to have dinner with Carl Lindner, a large investor and major stockholder in Penn Central. Near the end of dinner, Lindner said he was interested in our deal. He was a big player and would be a good partner. Carl is a class guy.

We flew on to Los Angeles after dinner, arriving at 2 A.M. (for us it was really 6 A.M.). Later that day we met with the GIG partners. They were satisfied with the way things were going, but I detected an undercurrent of doubt about the ultimate destination. They had a lot of money invested and wanted to see the finish line. We made our report and discussed the meeting with

Drexel, but we held back any information about Arco. It was just too sensitive to take a chance on letting it out of the bag. The Drexel idea for raising additional money would be expensive, involving commitment fees and a cut of the profit.

John Harbert thought we might consider taking some profits now. He was still unhappy about losing the proxy fight and saw no problem with our cashing in. "The stockholders didn't vote with us," he said, "so why do we owe them anything?" We talked it out and John said at last, "Let's keep moving. You guys are doing a good job."

John was testing me with his remark about taking profit. I think he wanted to see if I had the resolve to see it through. John and I have gained a great deal of respect for each other, and this was one of those key exchanges.

For a fleeting moment I thought the partners saw me as McCartt had seen me years before and doubted that I could make a big deal.

Anderson called me on February 2, the next day, and told me that he had offered Lee $70 a share. Whenever more than two people know something, there is likely to be a leak. It put me in a tight spot. I had to go underground and break my communication with the media. If there was going to be a leak, it would not come from me.

Lee had reluctantly agreed to discuss the merits of the royalty trust. I never thought it would come to pass, but we were scheduled to meet in Houston on February 6. We were both going to be there with our staffs, and it was going to be a working session. But now that he had the $70 offer from Anderson, the royalty trust session didn't make sense. I called Lee and asked if just the two of us could talk instead. He seemed relieved and said he would arrange a dinner meeting at the Gulf suite in the William Penn Hotel in Pittsburgh; he would have one of his security people pick me up at the airport.

The Gulf security man was very talkative; he said that a lot of Gulf's employees had sold their stock for $50 a share — an interesting bit of information.

Gulf's suite was at the end of a corridor high up in the William Penn. The doors to the rooms on both sides of the corridor stood open; a security man was sitting near the door in each room.

I knew that Lee wasn't happy to see me, but we were getting down to the short rows and needed to talk. He had no choice. By now he understood the facts of life: we were his largest stockholder and responsible for Gulf's hitting a new all-time high that day, $56. Jimmy hit a new high for his net worth, about $10 million. Only two months earlier, he hadn't been worth 25 percent of that.

"Well, Jim," I said when I walked into the suite, "how are you doing?"

"Pretty good, I guess, under the circumstances." He seemed exhausted.

"You probably look at me like the guy who saw his mother-in-law drive off a cliff in his new Cadillac."

He wasn't amused. We sat down to the dinner he had ordered some time before — cold broccoli soup and cold cuts. There we were, talking about a multibillion-dollar deal and eating cold food when it was 10 degrees outside. I wondered about Lee's abilities as a planner.

I asked if he was taping our conversation. He said no, but later it came out that I had been taped.

Finally I said, "What are you going to do about Bob Anderson's $70 offer?"

Lee was stunned. He'd hoped I didn't know. When he regained his composure, he replied, "That wasn't a formal offer. It was just exploratory."

"Bob Anderson and I had a meeting," I told him, "and I know he's damn serious."

Lee stared at me. He saw then that I knew everything.

"As your largest stockholders," I said, "we consider it a serious offer, and we want to know why you haven't disclosed it."

There was a long pause, and he put his hand to his forehead. "I wish you'd give me a couple more years."

"What would you do with a couple more years?" I asked.

"I believe I could have the price of the stock up to $60 or $65."

"Why would we want to wait two years," I asked, "when we have $70 offered right now?"

After another long pause he said, "I was afraid you were going to ask that."

"All you guys have made some money, Jim."

"But our stock options haven't matured."

"We won't challenge you if you want to accelerate the options," I said. "That's only fair."

It was our last meeting.

Not long afterward Gulf's board met and in a desperate move started litigation against us on February 10. It was their last gasp, halfhearted and with no punch. They would have sued us earlier, but they were vulnerable because of their past dealings and they were not sure how much we knew about their activities. Now everything had closed in on them, and they were suing us for allegedly having an undisclosed plan for taking over Gulf.

Just before they filed the litigation, Harold Hammer decided to cash in on 95,000 shares of stock at $57 per share. It was clear what he thought the litigation might do to Gulf's stock price. Ed Walker, the president of Gulf, had cashed in on his 160,000 shares several weeks before, at $47 a share. It looked as though he took his cue from the Morgan Stanley report. Lee also cashed in somewhere along the line. So the three top guys got to the finish line with only a small part of their stock. Judging from their actions, we had to assume they didn't know what the company was worth. There was no public announcement of their sales. They must have forgotten that church isn't out until the fat lady sings.

On February 14, they announced that Gulf was dedicated to continuing as an independent company, and that they were not having, nor did they intend to have, discussions with other companies about its possible sale. We knew they were lying; they had already called Chevron and Mobil to see if they could be possible white knights.

That same day, Gulf's motion for a temporary restraining order against us was denied in federal court in Delaware.

Both these announcements paled beside the story that broke in the *New York Times* about Arco's offer of $70 a share. I don't know who leaked it to the *Times*, but the finger points to the investment bankers. That call was worth millions to them. (GIG might have had the same incentive, but we had come a long way to start playing that game.) With the $70 Arco offer now public information, there would be tremendous pressure from the stockholders. We didn't want Arco to lose interest, but we had to keep the pressure on Gulf. We set up a meeting with Carl Lindner to talk about additional financing.

Lindner was in Florida, at Ocean Reef, and John Sorte, Peter Ackerman, and Steve Massad all flew down from New York with Batchelder, and Bea and I came in from Amarillo.

I joined David's group, and from Miami, Lindner's small plane took us to Ocean Reef. The members of the GIG team were the only people wearing suits and ties. For five hours we sat on a patio while the security people kept sunbathers at a distance. Lindner drove a hard bargain. One of the companies he controlled would loan us $300 million. Within four months, as it turned out, they made a profit of $47 million. It was a tribute to Carl and his group that we were able to make a deal that quickly. Lindner and I are both entrepreneurs; we understand each other, and we are both dealmakers.

We went back to Miami, where Bea was waiting. She said, "You need to call Jesse. Gulf's trying to greenmail you."

She was referring to Jesse Lovejoy, of Davis, Polk & Wardwell, one of our New York law firms. Lovejoy told me that Gulf had floated an offer of $70 a share for our stock. This would mean more than $500 million in profit to GIG if we took it.

"Are they going to take care of the other stockholders?" I asked.

"No."

"Then forget it."

"That's what I thought you'd say."

Bea and I headed for Amarillo; David and his group were off to New York. As soon as we had reached cruising altitude, she said, "You turned them down, didn't you?"

"I sure did."

"I knew you would," she said.

It had been a long day. I had half a dozen telephone calls to return, but I was tired of talking, and I napped all the way home. It was 1 A.M. when we arrived, and I had an urgent telephone call from Bob Rubin, of Goldman, Sachs. I return all urgent calls, especially from people like Rubin. I woke him up from a deep sleep. He said, "Wait a minute while I go splash some cold water on my face."

When he returned to the phone, he said, "I know what they've offered you." I knew Rubin well enough to realize that he had all the details.

"Boone," he went on, "you have great credibility on Wall Street. Don't make a mistake and accept their offer. It will destroy your reputation."

"Go back to sleep and don't worry," I told him. "Know I'll do the right thing."

We would have flown directly to New York from Miami if it hadn't been for the funeral of my old high school basketball coach, T. G. Hull. I would have come back from London if it had been necessary. Coach Hull had been a mentor to me, and the example he set made decisions like the one I made about greenmail easy for me in later life. I served as a pallbearer, and I wasn't sad during the services. Coach Hull had died in his sleep at eighty-three, a happy man, and all I had were happy thoughts about him.

Then we were on our way to New York. While we were at Ocean Reef, Gulf had arranged a $6 billion line of credit — another indication of their desperation. We brought the GIG partners together at the Helmsley and proposed a partial tender offer — our most logical move. It would be similar to our Cities Service tender offer and would require buying at least 13.5 million shares at $65 a share.

Two days later we announced our offer. Gulf tried to shut us down with another temporary restraining order, but the Delaware federal court denied it. Little David was landing a flurry of blows, and Goliath was staggering. Gulf claimed that our offer was inadequate, but its stock price had moved from $37 to $62 — an increase of over $4 billion in market value. As Harold Dunn might have said, "That ain't no chickenshit deal, boys."

Things were getting pretty wild. In Washington, Senators

Howard Metzenbaum, Democrat of Ohio, and Bennett Johnston, Democrat of Louisiana, introduced legislation to shut down mergers affecting the major oil companies. It was aimed at protecting Gulf and Getty. It was defeated. Our offer accelerated the inevitable. Gulf had to either restructure or sell out.

Monday, March 5, was judgment day, the day Gulf was to look at all the offers. The company put out the usual hot air, trying to appear as if it wasn't necessary. Everyone knew they had to make a deal: Goliath was flat on his back, and the referee was counting.

Shortly before noon a message came across the Dow Jones broad tape: Gulf had entered into a merger agreement with Socal, providing for a cash tender offer of $80 a share. Socal would double the value of Gulf management's stock options, which amounted to a $52 million payoff, but Lee, Hammer, and Walker had left millions on the table because they'd sold most of their stock early. Later, Socal's CEO, George Keller, told how the merger talks began: "The main thing that made us decide to try the acquisition was that I got a call from Jimmy Lee saying 'Help!'"

Good Ol' Boy power was getting ready to do a $13.2 billion merger.

But Congress was not through with oil company mergers. Metzenbaum, Johnston, and Warren B. Rudman, Republican of New Hampshire, announced their intention of introducing a bill that would curb large oil company mergers for six months — effective February 28, 1984. That would have stopped the Gulf-Socal merger. Meanwhile, I was asked to testify before the Senate Judiciary Committee, along with Jimmy Lee, George Keller, and William Tavoulareas, the president of Mobil.

It was the first time I had ever testified before a congressional committee. Lee and Keller were on the first panel, to be followed by me and another person, but they couldn't tell me who it was. I later learned it was supposed to be Tavoulareas, but he had refused to appear with me.

On the day of the hearing, Lee and Keller came into the room with a platoon of lawyers, accountants, and technical people. It was Big Oil personified; they took up the first three rows of seats. I saw this as the opportunity of a lifetime. I was going to be on by myself. I was fascinated by the challenge. It was the big guys against the little guy.

I don't mean to say I wasn't nervous; I was. But as my testimony proceeded, I got looser and looser. The committee was cordial but tough. At the conclusion, Senator Johnston, who had led the questioning, went for the jugular. He said, "Mr. Pickens, I read in the *Wall Street Journal* that when you were given the word that Socal made an $80 offer for Gulf you replied, 'Shucks, we lost again.'"

"Senator," I replied, "the article that you are referring to was in *Business Week* and I can't recall ever saying 'shucks' in my life."

Senator Johnston concluded with: "Mr. Pickens, you're a wily witness."

We lobbied for two weeks in an attempt to defeat the bill. I talked personally with at least half the senators and developed support on both sides of the aisle. Senators John Tower and Lloyd Bentsen of Texas both opposed legislation that would kill a deal in progress. We had been told that we had only 38 votes out of 100 — a pretty sobering count. After the first week we were told by the Senate staffs that we were making progress and that my testimony helped. I knew we were on the right side of the issue and that, as usual, success lay in getting our story told. I was now testifying at congressional hearings weekly.

The Reagan administration had announced that it was opposed to the bill. Metzenbaum et al. were losing ground and amended their bill so that it would take effect on March 21, which meant that the Gulf-Socal merger would be grandfathered. We had won. It was then that Senator Orrin Hatch of Utah grabbed me by the arm and said emotionally, "This isn't the sort of legislation we should be passing. I hope you'll keep working to defeat it." We stayed and helped.

The following week the vote came up on the floor of the Senate. The bill was defeated, 57 to 39. I took pride in having had a hand in defeating a poor piece of legislation. In hindsight, had it passed in its original form, the losers would have been Gulf's 400,000 stockholders.

And on June 15, at a special meeting of the Gulf stockholders, the merger with Socal was approved for $80 a share. The shareholders had made a profit of $6.5 billion. That was $6.5 billion that would have never been made if Mesa and GIG hadn't come on the scene.

The story had a final, ironic twist: we were the last ones to get paid. And two years later, in Washington, a senator told me I had greenmailed Gulf!

Gulf's largest stockholder, GIG, had made $760 million before taxes. I had almost forgotten that there was an even larger stockholder, the U.S. Government. It got more than $2 billion in federal income tax.

Not long afterward I gave a speech in Lafayette, Louisiana — Cajun country. A big, burly guy with a beard came up and hugged me.

I said, "You must be a Gulf stockholder."

"You better believe it, bubba. I appreciate what you did for me."

"How many shares did you own?" I asked.

"Five thousand."

I was glad it wasn't 10,000. He might have kissed me.

# · 18 ·

# *Phillips*

## The Battle of Bartlesville

The Gulf deal made Mesa a household word. It was the biggest corporate merger in history. During the spring of 1984 I made a dozen appearances before Senate and House committees. I made the point that it was not the government's job to protect weak managements and the oil industry should be left alone to restructure. The Senate had rejected a six-month moratorium on oil company mergers — a triumph of good sense and a victory for shareholders. That was my first experience with lobbying in Washington, and I gained a faith in the process that I had lacked. I learned that the Senate was capable of analyzing a complex business phenomenon, but that you damn well had to go and make your case. After all, the big companies had an unlimited number of lobbyists working full time.

I was convinced that the oil business was still headed south, but there were nevertheless a number of huge companies with big cash flows that should be considered for acquisition or restructuring. I knew one thing: it wasn't time to be exploring for oil. Acquisition made a lot more sense, and there was no reason to think it wouldn't pay off again.

We spent the summer getting ready for a deal that was yet to be identified. Drexel raised $500 million for us by selling our variable-rate subordinated notes. We then bought $500 million of the Mesa Royalty Trust stock. This offer marked the first time we didn't use investment bankers, and a very unusual thing happened. During the week and even the day before the tender offer, when the stock price usually goes up, Mesa Royalty Trust went down slightly. There had been no leaks.

It was an interesting deal in other ways, too. There was no weak management to get angry, so no problems, either. The stockholders were delighted. We offered $35 when the market price was $27. Some 89 percent of the stock was tendered, and no pressure was put on anyone. Everybody was happy but the press; it just wasn't newsworthy.

By the end of the summer we were ready to go. We had an extensive file on the oil companies and came up with several interesting prospects. Chevron, Texaco, Amoco, Arco, and even Kerr McGee were on the long list. We reviewed their balance sheets and reserves. Cash flow is the key, along with the location of the company's reserves: whether or not they were in the United States was important. We wanted a company that was flexible enough to restructure, one that didn't have too much debt. After all these factors had been considered, I offered my analysis of the company's management. We naturally picked the weakest managements.

Two companies kept showing up on everybody's short list: Phillips and Unocal.

Phillips was a special case for David Batchelder and me. Not only was I a former employee, but David grew up in Bartlesville, Phillips's headquarters, where his dad had worked; his brother was still working there. Bea and I were both native Oklahomans and had family scattered all over the state. We had even donated $1 million to Oklahoma State University in 1982. I could imagine living in Bartlesville again, and, although it was a hurdle for Bea, she understood its importance.

Unocal and Phillips were about the same size, but Unocal had less debt. Our decision hinged on the analysis of the two managements. Bill Douce, Phillips's CEO, was just a year away from retirement. I knew Bill and thought he would be easy to talk to.

Fred Hartley, Unocal's CEO, was . . . We'll talk about Fred later. Both companies had lagged behind the changing trends in the oil business. I doubted if either had even looked at the possibilities offered by royalty trusts and master limited partnerships.

Our final question was: What is the stock trading for, versus its appraised value? Both Phillips and Unocal made the final cut, and we started buying — both stocks.

My good friend Fayez Sarofim, a well-known money manager in Houston, did the initial buying for us. We had a system for keeping our purchases confidential. We borrowed the max on our bank credit lines and then moved the money around, leaving it in numbered accounts for a while and then wire-transferring it, similar to the Gulf deal. Again, Sidney Tassin had this responsibility. None of the banks knew where the money had been or where it was going. Before long, several hundred million dollars was in Fayez's numbered account, and he was steadily buying shares in Phillips and Unocal.

Bill Douce was a nice guy and an avid bird hunter. In 1982 I was in Palm Springs for an API function. Bill and his wife, Wille, were at the same dinner table with Bea and me and two other couples.

Bill had a few drinks and got on my case pretty good — it was just a few months after the Cities deal. "Why don't you make an offer for us, Boone? Come on, make an offer! We'll take a look at it!"

"Come on, Bill," I said, "get serious. We couldn't make an offer for Phillips. You guys are too big."

"Aw, come on, Boone. Aren't you getting ready to make an offer for us?"

"We're not getting ready to make an offer for anybody," I said, and added to myself, "at least not tonight."

Mesa and its partner, Wagner & Brown, bought almost 5 percent of Phillips. And we prepared a tender offer for an additional 15 percent and proxy material for the written consent of the shareholders to replace their board of directors.

We prepared to file our suit in Delaware on the standstill agreement in the General American deal two years earlier. Mesa had agreed not to buy any GAO stock or try to influence the company's management. Phillips had acquired GAO, and although the agreement didn't say we couldn't buy Phillips stock (it didn't even mention Phillips), we knew Phillips would try to use it as a defense. When management realized we were after them, a Phillips lawyer would just walk across the street to the district court in Bartlesville, where they had tremendous influence, and say, "Judge, old buddy, Boone Pickens is buying our stock. Two years ago he agreed he wouldn't buy General American stock. Doesn't it make sense that he can't buy Phillips, since we own GAO? So give us a restraining order."

As soon as we crossed the 5 percent threshold, Mesa Partners would have ten days to file with the SEC. Then Phillips would know the whole story. We hoped to cut them off at the pass by resolving the standstill issue early, and in Delaware rather than Oklahoma, where it was a sure loser.

By the end of November, Mesa Partners had almost 8 million shares of both Phillips and Unocal, and Sarofim was getting calls about his large purchases. He would only say that he was buying for his accounts, but Douce at Phillips and Hartley at Unocal suspected who the buyer was.

Both men went hunting in Spain in early December as guests of a construction company that did business with their companies. Texaco's CEO, John McKinley, was also there. They were shooting red-legged partridge. This was an acceptable corporate expense, of course, and each man had his company's plane flown across the Atlantic, at a cost of about $30,000 per plane. Remember, these were all damned important executives. Douce told me later that he and Hartley had talked about the possibility of Mesa's making a move on one of them while they were in Spain. Hartley couldn't get the subject out of his mind. He was worried about Unocal's being taken over — and with his record he should have been. Douce got tired of listening to him complain about me and finally said, "Let's try to enjoy the hunt. What will be will be." A few hours later, the truth of that statement came home to them.

They were having dinner late on December 2 when Douce received an urgent telephone call from the states. It was from Phillips's treasurer, who said that Mesa Partners was tendering for 23 million shares of Phillips at $60 a share. Even more disturbing, Mesa was going to solicit consents from the shareholders in order to replace the board. And they also said they would take over the company through a leveraged buyout at $60 a share. Douce must have known that there would be no more partridge hunts; no more trips abroad in the company jet if Pickens takes over Phillips.

Douce returned to the dining room to find Hartley having a drink. "Relax," Douce told him, although there wasn't much chance of that, even with a few drinks under his belt. "It's us."

Douce flew back to Bartlesville to deal with the problem, then went on to New York. He didn't understand the game he was now involved in, so he hired Joe Fogg of Morgan Stanley and Marty Lipton of Wachtell Lipton to deal with us and went off hunting again — this time to Phillips's camp in South Texas. It was the last year Douce would be able to use it, since he and the incoming CEO of Phillips weren't close, and Douce knew he probably wouldn't be invited once he retired. He had actually gone to Spain when there was heavy buying in Phillips stock. But nothing was as important as the hunting season! The stockholders owe that to the CEO for all his hard work.

Douce might have listened to me in the beginning, but he was talked into resisting by his bankers, who were lining up for a fat fee. You would think their fee would buy a little loyalty, but they laughed at the naiveté of the Phillips executives behind their backs.

We flew to New York, where we waited for the outcome of the litigation in Delaware and polished our tender offer.

We were at the Helmsley Palace, as were the Phillips people. Going jogging one morning, I ran into Douce at the elevator. "Hi, Bill," I said. We shook hands, but the other Phillips people wouldn't speak. "How are things?" he asked. The elevator door was closing, so I just smiled.

We had $1 billion borrowed on Mesa's reserves and were now

Phillips's largest stockholder. We were trying to get our offer going, but Phillips had opened up litigation and we were being frustrated by the Oklahoma court.

The consent process was a short cut, to be used instead of a proxy fight. It was not necessary to have a stockholders' meeting; all we had to do was get the consents from the shareholders. The management would not know when we were complete or what the outcome would be until it was over, and that scared the hell out of them. It was a little like impeachment, and they knew they were impeachable. They probably wondered why it hadn't happened sooner.

The consent process was important because it might keep the board from doing something stupid, like making a bad acquisition to dilute the company's value or issuing a load of "super voting" preferred stock to a "friendly" investor. But that would annoy Phillips's stockholders and make them vote with us. We were being "hometowned" in the Oklahoma courts, but as soon as we got that cleared up, Phillips would have a real problem on its hands. And the management was just saying, "Let Marty Lipton take care of it."

Phillips's suit in Oklahoma district court claimed we violated the GAO standstill agreement. The judge, of course, issued a temporary restraining order (TRO) prohibiting us from going forward with the tender offer.

Our lawsuit in the Delaware federal court, which took precedence over the proceedings in Oklahoma, wasn't getting the job done. We also filed in Delaware chancery court for a declaratory judgment that the GAO agreement didn't include Phillips. The Delaware court agreed to try the case and issued an order prohibiting Phillips from proceeding in Oklahoma. But the Delaware court did not choose to revoke the TRO in Bartlesville. Consequently, we couldn't launch the offer.

We were losing momentum just when it was dangerous to slow down. Phillips was getting more lawsuits filed by picking up the expenses and indemnifying the people filing the suits. It got two local jobbers — gasoline distributors — to file a suit in Oklahoma alleging federal antitrust violations by Mesa. The suit was a joke, but we had to deal with it. The judge gave Phillips another TRO anyway. Hometowned again.

Phillips's management didn't care how much all this cost. Fogg and Lipton seemed to have one order from the management: "Save our jobs." The price for that defense was a blank check.

Phillips's legal strategy was simple: do everything and anything to transfer the litigation to Oklahoma, where feeling was running so high that Mesa had no chance for a decision on the merits. One Sunday night Charlie Richards, our Delaware counsel, was told that we would be sued in federal court in Tulsa the next morning and that the hearing had been set for 7:30 A.M. Obviously, they thought that on a Sunday night there was nothing we could do about it. Within an hour, a Mesa plane with Joe Cialone and Mike Graham of Baker & Botts on board, among others, left from New York for Tulsa.

Meanwhile, Charlie was able to arrange a hearing at about 10:30 P.M. that same Sunday in the living room of Judge Joseph J. Longobardi III of the U.S. District Court for the District of Delaware. As they sat there before Judge Longobardi's Christmas tree, all trimmed and with its lights blinking, Charlie asked for an injunction against this new tactic by Phillips, which could have brought our offer to a halt. After the hearing, the parties went home while the judge decided how to handle our request. At 1:30 A.M. on Monday, only hours before the scheduled hearing in Tulsa, Judge Longobardi enjoined Phillips from bringing its new lawsuit. I knew we had a good team of lawyers, but their performance on this case was outstanding.

Phillips made us a greenmail offer through an intermediary. I got a call from my friend Joe Flom. He was still on retainer to Mesa, but he was also on retainer to Phillips. Joe couldn't represent either side, but he could act as a go-between and he called with the offer. They used Flom so that they could later deny they had offered greenmail if they were asked. Phillips was playing holier than thou to the press but was ready to pay greenmail from the beginning. As soon as management was threatened, they broke down like a $3 tent. We could have picked their pockets at $70 a share, which would have made us $300 million, if we had wanted to do it. Nobody in our camp was interested in greenmail.

"Forget it, Joe," I said. "We're not going to do that."

Greenmail had become a public issue, for several big deals had recently involved greenmail. (The Bass brothers of Fort Worth accepted a whopper from Texaco: A $400 million profit for the Basses and an equal loss for the Texaco stockholders.) But the public and the press didn't realize that the culprits weren't the people who took it but those who offered it.

I got a second call from Flom. "Forget the cash," he said. "What about buying a property?" He speculated that they would be willing to sell us an oil field for $100 million when it was really worth $200 million.

"That won't work either, Joe."

"Well, then, maybe you could sell them some Mesa property at an inflated value."

"No, Joe, even a dumb analyst could figure that out." Joe knew it, too; he was just trying to come up with an idea.

If Phillips could get rid of us, the empire would survive. All the sacred perks and power would still be in place. But when they saw we wouldn't go along they changed tactics, putting out the word in Bartlesville that Boone Pickens would destroy the company and the town. What was left would be moved to Amarillo. Bartlesville would be a disaster if the citizens didn't rise up against the invader! The locals bought it — hook, line, and sinker.

The Phillips management stampeded the employees and the townspeople like a lynch mob. The twenty-four-hour prayer vigils were popular. T-shirts with BOONE BUSTER logos were distributed to anyone who would wear them. All the major television networks flew into Bartlesville and interviewed townspeople who were sure that Mesa intended to destroy Phillips and Bartlesville. The Chamber of Commerce staged a "crisis forum." Anyone speaking up for us was in real danger.

In the short term, media perception is very important, and this time it was going against us like a tidal wave. The public saw us as something we weren't — that image was established in a matter of hours. No matter how well intentioned you are, you can't reverse that initial impression nearly as quickly. Phillips was cautious in its relations with the press. Douce later told me he had learned a lot by watching Gulf's blunders.

I told reporters that it would be ridiculous for Mesa to invest a billion dollars in a company and then destroy it. I also reminded them that my roots were in Oklahoma and said clearly that we had no intention of moving Phillips's headquarters out of Bartlesville. Phillips had some 6,800 employees in Bartlesville, and its 40,000 inhabitants were indirectly dependent on the company. Worldwide, Phillips had 25,000 employees, Mesa only 500, so there was no way we could displace its work force. We thought the announcement would diffuse concerns in Bartlesville about the future. We were wrong.

Cable News Network gave the story full coverage, but some important facts about Phillips were not mentioned. For instance, Phillips had let 10,000 employees go before we ever bought a share of its stock. High volume in the stock began before we got involved, indicating that someone else was accumulating the stock and that it was just a matter of time before something happened. If someone larger took over, Bartlesville might become a ghost town. I told Douce later that it was wrong to frighten people. He said it was part of Phillips's defense.

The unresolved issue was the standstill agreement, going back to the investment bankers Morgan Stanley, who had negotiated it on Mesa's behalf in 1982. Morgan's Joe Fogg filed an affidavit in the Oklahoma court claiming that he had told me, back in 1982, that the standstill agreement applied to Phillips. Other people involved in the GAO deal remembered it differently. Since Fogg was working for us at the time, it cost him and Morgan credibility on Wall Street.

Phillips's questionable tactics extended all the way to Amarillo. One day, going out to the Mesa hangar, I noticed a car parked on the service road and a man with binoculars. Phillips had hired someone to keep track of us, just as Cities Service and Gulf had done.

Phillips also filed a suit charging that I had given inside information to my friends in Amarillo, enabling them to buy stock ahead of an offer. This charge was without foundation and purely for harassment. Things were really getting crazy now.

An unidentified man tried to force his way into our offices and, when challenged, ran away. I put a guard at my house, just in case, but the Phillips campaign galvanized our people and made them even more determined. Attempts at intimidation by Big Oil were as old as the business, and Phillips was desperate.

I filed a lawsuit for intimidation against Phillips, Douce, and their investigator for asking a former employee where my children lived. I got my own temporary restraining order, and the investigator left for Bartlesville in a cloud of dust.

On December 20, the Delaware judge ruled that Mesa's "standstill" case won on the merits, but he refused to remove the TRO in Oklahoma that was holding us up. To win was a boost for us, and it looked as if we were about to get our offer under way.

We soon had most of our people in New York, including David Batchelder, Sidney Tassin, Drew Craig, Bob Stillwell, and Steve Massad. It was Christmastime, and the city was crowded with shoppers. Phillips was also there in force, along with its contingent of investment bankers and lawyers.

Mesa was a small band of people opposed by an army that had taken over the opulent top floor of the hotel for its top executives. Their gofers were billeted on the lower floors with us. What these guys wanted was to buy out their largest stockholder quickly so that they could get on to the hunting camp.

Drew Craig, another one of our top people, had just come in with me from Amarillo. We got on the elevator with a nervous man who obviously recognized us. We all got off on the forty-eighth floor and walked down the hall in the same direction.

When we got to the end of the hall, I said to Drew, "Are we going to the same place?"

"Looks like it."

The other man went into the room directly across the hall from Batchelder's door. While Drew and I were waiting, we heard some scuffling behind the door across the hall. There was some laughter, and the door opened. I recognized one of the group, Bob Jeffe, of Morgan Stanley. He was with some of the Phillips people. They must have been watching us through the peephole in the door. They reminded me of their detectives.

Jeffe came out and we shook hands. He was wearing an overcoat, and at the neck I could see the white band of a T-shirt. Jeffe said, "He wants to meet you," and pointed to the man who had ridden up with us on the elevator. "He's Phillips's treasurer."

I shook hands with him. Then I reached over and unbuttoned Jeffe's overcoat. He didn't try to stop me. Underneath the coat he was wearing a BOONE BUSTER T-shirt that he had pulled over his dress shirt. These guys were having a ball, and at the same time they were going to make $20 million off the Phillips stockholders. They didn't give a damn about the stockholders. The Phillips management didn't give a damn, either.

David brought me up to date: we were still on hold. We reserved ad space in the *Wall Street Journal* and *New York Times* for the tender offer announcement and then had to cancel it while we waited for the court to knock down the Oklahoma TRO. It was frustrating.

On December 21, Joe Flom called and said, "It's time to make a deal." I knew what he was talking about.

Phillips had lost on the standstill issue, so management was ready to talk. It sounded like more greenmail, but I agreed that David and Sidney would meet with them in Skadden Arps's offices at five. We decided to repeat our offer for a leveraged buyout. Either we would do it or the management could do it.

Bob Stillwell went along with David and Sidney. Representing Phillips were Joe Fogg, of Morgan Stanley, and Simon Orme, as well as Jeffe (without the T-shirt) and the First Boston M&A guys. Phillips had lined up a stable of investment bankers. It was the old rationale: if one is good, then two is twice as good. Marty Lipton, Phillips's outside counsel, was called "the king of takeover defense" or "the great defender of entrenched management." The story was that when he received a call from a terrified CEO about to lose his empire, Lipton would say, "My sign-on retainer is $2 million. You have ten seconds to make up your mind, because I have another anxious CEO holding on line two." I'm told that Lipton has never been turned down, and his sign-on fee will go up to $3 million in 1987.

David's opening remarks were brief. We wanted to do a leveraged buy-out (LBO), put in more than a billion dollars in equity, retain some of the management, and keep the company basically the same. They weren't interested. Remember, we were negotiating with their hired guns. There wasn't a single Phillips employee in the room, and we didn't have a single investment banker in the room. All of their representatives were being taken care of with fees. Meanwhile, we were offering the best value to their stockholders and at the same time providing security for their employees.

The Phillips reps were instructed to kill any idea of ours, and they proposed a recapitalization plan, a defensive alternative that would preserve the management. The plan would require the rank and file employees to bail out the company's leaders for their past mistakes. The employee stock ownership plan would pay a premium for a large percentage of the Phillips stock. Phillips would repurchase about 30 percent of its outstanding stock through an exchange offer and spend up to $1 billion in open market purchases during the next year. The company would sell some of its assets and reduce the debt, increase the dividend, and the Phillips employees would own 30 percent of the company. The investment bankers valued the deal at $53 per Phillips share. If this was such a good idea, why didn't the management think of it before we showed up?

They offered us $53 a share, significantly more than what the stock was selling for. Their main provision was that Mesa would get out of the Phillips stock and stay out. David made it clear that they had to take care of the other stockholders in a similar fashion. The other stockholders were different in that they did not have the expense or time in the battle, and they had not been given a standstill agreement.

When the Mesa team returned to the Helmsley, we talked

about it over a late supper in the room. I thought $53 was too low, but we were in the mood to make a deal. Bea and I were no longer interested in moving back to Oklahoma, and it was clear that the Phillips management was not going to work with us. I had a real concern about the price of oil in the spring. On the previous Monday I had met with an expert on the Mideast. He said, "Boone, don't pay too much for Phillips, and $60 a share is too much. Oil prices are headed down."

Our other choice was to keep driving. "Even if we don't take their offer," David said, "they've shown us their defense plan." The employee stock ownership could be a powerful defense.

I was afraid my friend was right about oil prices, and we could get in a spot on our financing in the spring of '85 that would eat our lunch. It was time to make a deal, and I knew it.

"Let's try to work it out," I said.

David said, "We have to get them to beef it up so that everyone will get $53." At $53, we were looking at a profit of $90 million.

David called Fogg around midnight and told him we were ready to talk.

Fogg said, "Tell me your wish list."

We wanted them to buy back 50 percent of the stock, not 30, commit to spending a billion dollars more to purchase shares in the market over the following year, and increase the dividend.

Fogg told David they would get a document to us by ten o'clock the next morning. We planned to leave for Amarillo right after we signed the agreement.

Our daughter Liz had come up from Washington, D.C., to catch a ride home. She had brought her cat, and she tranquilized it, thinking we were about ready to go home. We ordered some food, and waited. Liz went shopping and came back with a box of chocolates for the team and a Christmas ribbon for the cat, Huckleberry. He soon became known as Deal Cat, the most docile former tomcat in town.

Finally the document arrived. To our surprise, it contained almost the same numbers that Fogg had presented the night before. Phillips would buy back 30 percent of the stock, not 50 percent; this was the biggest problem. Then there was cheap stuff, such as the agreement's being governed by Oklahoma law. After our experience in the Oklahoma courts, this was a joke. We couldn't believe that Fogg was silly enough to put it in. First drafts always have goofy points, but this was too much.

David called Fogg and said, "You guys call this negotiating? We're packing our bags. We'll see you after Christmas."

Fogg couldn't understand why we wanted Phillips to sweeten the deal, i.e., buy a higher percentage of the stock and commit to open-market purchase programs. "Why do you care about the other stockholders?" he asked. "You're getting your $53."

"Let's quit screwing around," said David before he hung up.

I called Joe Flom. "Joe, they aren't serious about making a deal — they're just interested in saving their ass."

"I haven't seen the agreement yet," Joe said. "They'll come around. Fogg's just hard-trading you."

It was all part of Fogg's negotiating strategy: he would cut a deal with us and pretend to take it to the Phillips management; then he would come back for more.

"It's a chickenshit way to trade," I said.

Finally Flom agreed to call Fogg. When he called back he said, "They'll negotiate — I mean, really negotiate. The Oklahoma thing is out." He knew it was a silly point.

Lots of telephone calls were going back and forth between David and Fogg as David tried to move the deal off high center. Fogg was holding out for a smaller buy-back; the figure hung between our insistence on 50 percent and their offering of 30. Their strategy was to resolve everything but the buy-back percentage and then to hard-trade. We were trying very hard to get a good deal for all the stockholders.

Meanwhile, their lawyers worked on management's most important point, the standstill agreement.

We agreed to support their recapitalization plan when it was voted on by their stockholders. It wasn't as good as our $60 LBO, but it beat the hell out of what they had been doing for the shareholders.

"I don't understand why you're being so tough," Flom said toward evening. I could see the lights along Park Avenue and the endless stream of traffic, beautiful in the cold December twilight. But I thought of Bartlesville, and what Phillips's CEO had done to discredit me. I also thought of all the people — shareholders — who that night were finishing up their Christmas shopping, unaware of what the boys at the top were doing, how they had passed up a good deal for a so-so deal. It was ironic that we were labeled the hostile adversaries, negotiating with the "good guys" and trying to get them to let the shareholders have a chance at our $60 offer. These same "good guys" were telling me not to worry about those people down there on the street, that we were getting our money.

We argued back and forth until very late. Meanwhile, Deal Cat was all over the suite in his Christmas ribbon. At one point he came very close to going out an open window, forty-eight stories above the street. There was mixed feeling about this.

We got them up to 33 percent on the buy-back; they got us down to 45 percent. We sat around for another hour waiting for a final offer. Then we got the call, and David and Fogg sawed off at a 38 percent buy-back. Fogg said, "I don't think the Phillips people will buy it, but I'll call you back shortly." We knew the so-called Phillips people would do anything to get their ass out of the crack. Typical of Fogg, he didn't call back.

The next morning he did call and said, "You got a deal." It included a reimbursement from Phillips for our expenses.

The documents were being prepared when I got a call from Douce. "It looks like we have a deal," he said, and I agreed. He went on, "I think we should sit down and talk one-on-one."

I went upstairs to his suite and we shook hands. "I'm really surprised you did this, Boone," he said, referring to Mesa's move on "his" company.

"Well, Bill," I said, "what's done is done."

"You told me two years ago that you weren't going after Phillips."

"We weren't after you two years ago."

Soon after we sat down, Pete Silas, Phillips's president, came in with the chief financial officer. Neither man spoke.

I knew Silas, so I said, "Hello, Pete, how are you?" and stuck out my hand.

He took off his coat and walked to the closet and hung it up. Then he mumbled, "Hello." I stood there with my hand out just to see what he would do. He finally shook hands and left the room.

"Pete seems unhappy about something," I said.

"Yeah," said Douce, "he's pretty mad. You hurt Phillips."

"I helped the shareholders."

He got very serious, and looked me in the eye. "You said some things I didn't like."

"What was that?"

"You said I didn't own much stock. I know, because I had people taping your speeches."

I wanted to laugh. "Bill, what I said was that you make a salary of over a million dollars a year and you get a bonus of over a million dollars a year, and for two of the last three years the company has had down operating results. And you own hardly any stock." I added, "Then I look seriously at the audience and say, 'Wonder where Mr. Douce puts all his money. It surely isn't in Phillips stock.' This always gets a big laugh."

"Yeah, I know about the laugh," he said, adding defensively, "I own about thirty-seven thousand shares."

"Hell, Bill, a guy who's worked at Phillips for forty-one years and is paid more than $2 million a year should own a little more stock than that."

"To be fair, you should tell people that Phillips doesn't have a stock option plan."

I said, "Why not?"

"Hell, Boone, we never could make any money out of one."

"How can you go before a group of analysts and money managers and tell them Phillips is a good buy, when you won't even take a no-risk stock option?"

He thought for a minute. "They buy the stock because of the dividend."

"Bill, get serious. T-bills are paying nine percent, and the Phillips dividend is six percent. And you're depleting your reserves of oil and gas to pay the dividend. Nobody would buy Phillips for the dividend."

"You know, Boone," he said, "you've got a good point."

The deal was wrapped up later that afternoon, but only after more hard negotiating on the press release. We wanted Phillips and its investment bankers to agree that all stockholders would get $53 in value. This was finally accomplished, but only after we threatened to pull out of the deal.

Liz tranquilized Deal Cat again, and we were on our way to Amarillo. The next day was Christmas Eve, and none of us had been home for a while. Two Mesa planes were waiting. The Lear took Sidney home to Louisiana and dropped Stillwell and Massad in Houston. The rest of us boarded the Falcon for the Panhandle of Texas.

As we headed west, Liz asked, "How do you feel about it?"

"I'm so glad to get loose from Phillips, I don't know what to do. I felt the same way in 1954, when I quit."

But we weren't loose, not yet.

We had hit rock bottom in public opinion. I was seen as the financial barbarian with little regard for shareholders, employees, or consumers. It would take time for the economists in academia, government, and industry to analyze the situation sufficiently to prove me right or wrong.

On the replay, we could have made a profitable deal in a minute if greenmail had been our goal. It would have been easy to get $70 a share while the others got nothing. We had given up $17 per share — $150 million — but were blamed for greenmail anyway. As Joe Flom later testified before the SEC, "Pickens's getting tagged with greenmail is the bummest rap anybody ever got."

The *New York Times* said that the Phillips decline "undoubtedly sullied Mr. Pickens' reputation" in the arbitrage community and that the arbs felt "let down by the Texan." One of the arbs who lost money on the Phillips deal, interestingly, was Ivan

Boesky; he had no insider information on this one. I did care about the other stockholders, and I cared about what people thought of me, including the arbs.

The recapitalization plan was complicated and not well received by the institutional stockholders, and the press was thoroughly confused. Because Phillips was buying only 38 percent of the stock back, the blended value was perceived to be less than $53. Phillips should have done the 50 percent buy-back we wanted, and everything would have been fine. Now with the price down it was vulnerable again — not to Mesa, because we were out of the picture, but to some other entrepreneur. And the hunting season wasn't over yet.

The most likely suspects were Carl Icahn and Irwin Jacobs, both well-known takeover entrepreneurs. I was certain that they were watching the Phillips stock fall out of bed.

Indeed, Icahn moved in, as I supposed he would. He proposed a leveraged buy-out of Phillips for $55 a share, taking advantage of the company's vulnerability and shareholder dissatisfaction. The arbs began to buy Phillips stock in earnest; they had seen how weak the management was and knew they had a winner.

I wrote to Douce, suggesting that he consider a leveraged buy-out of Phillips at $53, and offered to help him do it. He wrote back a curt letter declining. Phillips had panicked again. I wondered how many times they were going to screw up. The management announced they would pay shareholders an additional $3.32 a share in preferred stock, to sweeten the recap plan, and that they were assigning "fair value" rights to all stockholders to protect the company from outside bids. Bullshit! This was a poison pill. When reporters asked for my opinion of the proposals, I said that poison pills are unacceptable, period, because their purpose is to protect inept management.

During Icahn's proxy fight, Icahn, Douce, and I were asked to testify before the Council of Institutional Investors. I was warned by friends not to expose myself to their hostility since we were now out of the deal, but David and I went anyway. The council represented big pension funds worth more than $100 billion.

Hostile questions were raised that implied we had taken greenmail. I explained that this was not the case and continued to answer questions. Finally, my patience wearing thin, I said, "We put fourteen points in the Phillips stock, invested a billion dollars, fought the lawsuits, and took the heat. Did any of you help us? Hell no. When are some of you guys going to put some points in the stock?" Everyone laughed, but I wasn't through yet. "You haven't done a goddamn thing but sit here and criticize me," I said, "and we helped you make millions of dollars." As I was leaving, several of them thanked me for testifying.

Phillips lost the proxy fight with Icahn. It was the biggest proxy fight loss by management on record. Icahn drove Phillips to a $62 self-tender for 50 percent of the stock. The shareholders now got more than our $53. If it had been done that way earlier, the deal would have been called a "creative major restructuring." But the negative publicity, Icahn's involvement, and the proxy fight left a bad taste in everybody's mouth.

Some 150,000 Phillips stockholders saw their stock go up $15 a share — a 40 percent increase and a market value enhancement of more than $2 billion — all in less than three months. We were Phillips's largest stockholder, and we were criticized for making $89 million, which was only 4 percent of the profit.

I regretted that Douce and I hadn't had a man-to-man session before he turned it over to his investment bankers and outside legal counsel. Bill and I had known each other for years, and I think he would have heard me out. Time has proven that our plan would have been best for the stockholders and employees as well as Bartlesville.

# · 19 ·

## *Unocal*

### "Is You Is or Is You Ain't . . ."

You can't talk about Unocal without talking about Fred Hartley, its CEO. Never has a company been more dominated by a personality: its operating philosophies and the character of its organization are a direct extension of Hartley's. I had been acquainted with Fred over the years through the American Petroleum Institute, where he was once the chairman and I — a token independent — was a director. Once a year the executive committee of the API goes to Palm Springs, California, for a meeting in the sun. I wasn't a member of the executive committee in 1980, but I was a member of Eldorado Country Club, so I was invited to participate in its one-day golf tournament. But golf wasn't the main entertainment. That was provided by Hartley.

I had heard funny stories about him from other CEOs. He fancied himself a musician and even had a piano installed in one of Unocal's jets.

Fred and I shared a golf cart that day. It was raining, so we played all day in rain suits. That may have affected Hartley's game, or it may have been the drinking the night before, but he got off to a poor start. Later, he asked how long I had been a member of Eldorado, trying to figure out who I was. When I told him, he asked, "Who do you work for?"

"Mesa Petroleum."

"Is that a publicly traded company?"

"Yes, we've been on the New York Stock Exchange since 1969."

"Well, what does Mesa do?"

"We're in the exploration and production end of the oil business."

That aroused a spark of interest. "How many people work for Mesa?"

"About six hundred," I said.

He wasn't impressed and started talking about Unocal's size.

"Fred, I saw recently that your domestic budget is about $700 million." I said. "Ours is about $400 million."

There was a long pause. "How many people did you say you employ?"

"About six hundred."

We got out of the golf cart and walked to the tee. I hit a pretty good drive down the fairway. It was Fred's turn.

"Goddamn," he said. "You've only got six hundred people — we've got twenty-two thousand."

"Fred, have you ever thought you might be overstaffed?"

He looked at me as if he were seeing me for the first time. His mouth opened, but he didn't say anything. Red-faced, he drew his club back and made a lunge at the ball. He got about a third of the ball, and it dribbled through the wet grass.

I later ran into Fred and invited him to have breakfast at Eldorado. I had been giving speeches about the advantages of royalty trusts, and I thought he would be interested in the concept. However, he was more interested in who paid for the breakfast.

"I'll pay for it, Fred," I said. "You'll be my guest."

We met at the club the following morning, and Fred ordered a lumberjack's breakfast. I started to explain the royalty trust concept and how we had spun off one at Mesa in 1979, but he interrupted me. "That's the dumbest thing I ever heard of — giving the oil and gas reserves to the stockholders."

"But they already own them," I said, "since stockholders own the company."

He just looked at me and shook his head. I could see that there was no point in going on with the discussion and excused myself to join my golf foursome. I looked back to see Fred sitting contentedly behind a large stack of pancakes.

That was a few years before all the publicity about Mesa. After the Gulf deal, I saw Hartley at the annual meeting of the All-American Wildcatters in Phoenix. I don't know how Fred ever got into the organization; it would be like my getting into the Hall of Fame as a defensive end. He wouldn't pay a dime to see a piss ant eat a bale of hay, and he sure wouldn't invest his own money in a wildcat well. Some executives think they're wildcatters because they spend stockholders' money.

He came over to me and said sarcastically, "I guess I ought to compliment you on the Gulf deal."

"Well, thanks, Fred. I appreciate that."

"Goddamn it, you put a fine old company out of business, that's what you did."

"No, I didn't put Gulf out of business. Their properties and assets are now a part of Socal, and that was a decision their board made."

His face was bright crimson as he looked around the room. He spotted Bob Anderson, Arco's CEO. "There's the shill that made the deal for you," he added, referring to the disclosure in the middle of the Gulf deal that Arco had made an offer to buy Gulf.

"Fred, I don't think Bob would appreciate your calling him a shill."

"Well, by God, that's what he was!" And he stomped off to get another drink.

Soon after the Gulf deal, rumors started to fly that Mesa was on the move again. At the outset of the Phillips deal, Hartley's hunting trip to Spain had been ruined when he wondered if we were going after Unocal, and he kept talking about that "no good son of a bitch from Amarillo." He had definitely gotten to know about Mesa since our golf game back in 1980.

Unocal was just like the other majors: it had more cash than investment opportunities, and was screwing off stockholders' money at an alarming rate. Unocal had an ongoing black hole for cash in its shale oil plant in Colorado. I don't think the company has ever told the whole story of that disaster. The shareholders have taken enormous losses, and there is a distinct possibility that the government will have to pick up part of the tab, courtesy of the old Synfuel Corporation, which was formed in the Carter administration. Mesa would have closed it by sundown, if we had gained control of Unocal, and not asked the government for a nickel. How big is the loss? Would you believe over $1 billion and growing?

Unocal's mistakes were covered up by its huge cash flow, fueled by OPEC price increases. Its dividend was the lowest of all the majors. (At Unocal's 1984 annual meeting, a man complained that he had been a stockholder for years and was getting tired of waiting for a decent dividend. Hartley responded, "You look like an elderly fellow. Why don't you sell your stock and go have a good time.")

Hartley was well known for his combative personality. During a speech made to the Oil Writers Association in San Francisco, he was at his best. There he was asked what would happen to the price of oil. He said he thought oil prices would stay up because the French were selling Exocet missiles to the "Iraqians" to bomb the Iranians. War eliminated a lot of competition, he added. And it was as effective as price-fixing.

In the late seventies, Hartley had sued a *Los Angeles Times* cartoonist for depicting him as a light bulb on an otherwise naked Christmas tree. It was during the oil shortage, and Hartley had diverted a tanker from California to Alaska, at a time when California desperately needed the oil. Hartley lost the suit and then sued Otis Chandler, the publisher of the *Times*. He lost that one, too, with Unocal's stockholders probably picking up the tab for both of them.

I had seen Fred perform over the years at National Petroleum Council meetings. Once a man seated next to me said, "Oh, God, we're going to have to listen to Fred today."

I asked, "How do you know?"

"He's got his hair backcombed and sprayed."

Sure enough, at the first opening Hartley was on his feet. Instead of asking a question, he made a five-minute speech. I hoped that we were looking at the end of an era for the oil business.

In January 1984, Fred came to the Cambridge Energy Conference in Houston, where I was the keynote speaker. One of the organizers told me, "Hartley's going to challenge you on your ideas about restructuring the industry. He's really going to work you over."

Hartley showed but didn't say a word. He sat at the back of the room and, instead of challenging me, turned his chair around and faced the wall when I spoke.

A year later I was back at Eldorado for an annual black-tie affair. John Connally and I shared the podium as speakers before 400 club members. After I had spoken, Hartley stood up, very red-faced, and said, "I know what happened to the Gulf stockholders. They all got rich and now live in Palm Beach. But what about Socal?" He proceeded to blame me for Socal's debt on the Gulf acquisition.

"Fred," I said, "do you think I work for Socal?"

"Well, you caused all the debt because they paid too much for Gulf. It's your fault."

"George Keller runs Socal, Fred. You know that. George thought the Gulf purchase was a hell of a deal. If I had tried to tell him how much to pay for Gulf, he'd have thrown me out of his office."

Hartley had a dozen chances to debate me but passed them all up. He treated not only stockholders with contempt, but also government and anyone else who crossed his path. If you didn't see things his way, he considered you stupid and told you so. I remember one of his speeches when he said he wanted to decontrol oil because it was best for free enterprise. Oil was then selling for $35 a barrel. In 1986, when it was selling for $15, he wanted the government to impose an import tax. Ol' Fred's version of free enterprise is like that of a lot of other CEOs in corporate America — self-serving.

*

Coming off the Phillips deal with a bad taste in our mouth, we were not anxious to return to the trenches. But we had a timing problem. By mid-February 1985, we would have to file a report with the SEC disclosing our securities ownership as of the fourth quarter of 1984. This would reveal our 4.4 percent ownership of Unocal. The question was: Do we sell it, or do we expand our holding?

In a lengthy session with our partners, Cy Wagner and Jack Brown, we decided to expand. Our strategy was based on the assumption that Unocal would have to follow the leaders and restructure. We weren't even considering making a tender offer, and in fact we viewed Unocal as we had Gulf — it was an investment. After the industry had been going through a year and a half of rapid change, we thought that even Fred Hartley could see the advantages of restructuring.

Our ownership passed 5 percent in early February, and we filed with the SEC, stating that our purchases were for investment only. We had to file amendments twice that month, as our ownership increased. We had 17 million shares — 9.8 percent of Unocal's stock — and we were now its largest stockholder. The price of poker was going up fast: Mesa Partners II had $770 million on the table. We still had no intention of making an offer for Unocal, but we did expect the company to make changes to fit the times and boost the stock price. We had every reason to be interested in constructive change.

Hartley wouldn't talk to me about restructuring or anything else. Instead, he went to New York and hired Goldman, Sachs and Dillon Read, hoping they could help him get rid of us. They also put the New York public relations firm of Hill & Knowlton on the payroll. Hartley was mobilizing for war — the last thing we wanted.

The Unocal advisers went over our past deals and decided that our weak link was the banks. Not a bad call. They zeroed in on Security Pacific National Bank in Los Angeles, which happened to be Unocal's lead bank and one of our weakest. We had been a Security Pacific customer for twelve years, but we didn't have the muscle Unocal and its friends had. The bank chairman begged to be free of our loan — only $54 million out of a credit line of $1.1 billion — so we brought other banks in to pick up Security's position.

Hartley was so mad that he sued Security. People from Hill & Knowlton were called in. They made copies of the lawsuit, Unocal's press release, and a letter Hartley had written to the Federal Reserve chairman, Paul Volcker, complaining about everything. This material was sent in unmarked envelopes to the homes of our other bankers and their directors. Hill & Knowlton's people called reporters and tried to get them to write uncomplimentary articles about Pickens, the raider.

Hartley said that Security Pacific's action "exemplifies a larger problem that affects us all . . . a takeover frenzy that strikes at the economic well-being of this country." In other words, when your ineptitude is challenged, wrap yourself in the American flag! He called me "a self-serving raider . . . acting in opposition to so-called entrenched management," and added, "I urge you to act now to curb this abusive use of credit."

The fact that he complained to Volcker seemed ridiculous, but maybe it wasn't. I have thought long and hard about why Hartley contacted the chairman of the Federal Reserve so early in the game.

It was no surprise, therefore, when Volcker rammed through some margin requirements for high-yield or junk bond financing used in "hostile" takeovers. The ruling did not affect friendly deals. (Whether a deal is hostile is only in the mind of the target company chairman.) It did surprise me that Volcker had had a three-hour dinner with Andy Sigler, the chairman of the Policy Committee at the Business Roundtable, the night before the ruling. I was catching on to how powerful the Business Roundtable was: the White House, the State, Treasury, and Commerce departments, the Office of Management and Budget, and the president's economic advisers had all encouraged the Fed not to pass the rule. To go against that lineup — wow, that's power!

Unocal was now applying more pressure to the banks. It reminded me of Phillips's scaring the daylights out of the people of

Bartlesville. Its message to our banks was clear: "Drop Pickens, or we're going to sue you, too." Bankers hate litigation.

We filed suit against Unocal for intimidating our banks. Hartley's attacks on what he called "raiders" were becoming more strident and bitter. He called me a financial barbarian and a "communist." He had also called me a crook in the presence of four other people at a Unocal retirement dinner. His behavior was disturbing to a lot of people. He was showing little regard for his newest and largest stockholder. More than one person asked me how long I was going to put up with him.

Meanwhile, Unocal's directors were frantically changing the bylaws to take away shareholders' rights. They were scared to death of us but were now damaging 100,000 other stockholders as well.

It was obvious that we would have to reconsider the original purpose of our investment. If Hartley refused to face reality, we would be forced to look at alternatives. We had big bucks invested and couldn't ignore what was going on. I had purposely kept quiet and not given Fred reason for further agitation by criticizing him in the press. But being called a communist and a crook was not something I took lightly.

On March 26, we flew to New York and met with Joe Flom to discuss our strategy. We announced the next day that we were going to solicit proxies to postpone the shareholders' meeting, and we filed a demand to receive the shareholder list. We needed more time to decide what course of action to take — proposing a restructuring plan or a new slate of directors, for instance, or maybe a tender offer. Because of the recent bylaw changes, if we were unable to postpone the meeting, it would be another full year before we could present a proposal.

Sidney and I flew to Los Angeles on March 27, and I gave a speech at Drexel's annual bond conference. That day, while we were en route, David bought a block of 6.7 million Unocal shares for $322 million, one of the largest block trades ever done. This raised our stake to 23.7 million shares — 13.6 percent of the company. We now had more than $1 billion invested. During the questions after my speech, I sidestepped anything related to Unocal. When I got back to the airport I called Fred, but he wouldn't take the call. I didn't want to ignore him while I was in town; things like that can upset people.

On April Fool's Day, Unocal sued us for alleged SEC violations and for contacting Drexel and others about possible financing to take over Unocal. David, Drew, and I went back to New York on Good Friday, April 5, and met with our attorneys and Drexel's people to consider alternatives. Drexel was confident it could raise $3 billion. After lengthy discussions, we decided that we would offer to buy 64 million shares, enough to give us a 51 percent majority.

Sidney was in Houston, being deposed on one of the Unocal lawsuits. Their strategy was to keep our people tied up because they knew we worked with a small group and no investment bankers. We planned to announce on Monday our intention to make a tender offer and follow up with the financing details by the end of the week. But that would give Unocal time to devise a counterstrategy or block the offer, as Phillips had done. "Why not go now?" said Joe Cialone, a smart Baker & Botts lawyer. We would need to complete our deal with Drexel and the banks, reserve ad space in the *New York Times* and the *Wall Street Journal*, and prepare and print our tender offer by Monday morning. There would be no Easter egg hunt this year.

Things could have turned out differently. Hartley could have announced a restructuring plan for the company, as we originally expected. But he was set in concrete; he wasn't going to do a damn thing Pickens wanted him to do. We were bucking corporate America's biggest and best-known ego. He must have assumed that we would push on and try to take over Unocal. Ironically, each of his moves narrowed our alternatives. His first strike against us, to intimidate the banks, hadn't worked. Rewriting Unocal's bylaws to prevent shareholders from calling meetings and bringing up new business had led us to launch our proxy fight. Now came the big battle over the tender offer.

Sidney finished his deposition in Houston knowing that we would launch on Monday. He told the Unocal lawyer that he needed to finish by 5 P.M. so he could catch a plane. He was joined by two Baker & Botts lawyers, and they all went to New York.

We called all the players who weren't in New York and told them to get moving. One of the bank lawyers said he couldn't make it until the next day because there were no flights available; David told him to charter a helicopter that night. We worked around the clock through the weekend with investment bankers and commercial bankers and lawyers, using several offices and conference rooms at Skadden Arps. We slept there and at the printer's where the tender offer was being prepared.

The announcement of the tender offer made Monday's *New York Times.* We offered $54 cash per share for 64 million shares — enough to give us majority ownership. The remaining shares would be purchased with debt securities valued at $54 per share — clearly not a two-tier coercive tender offer. Within a week Drexel had lined up 130 investors for $3 billion, and we raised another billion from commercial banks. Unocal was stunned. One of its executives later told the *Wall Street Journal,* in a rare moment of candor, "All of us were just shocked when Boone came up with that money. . . . Think of it! That's green for half the company!"

I was in Washington when Unocal started shooting back. They were coming with a self-tender for 50 million shares at $72, but they would buy only if Mesa bought first. That was a cute wrinkle, but it wouldn't work. The $72 was more than Unocal was worth, and they knew it. The high price was designed to keep shareholders from tendering into Mesa's offer. If we bought first, Unocal could then buy the remaining untendered stock for the inflated $72, pushing the company to the brink of bankruptcy. These were scorched-earth tactics. Any rational stockholder would want to tender to the highest offer.

And now for the coup de grace: they were excluding their largest stockholder, Mesa Partners II, from participating, a clear violation of the legal principle stating that all shareholders must be treated equally.

The offer was illusory. Unocal wouldn't buy unless we were excluded and unless we bought first. And they knew we couldn't buy first when, sitting right behind us, was Unocal's "debt bomb" — their ability to bankrupt the company by paying too much for the shares tendered to them.

"Now that's interesting," said David when he called. Interesting, I thought, and dangerous.

Flom was in New York, and we discussed what to do. Excluding Mesa from Unocal's self-tender was clearly indefensible, so if Unocal had to do a buy-back, Mesa would have to be included. If they disagreed, we assumed we could stick it to them in court. Our strategy had been to make decisions fast and put the ball back in their court before they could relax. We decided what Mesa's position would be: we wanted Unocal to commit to the buy-back, whether Mesa bought or not. That way, we would force Unocal's management to do something for their stockholders for the first time that anybody could remember.

We put out a press release that day denouncing the exclusion of Mesa from Unocal's offer. In the release I said, "If the Unocal board is really interested in providing shareholders with $72 per share, they should do just that. They should drop the condition that Mesa purchase 64 million Unocal shares. Unless Unocal drops that condition, shareholders should regard Unocal's illusory offer as just another poison pill in a new bottle."

Another defense Unocal used was a claim that Mesa's financing violated the Federal Reserve Board's margin requirements. It was a crazy allegation, yet one that would eventually go to the Federal Reserve Board and find a sponsor in the chairman himself — another indication of the Good Ol' Boy power that Hartley was able to tap when he was in trouble.

We sued Unocal in Delaware and in Los Angeles on the exclusion of Mesa Partners II, certain that the courts would rule in our favor. Unocal announced that they were now "studying" master limited partnerships, but it was obvious they would do anything to avoid restructuring. Hartley, on deposition, admitted that he had never heard of MLPs until shortly before he was deposed, although they had been around for several years. This guy was clearly living in the past.

Throughout this period, the proxy fight to delay the annual

meeting continued. We thought Unocal's refusal to commit to repurchasing the stock would turn off the institutional investors who had a large stake in the company. This refusal reinforced the general concern that management would leave the shareholders stranded if they could somehow get rid of Mesa Partners II. One institutional investor, Arnold R. Schmeidler, filed an affidavit in U.S. District Court in California saying that he had received an assurance that Unocal would go through with its offer regardless of what Mesa did. Gilbert Schwartz, a partner of Schmeidler, said he had been told by a Unocal director who was soliciting his vote for the shareholders' meeting that the board "had grown up a lot" since the fight began and was "definitely going to take care of Unocal shareholders from now on." But Unocal still refused to commit publicly to the buy-back.

The press was having a field day, and not all the coverage was positive. There were plenty of people in both the media and the financial community who didn't like Unocal's management, but others thought that we were moving too quickly against the big oil companies, and much of the public was confused. The sad part was that most people, the media included, didn't understand what was happening. The industry was changing very fast, and it was difficult for us to get our message across. Also, during the Phillips deal we had lost our underdog role, and although we were small compared to Unocal, many people saw the contest as two giant oil companies battling it out. If we hadn't gone for Phillips earlier, the Unocal deal would have been perceived much differently, and Hartley would have stood out like a sore thumb.

On the exclusionary feature of their self-tender, however, there was little disagreement in the financial community or from anybody else. It simply violated the principle of equal treatment for all. The fact that Unocal had even attempted to exclude us showed how desperate they were. It was a long shot that only a novice would have tried.

Bea and I had lunch with the editorial board of the *Los Angeles Times*, and when they asked if we would move to Los Angeles if Mesa Partners II acquired Unocal, Bea said, "Let me answer that. I would a lot rather live in Los Angeles than Bartlesville or Pittsburgh."

We appealed to the SEC to file an amicus brief supporting us on the exclusion provision of Unocal's offer. The SEC agreed with us, but the agency was too unwieldy to act on relatively short notice, so we got no support from them. In federal court in Los Angeles, Judge A. Wallace Tashima ruled that no federal law specifically prohibited exclusionary tender offers.

The court in Delaware, where Unocal was incorporated, was much more important. The chancery court there ruled in our favor, but Judge Andrew G. T. Moore II, on the supreme court of Delaware, asked Vice Chancellor Carolyn Berger to review her decision. We had no doubt that we would win.

Then we got our only break. The stockholders' meeting was scheduled for April 29, but Judge Tashima, in Los Angeles, ordered Unocal to delay the meeting for two weeks while Unocal and Mesa Partners refiled proxy materials to correct "misstatements" in the original material we had both sent to stockholders. In the meantime, Unocal continued to keep 700 employees on the phones getting proxies; it had learned this trick from Gulf's 1983 proxy fight. It is incredible that managements can turn their headquarters into phone banks directed against their largest stockholders.

Unocal still refused to commit to buy shares if Mesa was included in the self-tender offer, despite our victory in the Delaware chancery court. In speeches in both New York and Los Angeles, I urged the stockholders to tender their shares into Unocal's $72 offer. This was absolutely necessary if the stockholders were to protect themselves. The price was so outrageously high that it would be foolish not to tender in case Unocal bought.

Our plan was to tender our shares into their offer as well, then come back with a new offer for the company at a lower price. Combining what Unocal would purchase at $72 and what we would buy at the reduced price, shareholders would still receive a "blended" $54, the same price as our original offer.

I had given up trying to talk to Hartley. He hadn't returned my calls, and his public ranting seemed to preclude any kind of meeting. Then, a week before Unocal's annual meeting, I got a call from a mutual friend, who offered to act as a go-between. It was Oscar Wyatt, the CEO of Coastal Corporation, and he said that Fred wanted to buy Mesa. This was a real surprise.

It somehow didn't make sense, but if Unocal wanted to make an offer for Mesa, then we would make sure that our stockholders got a chance to see it. Things were getting screwier by the hour. I told Oscar that talking to someone as irrational as Fred seemed useless, but he said he knew Fred a lot better than I did. They had been friends for a long time.

The annual meeting was finally held at Unocal's headquarters in Los Angeles on May 13, 1985. While the Drexel and Mesa people met for breakfast at the Sheraton Grand, I received a call from Oscar. He told me Fred was serious about buying Mesa as a way to end the battle and suggested that I listen to his offer. I didn't believe Fred would make an offer, but I wasn't about to ignore it. I said, "Put him on the phone."

Oscar had me hold while he patched Fred into a three-way hookup. As soon as Fred got on the line, I told him that I couldn't hear very well and that he should call me back directly. He called back in three minutes and said that he had an idea and wanted to talk. We agreed to meet after the stockholders' meeting. He was to call me at the hotel.

The stockholders' meeting was as stagy as the one with Gulf had been, maybe even worse, but we were in movieland, after all. Bea was with me, as well as David, Sidney, Bob Stillwell, and a few others. We found seats on the side of the almost dark auditorium and waited for the show to begin. A voice announced, "Live from Los Angeles . . ." Skillfully made up and immaculately coiffed, Hartley was on center stage, and when he started to speak from his TelePrompTer, the lights were lowered and a spotlight focused on him. Employees in other cities watched the proceedings, televised by satellite.

"We're now two weeks and two minutes late starting this meeting," Hartley said, referring to the court-imposed delay. He mentioned Unocal's self-tender. "I have given the board of directors' position as to why we are convinced that Mesa's proposal should be defeated." All we asked for was a delay of the annual meeting for sixty days.

He reviewed Unocal's worldwide operations and went on to praise the management. I was given an opportunity to make a statement, and then he opened the meeting to questions. We expected hostile questions, but what I saw was a genuine interest in our plan. One man asked if I was capable of running a company with 22,000 employees. I told him to look at my record. "I don't think you'll have any doubt when you compare my record to Mr. Hartley's that we have performed better for our stockholders and our employees." There was no reason to ride hard on Fred — this was not the right forum — and I think Fred had made the same decision.

A woman who worked for Unocal expressed concern about my motives. She said that I had not kept my word because I had originally stated that our interest in Unocal was for investment only. For a moment the microphone went dead. When it came on again, she asked, "Are you still there?"

"You may be surprised how long I stay around," I quipped. That got a laugh.

Then she said, "What about me?" and that got one, too.

I explained that since our original investment, Unocal's management had changed the bylaws, inserted poison pills, and attacked Mesa and me personally. In short, the situation had changed dramatically.

An elderly man asked the key question of the day: "What does Unocal intend to do if Mesa Partners is included in its offer? In other words, will Unocal commit to buy?"

Hartley said, "What you mean is, 'Is you is or is you ain't my baby.'" There was a long silence. No one knew what he was talking about.

Finally the man said, "I'm not your baby, Mr. Hartley. I'm older than you are," and repeated his question.

"*Is you is or is you ain't my baby?*" Hartley repeated, trying to make a joke. He pointed out that the words came from a Broadway show years before and went on to the next question.

Another man asked whether he should tender his stock into the Unocal offer. He was asking for advice, he said, because of Mesa's and Unocal's offers and the complicated timing issues involved. Instead of giving advice, Hartley told him he could do whatever he wanted with his stock. "You're free, white, and clear," he added — an incredible answer. Hartley really *was* from another era.

An attractive woman in her early sixties asked Hartley why there were no women on Unocal's board. He was stumped; he didn't have any more cute remarks, so he said, "I had one lady in mind, but she died." There were loud groans.

Hartley was coming off as bigoted and abrasive, and clearly his blood pressure was rising. Just before the meeting broke up, one of Unocal's runners came in and whispered to the general counsel sitting across the aisle from us. As the word was passed down the row of Unocal brass, we could see their faces drop, one by one.

Bob Stillwell leaned over to me and whispered, "They've just heard they lost in the chancery court again."

Five minutes later the news was confirmed. The Delaware chancery court had upheld its earlier ruling that it was illegal for Unocal to exclude Mesa from its self-tender. It seemed odd that the Unocal executives were surprised. Surely they knew what a long shot that lawsuit was, but then I wondered if they knew something we didn't.

We returned to our hotel to wait for Unocal to have its board meeting. Fred finally called and said that the two meetings had worn him out, and he wasn't up to another one. He sounded exhausted.

We planned to meet the next morning at the New Otani Hotel, in L.A.'s Oriental district. Our team spent the evening at our hotel, talking strategy and trying to anticipate the next morning's discussion.

At one point Sidney asked me, "How long are you going to listen to Hartley's philosophy tomorrow?"

"No more than ten minutes."

We all knew we were dealing with an unpredictable person,

but we were optimistic that something could be worked out. They had no prospect of winning the legal battle, in our opinion. Within a few hours of the chancery court's decision, Unocal's lawyers went to Judge Moore, of Delaware's supreme court, and convinced him that the court should hear the case. Unocal was getting close to the end. If it couldn't exclude us from its self-tender, then it had lost. I couldn't believe that Hartley would bet the farm on a 100 to 1 long shot.

Within twenty-four hours of Judge Moore's decision to hear the case, Mesa's Delaware lawyers, under the leadership of Charlie Richards, worked all night to have a ninety-five-page brief in the judge's hands. We asked the SEC to file an amicus brief in Delaware, too, upholding the tradition of equal treatment for all shareholders, which might have stopped Unocal dead in its tracks, but the bureaucracy still couldn't respond.

Hartley showed up an hour late for our meeting and announced that he had spent the previous evening watching himself on a videotape of the stockholders' meeting. He had brought along Claude Brinegar, executive vice president, Phil Blamey, the vice president of finance, and Sam Snyder, his number one company lawyer. Hartley was wearing a twenty-year-old suit with cuffs on the sleeves and a fabric belt. My men were too young to have ever seen an outfit like this before.

Hartley's face was red, his eyes puffy and bloodshot. He made a remark about our showing up at the hotel "in a goddamn stretch limo." I ignored it and introduced our group, including David and Sidney, and our lawyers, Bob Stillwell and Mike Gizang, of Skadden Arps. Hartley proceeded to insult each one of my men. He told David, "You sure seem to have a lot to say to the press, don't you?"

When he couldn't get a rise out of us, he made a crack about Mesa's lawyers. It seemed to bother him that we had lawyers from outside the company. "Don't you have any company lawyers?" he asked.

"We've got four," I said.

Unocal must have had dozens, with all their lawsuits. I had known Sam Snyder thirty years earlier, when he was a Unocal division attorney in Midland, Texas. Sam was dressed about the same way as his boss; the only difference was, his socks drooped around his ankles.

Sure enough, Hartley launched into a diatribe on the oil industry and his "philosophy." We were treated to an update on the $800 million shale oil disaster and how they had it on production for all of two hours. I wouldn't have bragged about a two-hour test on a project two years behind schedule and $300 million over budget.

After a few minutes I said, "Fred, we've heard all this before. We need to get on with the meeting."

Fred said he had a proposal that might be the basis for resolving our differences. Unocal would permit Mesa to participate in its self-tender, and it would commit to purchase 50 million shares at $72. Unocal would follow through on plans to create a master limited partnership. The board also offered to pay our expenses in the deal. Fred never mentioned anything about an offer for Mesa. I wondered why he had told Oscar Wyatt that he wanted to buy Mesa.

We countered by saying that any recapitalization would have to ensure that the shareholders received a value comparable to the $54 we were offering. We also insisted that any settlement would have to be voted on by the shareholders. With that groundwork laid, we proposed that Unocal repurchase 75 million shares instead of 50 million and that it commit to maintain its common dividend and to distribute at least $250 million annually, in units of its limited partnership, to shareholders as additional dividends.

Fred reacted violently to the idea of shareholder approval, fearing that to be hung out during the approval process would invite a competing offer. We assured them that if the deal was good enough for the shareholders, there would be no room for a competing bid.

After five hours it looked as though we had made some real progress. We were only about $400 million apart — a big number, but not in a $10 billion deal.

During the negotiations, we would periodically leave the room and walk into the hall to discuss things. Sidney brought up an interesting tax point. If we made a deal along these lines, in which we would tender our stock along with all the other shareholders, we could take advantage of an obscure tax provision. It was complicated, but if we participated in what was called a proportionate redemption with other stockholders, we could get favorable treatment on the proceeds. It could be treated as a dividend, and a corporation could exclude 85 percent of dividends from taxation.

There was only one catch: we would have to hold the stock for a year. We had to be very nimble and not alert them to the importance of the holding period. We were like Br'er Rabbit, saying, "Don't throw me in the briar patch."

Back in the meeting, David said, "After you buy shares under your $72 offer, we'll hold your stock for six months before we sell. That way it won't disrupt the market."

"No," said Hartley, "you've got to hold it for a year." It was music to our ears.

At that point Blamey, who had been sitting there sullenly, got excited. "I know what you're up to!" he said. I almost fainted; I was sure he had figured it out. He took out his calculator and began punching in numbers, looking up now and then to glare at David. Nobody could figure out what the hell he was up to. Finally he said triumphantly, smiling at Fred, "I can tell you why he's willing to stick around for a year. I can tell you exactly why. Because with our dividend, and the limited partnership distribution, you're going to get a thirteen point two percent yield, that's why!"

I could have kissed him.

"Phil," David said, "you've broken our code." We had to laugh. "If we can't make more than thirteen percent working for Pickens, he'll throw you out."

Scowling, Blamey tossed his calculator back into his briefcase and locked it.

At about three o'clock Hartley started to sag. He couldn't concentrate and suggested we break up so that his team could go "run some numbers" on our proposal; we offered to meet again at six or later, but he refused. He said he had learned long before "never to negotiate after sundown, or you get screwed." We said we would meet the next morning, and he said wearily, "Well, we did pretty good today."

I agreed. "You didn't call me an idiot once."

"You didn't say I was arrogant, either."

As we were leaving, Brinegar said, "Don't feel bad about his calling you an idiot. He calls us idiots all the time." Brinegar was serious.

I wanted to get the deal wrapped up and proposed that we meet at eight in the morning. Hartley wanted to meet at nine-thirty. We compromised on nine o'clock, but Hartley was late again. When he arrived he was abrupt and got right to work — a big change from the day before. One of his short-boys passed out a two-page document, which Hartley read aloud, word for word. He was a slow reader, and his arrogance was stifling.

Everything we had agreed on the day before was out the window. He was reading a new proposal, and we were back to a 50-million-share repurchase, no commitment to maintain the common stock dividend or to do a limited partnership distribution, and no approval by shareholders. It was a "take it or leave it" proposal. Hartley had a reputation for not keeping his word, and I sat there trying to figure out what had happened overnight. I began to wonder what he knew that we didn't.

In conclusion, he said, "Do you have any questions?"

I told him we would step outside and talk about it.

"Oh, we have a room reserved for you next door."

"I know. You had it yesterday, too."

After what happened in the Gulf deal, I was jumpy about using Big Oil's hotel rooms when talking about confidential points. When Bob Stillwell and I talked during breaks in the bathroom, we ran water or flushed the toilet repeatedly and spoke in low voices. This time our group left the room and walked down the hall to the elevator lobby, where we could speak privately.

David said, "It's like yesterday never happened. What's going on?"

I couldn't answer him. Maybe Hartley's lawyers had advised him not to make a trade until they heard the Delaware supreme court decision. Something unusual was happening, and we couldn't get a handle on it.

"Well, what do you guys think?" I asked.

It took all of two minutes to poll the group. Sidney, David, Stillwell, and Mike Gizang all agreed: the new proposal was unacceptable.

We went back to the meeting room and surprised their investment bankers and outside counsel, who had slipped in while we were out. Hartley had criticized us for having a couple of outside lawyers, and here he was surrounded by not only lawyers but investment bankers as well. They had been stashed in the room next door and thought we would take longer to make our decision. Peter Sachs, of Goldman, Sachs, jumped out of his chair as if someone had stuck him in the ass with a hot poker.

"Keep your seat," I said. "We're not going to be here long enough to sit down. Fred, if this is what you call negotiating, forget it. I've already changed my watch to Central Time."

We were on our way to Amarillo. And we were also on our way to taking over Unocal — we were tired of screwing around. We were winning in Delaware. We had the money lined up.

I was due in Washington the next day, May 16, for the President's Dinner. This was the fund-raiser for the Republican House and Senate races for the upcoming year. David went with Bea and me. We stayed at the Hay Adams, and Joe Flom came down from New York for the dinner and to strategize about Unocal. The day before, Charlie Richards had argued Mesa's case before the supreme court of Delaware for two hours. The verdict of the three-judge panel was due the following day. I was ready to bet 100 to a doughnut that the ruling would uphold Judge Berger's decision in the chancery court.

The next morning I had breakfast with Flom and Batchelder. I had scheduled a racquetball game, but as I was leaving the hotel room the phone rang. David took the call. It was Charlie Richards, and after a minute David said, "Well, I'll be damned," and gestured with his thumb down.

"Is he kidding?" Flom asked.

I knew David wasn't kidding; we had lost in Delaware.

"I can't believe it," Flom said. He got on the phone with Richards, shaking his head. We couldn't believe it, either.

Flom hung up. Judge Moore had described Mesa's offer as a "grossly inadequate and coercive two-tier front-end loaded tender offer." The only explanation I can come up with is that a lot of pressure had been brought in Delaware. This meant that Hartley didn't have to offer Mesa anything. He could buy back the stock from all the shareholders but us, decreasing the value of the remaining Unocal stock. If Unocal bought back 70 million shares at $72, that left 100 million shares that would be worth a lot less, including all of the Mesa Partners holdings, which would drop to around $30 a share after the buy-back. Our stock would then be worth less than $700 million — a loss of about $300 million.

This new ruling was unprecedented, but there was no use crying about it. We had a choice: we could make a deal with Unocal, or after they concluded their tender offer we could make a 100 percent all-cash offer for the company. We got a call from Drexel asking us not to fold. They had raised $3 billion and were ready to raise the additional funds for us to make a 100 percent offer. It was an unqualified endorsement of Mesa, and it naturally gave us a lift.

It would be a great campaign, no doubt about it, but the risks were getting very high. It wasn't the time to get emotionally involved. It hadn't been a year since we had gotten out of a $300 million jam, so I wasn't ready to step up to the table and put everything on 7 and call for the dice. It might work — but it might not. If Mesa went all out for Unocal, Hartley would probably pull the same exclusionary self-tender the second time, and then we would be back in the Delaware court. We had been nailed once, and that was one time too many.

We could force Fred to take on even more debt, and he was gagging now. But there was no guarantee we would win.

My father summed up the situation when he said, "It looks like you've got them by *your* balls, son."

It was time to make a deal.

We talked to Stillwell in Houston and decided that he would call Peter Sachs and tell him that we were ready to talk. Sachs was noncommittal. He said he had no idea what Hartley might do, but he wanted to know what we had in mind. Stillwell told him we would have to be included in their tender offer or take action to protect ourselves. Sachs said he would pass the word along.

On the trip back to Amarillo we had a pretty stoic group. I think each of us wanted to take Drexel's offer and go for 100 percent. That would blow Hartley out of the tub. I kept thinking, "If only the SEC had intervened, how different things might have turned out."

Unocal could now complete its offer to buy 50 million shares at $72. And we would have a $300 million loss.

Sunday morning we heard nothing from Unocal, and David and Sidney took their families to the lake for a barbecue. I kept thinking about the unusual decision in the Delaware supreme court, piecing together bits of information I had picked up. The supreme court had heard oral arguments on May 16. There was a party that evening for a retiring supreme court justice, and it lasted until almost midnight, so the judges had had very little time to work on their decision. They met the next morning for a few minutes and ruled against us. That was that.

Stillwell got a call from Los Angeles on Sunday afternoon. Hartley was ready to talk. He would agree to Mesa's demands but had one of his own. He wanted us to pay Unocal's expenses — a silly request but a big point to Hartley. If he could get us to pay his expenses, he would never let us forget it. We still had our tax treatment "ace" up our sleeve. If we were included in Unocal's offer and held the remainder of our stock for a year, we would make around $80 million after taxes. The trick was to keep Unocal from figuring it out.

I stayed in Amarillo and left the negotiating in Los Angeles to Batchelder and Stillwell. They took Joel Reed from Wagner & Brown with them and went directly to the offices of Gibson, Dunn and Crutcher, Unocal's attorneys, in Crocker Plaza. They didn't bother to check into a hotel, but left their luggage in the limo and told the driver to wait. It was 4 A.M. before somebody remembered that the car was still waiting.

Mesa was assigned offices on the forty-ninth floor, Unocal on the forty-eighth. They got together about every other hour to negotiate and stayed with it throughout the night. There were people up all night across the country, too, waiting for calls from David and Stillwell on crucial points. Sidney and Bill Griffith, with Baker & Botts, fine-tuned the tax treatment as the deal was shaped.

Sam Snyder and Peter Sachs were there, as well as Unocal's lawyers from Gibson, Dunn. David kept them on the expense issue and the standstill agreement, neither of which was really important to us. Snyder knew he could earn points with Hartley if he could get us to pay Unocal's expenses, and that issue became all-important to him. We had to keep them from figuring out what our tax objectives were and at the same time not give up anything on the other points. But the tax question kept things very tense.

We finally agreed to a twenty-five-year standstill. We would be included in Unocal's offer and would have to hold the remainder of our stock for about a year. Snyder made one last push for the expenses, and David told him, "We're not paying Unocal's expenses, and that's all there is to it, Sam." He finally gave up.

At five minutes to seven Los Angeles time, on Monday morning, May 20, Unocal called the New York Stock Exchange and told them that settlement talks were under way and that trading in Unocal and Mesa should be suspended. There had been a lot of speculation over the weekend, and Mesa's stock had suffered in late trading on Friday, after the court decision.

Snyder told Hartley to call a board meeting. Unocal's negotiators had lunch with the board. We waited to see if we were going to clear the last hurdle. Then we got word that they had approved the deal. We were almost at the finish line.

Our team signed the deal and flew home on Monday night. The Mesa-Unocal deal was history. Hartley was soon crowing that he had defeated Pickens and tied up Mesa for a year because we had to hold their stock. He claimed we had lost $100 million. It was just the opposite. We were going to make money, but we couldn't announce it until our auditors, Arthur Andersen, had signed off. We also wanted to receive the proceeds from Unocal before announcing any profit. That meant waiting sixty days or so, but we just didn't trust them.

I could barely keep quiet as I read Hartley's claims of having "beaten" Mesa. Then, two months later, the Unocal bonds in hand, we enjoyed the last laugh — $83 million profit after taxes, twice what we had made in the Phillips deal.

When you have to explain a victory, it becomes something less. Gradually the financial community, the press, and the academicians came to understand what we had done.

Unocal didn't communicate with its stockholders the way it had in the proxy fight, and consequently 12 percent did not get the $72 a share for one third of their stock. This translated into a $300 million loss to these stockholders.

I was still bothered by what had happened in the Delaware courts, and so were many other people. When I was asked to speak to the Delaware Bench and Bar in Wilmington on June 4, 1986, there was speculation that I would attack the supreme court and its decision regarding Mesa. Instead, I didn't mention the decision in my speech but, in response to a question from the floor, I said that I believed in the judiciary system in this country, and although I didn't agree with every decision that came out of it, I still supported the system. "Some you win," I said, "some you lose, and some get rained out. This one we lost."

But in fact we hadn't lost. Besides our profit, moral vindication came in the summer of 1986, when the SEC finally came out with its ruling: exclusionary offers like Unocal's were unacceptable because they discriminated against selected stockholders. It was a sweet victory, but it came too late to help us.

Unocal will always be the one that got away.

*Five*

# THE LONG VIEW

# · 20 ·

# *Money*

I can't remember a year when I didn't make more money on outside investments — the stock and commodities markets — than on my Mesa salary. I once parlayed $34,000 into $6.6 million in six months, on live cattle futures.

That was 1973. Near the end of that six months I was playing in the Canadian Oilmen's golf tournament at Banff Springs, Alberta, when the cattle market went into a nose dive. I was trying to hold on for thirty days to turn a short-term gain into a long-term capital gain. On the first day of the tournament, while I was out on the course, the price for fed cattle collapsed; I lost a million dollars in just a few hours. It was time to take the remaining profit. The market had closed for the day, so I planned to put in the sell order the following day.

The next morning, all the phones were out of order but they were supposed to be operating by noon. Tee off time was 11 A.M., and by the time I got off the course at 4 P.M., the market was closed: another million dollars.

This was getting serious, and to top it off, the phones were down again the next morning. I wasn't much of a golfer the third day. Every time I stood over a putt, I wondered what was happening to cattle prices. If Jack Nicklaus thinks he has pressure putts, he should try eighteen holes after he's lost $2 million in two days, wondering how much more he's losing with every tick of the futures market.

After the round, my opponent said, "You hit the ball pretty good, but you putt like you've got something on your mind." Did I ever — I took another million-dollar hit that day. I finally got out with a $3.6 million profit.

At the same time I was in cattle, I was also in corn futures. My old friend Ed Watkins and I had been watching the corn crop in the Midwest from a distance. The summer had been hotter than hell and there had been very little moisture, but the corn price had not moved up, which it should have with those fundamentals.

On a hot Saturday afternoon, after golf, I suggested that Ed and another friend, Howard Rogers, might drive through the corn belt to see if the crop was as bad as we thought. They were on their way to Iowa early the next day. By the end of the week, they were satisfied that the crop was even worse than we thought. The price for corn should go up in the fall, or sooner.

It was decision time, and we took a substantial position in corn futures. After several weeks and a good move Ed remarked, "To make $500,000 for just driving around looking at corn fields isn't too bad."

A commodity futures play is one of the purest forms of entrepreneurship. The keys to success are an accurate analysis, a willingness to take risk, and the ability to act. Once you've made the decision, just stand by, because you're likely to get your answer quickly. Although I enjoy many types of investing, there's nothing like a commodity play for fast action.

I am impatient by nature. And by and large, commodity futures tend to satisfy that impatience.

My banker once asked my broker what kind of a commodity trader I was. The broker said, "One of the best because he knows when to quit." To be a good trader, you have to be disciplined and pull out when your analysis goes against you.

In November of 1985 Mesa shorted about 2 million barrels of crude oil, anticipating a market break. I discussed what I wanted to do with David Batchelder, the president of Mesa Petroleum Co., and Paul Cain, the president of the Mesa Limited Partnership. They listened intently and said they couldn't fault the logic. We discussed our alternatives. Mesa was going to produce 4 million barrels of oil over the next twelve months, and the 2-million-barrel short would hedge half of our production. We sold the 2 million barrels for $26 a barrel. The price moved up almost immediately to $30, so we had $8 million in margin calls. Batchelder and Cain were a little nervous; it was their first introduction to commodities. If the contract closed out at $30, we would have sold half our oil for $4 a barrel less than anybody else.

I went to Europe to speak in Zurich and London. One of the reasons for the trip was to check with friends in Europe about OPEC's production and tanker movements from the Mideast. We get reports here, but what we were up to needed confirmation. We had heard, for instance, that the Russians were cutting back and oil might go to $34 a barrel. But when I came back from Europe, I called my team together and said that things were headed south. I told them why and we discussed the situation in detail. They agreed with me and we shorted another 2 million barrels; now we were fully hedged. It didn't take long to realize we had made the right decision, because oil prices plummeted. In a matter of thirty days our analysis had been proven correct. We had sold our oil at $26 when the rest of the industry was going to sell theirs for at least $10 a barrel less. We had saved ourselves $30 million.

If you are a consistent moneymaker, you will be a good decision-maker. Sometimes the window of opportunity is open only briefly. Waiting isn't a decision, although many people think it is.

I don't play many commodities. I keep up with two or three — oil, cattle, and pork bellies, for instance. It doesn't take an hour a day to stay current once you get the foundation. I am always alert as to how I can make money. One day not long ago, when we flew from Amarillo to Oklahoma in a small plane at low altitude, I kept my eye on the ranches we were passing instead of reading, as I usually do.

"What are you watching for?" Bea asked.

"I'm counting cattle," I said. There were very few on the

ranches, which meant fed cattle would be in short supply six to eight months hence. It was like taking a poll. The following Monday, after doing some further checking, we went long 50,000 head of live cattle.

It's a game with us. When OPEC starts talking about how the cartel won't work, that's when it's likely to work. They agree to disagree, as in the summer of '86. Someone was saying to me that oil was going to $5 a barrel. I said, "That's the OPEC shill they have out talking," to scare the pants off everybody, and he did a pretty good job of it.

We use several consultants, all over the world. One of them called and said that OPEC wasn't going to reach an agreement, which meant the price of oil would stay down. He said there was plenty of oil on the water, headed for the United States, which was even more bearish. I talked to David Batchelder, and he said, "This guy has been wrong five out of five times."

I wanted to find out how firm our adviser was. As he was apologizing for being wrong before, I told him, "That's okay. Just be sure about what you want us to do." This time he was convinced the price of oil would fall, so we doubled our long positions — the opposite of his advice. I have been out of step on a commodity, and now one of our consultants was out of step.

When you're winning it's great fun. The more objective and the less emotionally involved you are, the more successful you tend to be.

Commodities is a leverage game. The first time I got into the futures market was in live cattle, and I was intrigued by the leverage factor. I could own thousands of head of cattle for a fraction of what it would cost to own them in the feedyard or on the ranch. Many unsophisticated investors don't realize that it doesn't matter whether you own cattle on paper or in the feedyard; either way, you are speculating. Any time you have your money at risk, whether in commodities, stocks, or whatever, you are a speculator.

Leverage is nothing more than debt. I think almost everybody understands return on capital. If I can borrow and get a good return on my funds, it's more satisfying to me than getting a good return on equity. It's like a bonus, or shooting once and having two quail fall. On the other hand, if you are highly leveraged and lose, your losses are compounded.

My record is perfect on the repayment of debt. I have never borrowed with the thought that I would let the lender shoulder some of the risk; in other words, I always knew I could pay back what I borrowed. Interest rates don't bother me as much as they do some businessmen. Now, I don't want to pay more for money than someone else, but if one half of a percent is going to make a difference, then I shouldn't be borrowing the money anyway. And I'm always confident that I can make several times what the money costs me.

I owe more money today — $55 million — than I have ever owed in my life. All I have ever known is debt, both personally and as CEO of Mesa. It was expensive for me because of taxes to spin off the Mesa Royalty Trust in 1979, and I had to pay even more taxes when we liquidated Mesa Petroleum Co. into the Mesa Limited Partnership in 1985, but taxes are a high-class problem. Generally speaking, you're paying more taxes because you're making more money, and I like that better than the alternative.

My long-term plan is to monitor the oil and gas industry and decide over the next five years whether or not to alter my position by selling some of my Mesa Limited Partnership and reduce my debt or to stay the course. What is the payoff for taking on the debt? Bea and I own about 5 percent of MLP, which represents about 130 billion cubic feet of gas. If you assume that gas will sell for an average of $4 per million cubic feet, that will be $520 million over the next thirty years.

My banks have ample collateral as well as a cash flow that will pay off the debt in 1994 under the worst case. Today — September 30, 1986 — I am worth $107 million — much less than most people assume.

*

I am a gambler, but I don't give a hoot about going to Las Vegas. I would rather go to the Amarillo Country Club and play gin rummy with Doc Watkins or with David on the company plane on the way to make a deal. I sometimes bet on football games with my friend Howard Federer, and I once dropped $15,000 on the Super Bowl, but usually the bets are much smaller.

Whether it is business or personal, we keep up with our deals closely and, if we get off track, sometimes make radical adjustments. On the other hand, if I put some money with somebody to invest for me, then I leave them alone and wait for the results.

I invested $5 million with an oil operator several years ago and almost lost the whole roll. Over the three-year period I didn't talk to him ten times — maybe I should have watched him closer.

Many managers won't face reality when assessing their own deals. They either panic and jump out of the boat or refuse to admit they have a problem. Stupidity may be part of the problem, but ego is probably the biggest obstacle.

Some people can't stand risk. I can remember the government auditor who, after reviewing the Mesa pension plan, gave me a lecture about my investment philosophy and fiduciary responsibility. I was the sole trustee for the Mesa employees' profit-sharing trust and had done extremely well on our investments for ten years. When the auditor checked our performance, he complained about the leveraging of the fund. We had structured the fund so that we could leverage up to 100 percent of the stock portfolio. He agreed I had stuck to the rules, but he wanted me to know that what I was doing was "very risky."

I pointed out that we had made $8 million one year on $5 million equity. He didn't argue with me. His advice was to stop doing it because I had just been lucky. I suspect that he hadn't made $20 on an investment in his life, and I wondered what compelled him to give me this kind of advice. I said, "Why don't you come back and see me when I have a bad year." That was seven years ago, and I haven't seen him since.

I sometimes get concerned, but I don't get nervous. You can't make money consistently if you're uptight. If you don't watch out, you'll spend twice as much time on the losers as you do on the winners. You shouldn't take a risk in the first place if you can't handle the loss, because you're not always going to win.

I hate losing, but I know that an aggressive investor is going to take some losses.

I am often asked what I would do if I suddenly became penniless. I would get a stake and get started again. If I was not able to come back, I would still consider myself wealthy — for all the people I have met and the friends I have made, and the fun of the whole thing has been great as well. I'm not a promoter by nature, although I have promoted deals. I prefer to put up my own money and take my chances. From very early in my career I never expected people to invest with me unless I was putting up some of my own money.

People with inherited wealth are often terrified that they are going to lose it. Their fathers have scared them to death by telling them how hard it was to make. I think that's one of the reasons that so many wealthy heirs just sit on their money. They're afraid that if they lose it, they'll never be able to make it again.

We talk about the ripple effect on our family of the wealth I'm creating. I've seen old money take away incentive. I would hate not to leave my children anything, but they would probably be better off if we didn't. As our wills are now written, half of our combined estate will go to charity. Our children all work for a living. I believe that one of the worst things you can do to children is deny them the opportunity to bring home a paycheck.

After I graduated from Oklahoma State, my father told me, "We're proud of you."

"I appreciate your giving me a college education," I said in what was an emotional moment.

"We have something else for you, son."

I thought Dad was going to give me a few hundred dollars but he just smiled and said, "Good luck."

What happened to me has happened to others all over the country. There are plenty of entrepreneurs who started companies and took risks. Some may have played it straight and some may have cheated, and even been ruthless and hard-nosed. Nonetheless, something meaningful has been developed by most of them.

I get a thrill out of playing by the rules and winning. I like to see everybody make money. I've never considered myself a tough negotiator. I usually know about where a deal should be made, and if the other side isn't realistic, then forget it. I have found damn few executives who know where a deal should be made. The big boys turn it over to their investment bankers and lawyers and have them report to a committee — it's easier than knowing what's really going on. I've made some bad deals, no question about it, but when it happened I didn't cry or attempt to retrade.

My grandmother's lesson has served me well: a deal is a deal.

Money is a report card. Many people set limits on what they want to achieve. For some, making $50,000 a year is enough, and after reaching that goal their momentum falls off rapidly. I've known many men who set a million dollars as their net-worth goal, and after they became millionaires they gave up making money and chose full-time hunting or golfing. I think that's fine, but it isn't what I want to do. Three days of golf in a row are about all I can stand.

Be careful of the limits you set for yourself. Psychological limits can be as effective as those you recognize formally. Personally, I don't have a limit.

Despite what I've said, it isn't easy to make money. I book my share of losers. Money is to be respected; one of the worst things you can do is to handle another person's money without respect for how hard it was to earn. My grandmother and mother often said, "Always get your money's worth, and don't buy things you don't need." I'm good at getting my money's worth.

I don't let money sit around. I either invest it or give it to a worthy cause. Most years, our charitable and political contributions exceed my Mesa salary. I give about a hundred speeches a year, some of them for honorariums of up to $15,000, and this is also money that goes to charity. I get a big thrill out of making money, but I don't get much of a thrill out of spending it. My business is as much fun as my hobbies. Wales Madden once asked me when I was going to quit, and I said, "When it ceases to be fun."

My needs haven't changed much over the years. I used to say that if I had two suits — a dark one and a light one — a couple of bird dogs, and a good shotgun, I would be happy. Now I seem to need fifteen suits, two dozen bird dogs, a good shotgun, and a set of golf clubs.

I drive an eight-year-old car (a blue Mercedes, bought used). Once, when we gave a million dollars to Oklahoma State, Bea said, "Why don't we give just $970,450, and you can go out and buy a new car?"

When I need new shirts, Bea has a tailor come in and fit me. I have worn the same size suit since 1972, when I was fitted by Oxford in Chicago. They have my measurements, and a couple of times a year I will go into a store somewhere in the country and pick out several swatches of Oxford's material; they'll make the suits and send them to me. I still wear a couple they made in 1972.

It seems as if everything I do is geared to saving time. I used to get a lot of speeding tickets when I drove the 90 miles from Amarillo to the ranch. Now we fly in a small airplane. It's faster — and it cuts out the tickets.

My barber, Keith Clark, comes to the house every couple of weeks to cut my hair. Keith is a good friend and has been my barber for more than twenty years. The first time I tried to pay him, he refused. I had put him in a deal several years before in which he had made $50,000. He said, "You have a lifetime of haircuts coming."

I spend very little cash. When I win at golf or cards, I put the money in my desk and use it until it runs out. Years ago, I won $300 playing cards and the next day went out and bought an expensive suit. Two weeks later I lost $300; I hated that $300 suit.

I had a new secretary who had been working for me for six

months before I cashed a check. She couldn't believe that I didn't need money more often. Then I hit a cold streak; she wore out a pair of shoes going to the bank to cash my checks.

Our ranch is not a showplace, just a well-run operation. We will build a new house at SenTosa and it will be Bea's greatest creation. But we aren't ready yet. We like things like this to evolve gradually, with a great deal of thought and planning. That way they last in your affection and in the affections of those who follow you.

· 21 ·

# *Leadership*

A lot has been written in the last few years about management: theory X and theory Y, grids and objectives. Lately there has even been a book telling managers how to do it all in a miracle visit of one minute, like a holy man conferring a blessing on the workplace. Other books tell us how to dress, arrange our office furniture, even what to order for lunch. Frankly, I think most of this is a waste of time.

There are three kinds of managements. Some see changes coming well in advance and may even accelerate the process. Some see changes coming just in time to adjust before it's too late. Some never see changes coming, so they don't adjust. The last group gets run over by change, and it almost always comprises the arrogant, iron-headed managements who have had it their way for years and, by God, they are going to keep it their way. Good-bye to the management that can't adjust.

A management style is an amalgamation of the best of other people you have known and respected, and eventually you develop your own style. The Boone Pickens management style started back in the oil fields of the Panhandle, Gulf of Mexico, and Canada and progressed through a long series of financial dealings.

A wise woman, Grace Hopper, now retired, was the best known female admiral in the U.S. Navy. She expressed my management philosophy succinctly when she said, "You don't manage people, you manage things. You *lead* people." She was right.

I never consciously manage anybody. I try to lead people.

Leadership is hard to define. You know when you're around it and when you see it. I've experienced many good leaders, from my old high school coach to Ronald Reagan to some of the young people who work at Mesa today. I've watched them inspire and galvanize others. I know that the important part of being a leader is what goes on inside your own mind — what you do to yourself, not what you do to others.

Part of leadership is taking risks and building confidence in yourself. You have to serve many apprenticeships throughout your life. Show me somebody who won't serve an apprenticeship, and I'll show you somebody who won't go very far. If you take up golf, you're going to serve an apprenticeship learning to play; you're going to serve an apprenticeship when you break in with a new group of people. Those who lack confidence will seldom serve an apprenticeship; they're afraid they'll fail. But a few people take it in stride and move on.

In corporate America, those who lack confidence surround themselves with people who continually stroke their egos. If my style were to jerk people around, you can bet your life that it would be practiced throughout the organization. At Mesa, people who are good, strong players find their apprenticeships to be surprisingly short. You can move up quickly, for there is always room at the top.

Leadership is the quality that transforms good intentions into positive action; it turns a group of individuals into a team. I learned early, in business as well as politics, that people love a leader. They like decisive action.

You lead by example. You don't run over your personnel, but you don't pump them up with false praise, either.

We work hard at Mesa — long hours, intense analysis. When House and Senate conferees agreed on a compromise for the new tax bill on Saturday, August 16, 1986, five of our men were in the office early the next morning to see how it would affect us. We worked most of that Sunday — and I wasn't the one who called the meeting. On any weekend, there are always cars in the garage while their owners take care of business that won't wait until Monday. It goes with the territory, and the rewards are proportionate — both financially and in terms of professional satisfaction. If you aren't a worker, you won't make it with me.

You can do some things to set up an organization so that leadership will flourish on all levels.

• Concentrate on the goals, not the size of the organization. You can't measure a place by size unless it's a football stadium.

At Mesa, we work short-handed. That way people have a greater opportunity to advance and less time for office politics. If you are worrying about keeping your head above water, you're not going to spend a lot of time trying to figure out how to do in a colleague. I want people to be challenged and to have the opportunity to advance.

It's unusual to find a large corporation that's efficient. I know about economies of scale and all the other advantages that are supposed to come with size. But when you get an inside look, it's easy to see how inefficient big business really is. Most corporate bureaucracies have more people than they have work. Large corporations were great at setting up massive assembly lines, but terrible at modifying those same lines to fit changing conditions. Insulated from the real world, most executives don't even notice what is happening. There are few visionaries at the top of our major corporations. "America has a pioneering spirit, a spirit of innovation we have to beat," a Japanese official said in 1939, recognizing the real strength of our brand of capitalism. Not many years later, inertia had replaced innovation in corporate America, something that became painfully clear once the foreign companies were competing on our turf.

The automobile industry is a perfect example of an industry paralyzed by bureaucratic inertia. The Japanese and Germans concentrated on building a better automobile while the U.S. automakers added a little trim and rested on their laurels. Then, when the rest of the auto world caught up, Detroit ran to Washington for bailouts and protection. All their preoccupation with bigness got them was vulnerability.

At Mesa, our goal is to have fewer people managing more assets; profits are a much better indicator of business acumen than size. I decided a long time ago to hire the best people, pay them well, get the best equipment, provide the best working conditions, and let size take care of itself. I have the best people I have ever had; it took years to put this group together, but it was worth it.

• Forget about age, which means giving the young people a chance. I have a bias toward youth, but I also think that youth is a state of mind. I am interested in whether a person can do the job. Mesa personnel know this well, and it is a great boost for morale. The average age at Mesa is thirty-six years old. (The joke is that if I would retire it would drop to thirty-one.)

Young people are a little rash sometimes, but they often make up for it by generating good ideas. I choose employees for their intelligence, attitude, and enthusiasm. I'm convinced that you can be old at thirty or young at seventy — it's all up to you.

Years ago, a CEO of a major company asked me how I included my young people. My answer was: "Just invite them in; it's easy."

• Keep things informal. Talking is the natural way to do business. Writing is great for keeping records and pinning down details, but talk generates ideas. Great things come from our luncheon meetings, which consist of a sandwich, a cup of soup, and a good idea or two. No martinis.

Communication is crucial — not the formal stuff but frequent conversation among the people who make the decisions. The dialogue should take place regardless of where you are. I talk to David Batchelder and Paul Cain at least twice a day no matter where we are. When Bea and I went to Africa, I was supposed to be incommunicado for two weeks, but I was on the phone to David after just three days from Maun, Botswana.

People know that they can talk to me, no matter how busy I am. My accessibility keeps me up to speed on our projects, and when it's time to make a decision I'm ready, with no need for lengthy presentations.

With good communication, there are no surprises. I hate surprises. I feel as though I'm not on top of things if I get surprised.

You don't have to rise through four levels before you make it at Mesa. David Batchelder said he couldn't believe the meetings he was in soon after he joined Mesa; he was only twenty-eight at the time. When we're involved in a big deal, there's so much going on that almost anyone can step up and say, "I can do that."

When people disagree with me, they do it openly, respectfully, but directly in front of the others. You've got to remove any fear of disagreeing with the CEO. It forces everyone down the line to use the same technique. You either speak up if you don't like it or forever hold your peace.

When I started PEI in 1956, one of the first things I did was to put each day's correspondence on a clipboard for anyone in the company to read if he or she wanted to take the time. As our business grew, it became impractical; but the message was clear: I want everybody informed; that way we don't have office rumors and speculation.

There are many ways to avoid mistakes, but the best way to sidestep the disasters is to be available. You don't have to make every decision, but you should always be accessible. If your people are smart they will keep you informed, and if you're informed, you're a part of the decision. With that in place, it's easy for you to back your people and it eliminates second-guessing.

• Play by the rules. Every year, I speak on about twenty campuses to ten thousand or more students. I'm interested in their ideas, and they're interested in the range of experience I bring to them. More than anything else, I emphasize that they don't need to cheat, or even bend their principles, to succeed in business. I tell them that pursuing a career is no different from playing golf or tennis. It's no fun to win by breaking the rules, and they can beat the competition and still stick with everything they believe in. As simple as it sounds, students really seem to appreciate hearing that advice. Maybe no other businessman tells them that they can win without cheating.

The oil business is rife with opportunities to bend the rules, but that is short-sighted. We plan on being around for the duration, and even though we might be tempted to take a short cut, it could ruin the good reputation that we're determined to build and keep. Playing by the rules applies to life within the company, too. I'm disturbed by what I've seen in the last several years, with people being asked to take "early retirement" in their fifties while the CEO stays on past the mandatory retirement age of sixty-five. Are any of us so valuable to an organization that we should be exempt from the rules?

• On hiring and firing. What I am always looking for is people who can do a job better than I can. When I find them, they are damn sure going to get that job. I never load myself so that people under me aren't challenged. Years ago, a man I was interviewing for a vice presidential post said, "The position doesn't have a good job description. I'm not sure I'll be challenged." I told him, "You won't ever have to worry about having plenty to do at Mesa."

When someone tips his hand and gives you an insight to his character, good or bad, don't forget it. When I look back over the people who have worked for me, it's surprising how close my initial evaluation was to my final one. A good manager will follow his instincts.

Of course you make hiring mistakes, and people sometimes have to be fired. I'll live with a bad situation just long enough to know there's no other choice. The rest, believe it or not, is easy. People know when they aren't doing the job, and the kindest thing to do is to release them.

There are three things I will fire someone for on the spot: drinking on the job, stealing, and carrying on an interoffice relationship, all of which are very damaging to morale, not to mention the work habits of those involved.

Some people are not comfortable in a fast-moving operation. They want more time to think or maybe procrastinate. It won't work here. You have to think fast and not let the decisions stack up. My advice to our people is: if you aren't happy, then you should leave. I can't imagine going through life in a job that I didn't like. The wear and tear year after year on me and my family would be unbearable. I would go back to field geology rather than serve my time in an unhappy situation, no matter what they paid me.

• Keep fit. Physical fitness is an essential part of the best-run companies, for it has economic as well as spiritual and psychological benefits. Its popularity will continue to grow over the years.

In 1979, we built a first-class athletic facility equipped as well as any commercial health center. A fitness center is a great asset for any company that cares about its employees and wants to stay competitive.

As early as the 1960s, Mesa paid for employee memberships at the Amarillo YMCA, but I wasn't a regular participant. I never had a weight problem because I did things in moderation. The gene mix was also to my advantage. My father has done very little exercise in the last twenty-five years, and he's still going strong at eighty-eight. But I gradually got out of shape, which is easy to do in your late thirties or early forties.

It wasn't long after I married Bea, in 1972, that a friend introduced me to racquetball, a new game that was sweeping the country. I began working myself back into shape. I jogged and took up racquetball seriously. Today, I may be the best fifty-eight-year-old racquetball player in America (there aren't many players my age).

I discovered that all those things you hear about being in shape were true. I felt better. My stamina improved and so did my powers of concentration. I was getting a lot more done each day and still had energy to burn.

About three quarters of Mesa's employees participate in the fitness program. It's like having an ongoing research project in your backyard. We've been keeping statistics since we opened the center, and the results are spectacular. The Fitness Center saves Mesa more than $200,000 in insurance claims annually. We know that employees who exercise regularly average $173 in medical bills a year, whereas it costs $434 for inactive employees. Exercisers average 27 hours of sick leave per year; non-exercisers, 44 hours.

You can quantify the insurance savings and even the sick time, but there are also many intangibles. For one thing, I am a regular participant at the Fitness Center, and this is good for overall morale. In 1985, Mesa was named the Most Physically Fit Company in America, winning the National Fitness Classic in Houston. Once again, we were out in front of the pack. But when you're a little guy in a big game, you'd better be out front or you'll get run over. I continually promote this theme.

"A small band of fit people" can do most anything. As one of our people said, "We are like the French Resistance."

• Make sure that as many people as possible have a personal stake in the company. Some 95 percent of Mesa's employees own stock in the company.

As I look at corporate America today, it's clear that one of the basic problems is the separation of ownership and control. Executives and employees who have a financial stake in the company tend to think and act like stockholders. The typical CEO of a large corporation owns very little stock, yet he has absolute control over assets worth billions of dollars. As a result, the goal of the professional manager is like that of a bureaucrat. The emphasis is on bigger budgets and expanding empires, not on serving the interests of owners.

Early on, I set up stock options and a profit-sharing plan for Mesa's employees. In 1984, *Money* magazine listed Mesa's benefits among the ten best plans in the nation, ahead of all the other oil companies. *Forbes* listed Mesa at the top in net income per employee in 1985 and 1986.

Not everyone can or should be an entrepreneur; most people work effectively for another person, or a corporation. Security is a reasonable and proper concern for most people, and working for a corporation is probably better than working for the government.

The desire for security, which led so many people to the corporate life, also developed a corporate culture that more closely resembled a government agency than a business operation. In the last two years, corporate bureaucracies have been shaken to the core. They have finally realized that they have to get competitive, and that means cutting out several layers of management. This will be good for all the employees because for the first time they'll see what decisiveness is all about.

Additional pressure is coming from the entrepreneurial movement that is sweeping the country. The young people moving up are becoming adamantly opposed to large organizations that they could get lost in.

Corporations were never set up to meet all the needs of their employees or management — they were set up to make money. That is their primary objective and it should also be the objective of management. Good managers make money for stockholders, serving both employees and consumers in the process.

• Finally, enjoy it. We may work hard, but there are no stomachaches. We laugh a lot. If we screw up, then we all screwed up. We move quickly, which often creates an advantage.

It's like racquetball, when you move in and cut off a shot. Your opponent thinks you're going to let the ball go to the wall, so he thinks he has a second to regroup. You may not be set up, or your feet may not be exactly right; you might not be best at an overhead shot, but the fact that you took the shot right then may ruin your opponent's timing. It works the same way in business.

Some companies operate on a two-, five-, or ten-year plan. At Mesa, we're a different company every two years. Once committed, we don't appoint committees and have more studies and discussions; we don't have beautiful slide presentations. We decide what we want to do and then do it.

People sometimes get too serious about business. Business isn't life itself: life is tragic, but business is not. There are no disasters in business that you can't avoid — if you see them coming and make the adjustments. If you understand markets, you can do as well in a down market as you can in an up market. Business, like racquetball, is fun.

· 22 ·

# *A New Breed*

There comes a time when the meaning of success changes. By my mid-fifties I had been working most of my life and despite setbacks had accomplished more than I had once thought possible. But then I found myself taking a longer, broader view of things.

For more than thirty years I had witnessed mismanagement in American corporations. It wasn't getting any better — indeed, in America's largest companies it was getting worse. Managements were systematically disenfranchising stockholders. Top executives invented scheme after brazen scheme to protect their own power. The temptations were too great for the weak, and now some of the strong CEOs were breaking down. And the nation's economy was suffering as a consequence. There had to be some way to mobilize against this powerful enemy.

It began to seem overwhelmingly important to get our message out to the public, and so I took to the road, giving more than one hundred speeches a year. It was clear that the recent turmoil in corporate life *had* awakened many people to the problems we face, but there were many misconceptions, too.

A couple of questions — good questions — came up again and again, and I answered them straightforwardly.

"What about the long term?" someone would say. "Takeovers and restructuring may raise stock prices, but what about the effect on concerns like research and development?" It's a good question — but there's a better answer. Stockholders aren't dumb. They try to learn about the companies they invest in. If a company really *has* a long-term plan, management should sell the plan to its owners or prospective stockholders. Plenty of companies do. Many companies have a good price without having any profit — because shareholders believe in its future. And, strangely enough, most of the noise over the "long term" comes from companies that have been in business for many years; they've had plenty of time to put their long-term plan into effect. Their shareholders ought to be enjoying the results *now*.

"What about junk bonds?" someone would say. "Doesn't restructuring create a lot of debt?" First of all, these so-called junk bonds tend to sell in denominations of $1 million or more, and they're bought by the most sophisticated financial institutions and individuals in the country, so it's not a case of the unwary investor taking unnecessary risk. (Incidentally, the great majority of high-yield financing goes to small, young companies that can't get backing any other way — the very companies that have been the engine of growth in our economy.) Less than 10 percent of the junk bonds have been used in takeovers. As for the question of debt, it's true that restructuring often turns equity into debt. But where is that money going? It's going right into the hands of stockholders, who then use it to make purchases or investments that invigorate the economy. I'd much rather trust that money to several hundred thousand stockholders than to the board of directors of a moribund corporation.

Finally, someone would say, "You talk a lot about stockholders, but don't corporations have other constituencies, such as employees, the consumer, society itself?" Sure they do, but those constituencies are not in conflict. In fact, they should overlap. First of all, employees ought to *be* stockholders. And if you satisfy the consumer the company does well. The stockholders are happy, the employees are secure, and society is served. I don't know of a better index of a company's success than the price of its stock.

As I traveled around the country, it seemed there was a place for a new kind of organization, established specifically to defend the rights of shareholders. I didn't have much experience with nonprofit ventures, but I decided to give it a try. Some 47 million Americans own stock in publicly owned companies — a potentially powerful constituency. But I could not be sure of how much support I had until we actually formed the organization and asked the shareholders to join us.

First we decided to put our money where our mouths were. I committed personally to underwrite the first year's budget of $1.3 million to launch the effort, which we called the United Shareholders Association — USA — dedicated to "a more competitive America." We distributed the first copy of our newsletter, *The Advocate,* in the summer of 1986.

In the newsletter we made a "public offering": annual membership for $50 in a community of shareholders as varied as American society. The newsletter pointed out that corporate abuses "hurt all Americans. They hurt employees who are denied the dignity of exercising individual initiative. Worst of all, they threaten the security of all Americans by crippling this nation's international competitiveness. The lack of accountability in corporate America is at the heart of this failure."

We scheduled a press conference in Washington, D.C., for August 26, 1986, to kick off USA. It was at the National Press Club, and I hoped there would be enough interest for a few reporters to show up. We expected a dozen or so and were surprised when we walked in to see the room filled to overflowing with more than a hundred print and broadcast journalists, along with cameras, tape recorders, and hot lights.

I stepped up to a podium bristling with microphones and told them why I had come to Washington. "We need a shareholders' association," I said, "because corporate America has drifted away from the principles on which it was founded. Owners, and that means shareholders, are unorganized, intimidated, and treated like second-class citizens, and these are the people putting up the money."

I pointed out that the managements and directors of the two hundred Business Roundtable companies owned less than one

one-tenth of 1 percent of the stock in their own firms. A recent study revealed that 387 of Standard & Poor's 500 companies had adopted anti-shareholder proposals. Some 170 companies had changed their bylaws to restrict their shareholders' ability to make charter changes. Forty-three had instituted poison pills, and more than two hundred had classified boards. "Public corporations are the only place in America where you sign your ballot, send it to the incumbent, and ask him how the election turned out. These executives," I said, "are digging their foxholes and loading their mortars. But it's too late."

Most shareholders are not rich, I pointed out. They make up 20 percent of the population. Their average age is forty-four, and their average yearly household income is about $37,000. The average stock portfolio is worth about $6,000.

"These aren't 'fat cats' we're talking about. These are hard-working Americans," I went on.

I offered to take questions, and two dozen hands shot up. Most of the reporters were interested in my battles with large corporations and wanted to know if USA was to help me in future encounters. I explained that the association was designed to help all shareholders equally. "We want to establish one thing," I said, "and that is that stockholders own companies, and management are employees."

"Isn't it true," asked another reporter, "that jobs are lost and that pensioners are hurt in companies that have been broken up?"

"Pensioners are not hurt because they are protected contractually. And if you break up a company, the pieces have to employ people, too. Often they employ more people and are more dynamic."

The impression that people are harmed by takeovers, I added, was purposely created by the Business Roundtable, which had hundreds of lobbyists telling their story while the stockholders had none. "Congress needs to be aware of what's going on," I said. "Look at the Business Roundtable for a minute. It's made up of the two hundred largest corporations in America. Who goes to their meetings? The CEOs. They meet several times a year here in Washington, behind closed doors. Do you think they're working in our interests? I don't think so."

Here were some of the most sophisticated financial journalists in America, and I could tell, watching their faces, that most of them had never thought about some of these things. I probably wouldn't have, but I had been so close to the action since 1982.

The next day, the USA office in Washington was deluged with phone calls from people wanting to join, to donate money, to help in any way they could. Our office in Amarillo received close to a hundred calls the same day. I could tell that the message had touched a chord. The stockholders needed and wanted to be heard, and USA was going to do the job for them. We had more than 3,000 members in three months.

There's a place for businessmen in politics and that place is right out in the open, saying what they believe. As CEO of Mesa, I don't hesitate to send letters to the stockholders urging them to vote for whoever I think is a good candidate. I get a few hot letters back, but that's fine; I want to know where stockholders stand. If I think something will help this country, I'll offer my opinion.

In 1985 and 1986, I was one of the organizers of the President's Dinner, to raise money for the House and Senate races. In 1986 we raised about $7 million — a record. At the dinner President Reagan said, "Boone, that's enough for us to take over a small oil company, isn't it?" The president has been supportive of the battles for corporate control.

I want more politicians to develop the starch to tell corporate America's CEOs, "Don't come to Washington and expect to get any better treatment than anyone else." They fly in like kings, announced by their lobbyists, and Congress rolls the red carpet all the way from the Hill to National Airport. These guys don't do a damn thing for either party, and what they're up to doesn't help this country.

They have access to key people in Washington because they head large, powerful corporations. But that may be changing. I have encouraged politicians to look at the situation closely and ask, "What is it that these people have to offer?"

I haven't heard one elected official defend them. CEOs don't have to stand for reelection every four years. We are all tenured. There are damn few CEOs who could find a comparable job if they were turned loose; in fact, a lot of them couldn't even get a job. They are entrusted with billions of dollars' worth of assets, and at the same time some of their companies have taken over a billion dollars of write-offs. Twenty years ago, if a company took a billion-dollar write-off, its stock would have gone through the floor and a CEO would be on the street. That's not the case today. Why should politicians and decision-makers listen to these mediocre performers? Just recently there was a rumor that the CEO of a big oil company had died — and the stock went up 2 points. Later in the day the rumor proved false, and the stock dropped 2 points. That says a lot about corporate leadership today.

We must reduce the influence of big business in Washington. People are tired of it. The people cry for leadership — in government and out of it. They want to see our companies take the lead and get competitive again. The way to do that is to kill the protectionism game. Send the executives back to the workbench — that includes oilmen. An import tariff on crude oil is not the solution. Senator Bob Packwood said in the spring of 1986, "Boone Pickens is the only businessman I know that if Congress would leave him alone he would never come to Washington."

Late in 1986 Ivan Boesky, Wall Street's best-known arbitrageur, was accused by the SEC of getting inside information on takeover targets and using that information to take illegal stock positions. Boesky agreed to pay a record $100 million in penalties and to cooperate with the SEC in its investigation of other people with whom Boesky may have conspired.

I was shocked by the revelations, like most everybody else. I considered Boesky a friend and a very astute investor. I had been on several panel discussions with him and was impressed with how smart and attentive to detail he was. I also noted an elfin quality about him. He always smiled, no matter what he happened to be saying. At first I thought it was nervousness. Then I realized that only his mouth was smiling — his eyes were unaffected. The smile was probably an indication of his self-control.

Boesky once invited Bea and me to "Sunday supper" at his home in Westchester County, New York. We had been specifically told to dress casually, so I wore an open-neck shirt and blazer; Bea wore slacks. We were surprised when our host met us at the door in a double-breasted navy blue suit. We soon realized that it was a seated dinner for twenty people. He asked me if I wanted to borrow a tie. "I don't borrow ties or shotguns," I told him. I think ol' Ivan enjoyed setting up a country boy from Texas.

Boesky made some money from investments in Gulf stock when Mesa was battling Gulf, and he reportedly lost money speculating on two other deals involving Mesa, Cities Service and Phillips. It's too bad he did what he did because he didn't have to cheat to win. It left the public confused and angry, but even more important, it gave the Good Ol' Boys — the Business Roundtable — an opening they didn't deserve. They immediately tried to link activist shareholders and arbs. It will take the media and the investing public a while to sort it all out, but it won't take too long, because corporate America's executives lost their credibility a long time ago.

The roles of activist shareholders and arbs in the restructuring of corporate America are related but independent. Activist shareholders come forth to battle for control of mismanaged corporations and to put the assets of these corporations to better uses. Arbs provide liquidity for shareholders who are concerned that entrenched management will defeat the activist shareholder and cause the assets of the corporation to be put to less valued uses.

Arbs are not essential to a takeover, but they do perform a useful function. They step in to the market with very sizable investments after a deal has been announced and absorb a substantial portion of the risk that the deal will be defeated. It is a risky business because sometimes a deal *will* collapse — like the Gulf–Cities Service deal back in 1982 — with enormous losses being shouldered by the arbs. That's why they are called "risk arbitrageurs." But they aren't reckless. They retain some of the finest legal talent in the country to help them assess both the legal and political risks in the deal. They also possess considerable acumen in economic analysis.

The panicked reaction in Washington to the Boesky affair was predictable. What is surprising is seeing two Democratic senators, Proxmire and Metzenbaum, talking about legislation that would entrench managements further. This is a great opportunity for the Republicans to unload an anvil that they have carried too long — big business. They should let the Democrats carry it for a while and see what it is like to be forever explaining their link to big business.

A bright spot in the Boesky situation was the SEC, which moved quickly and forcefully to crack down on insider trading. It is one government agency that deserves praise — and some additional funding to beef up its enforcement division and keep pressure on those who break the rules.

We don't need more laws hamstringing honest investors and stockholders. What we do need is vigorous enforcement of the existing rules. What's going on in corporate America today is too big to stop. The Boesky case is a side show — and a pretty poor one at that. The main event is the ongoing restructuring of corporate America to make us more competitive in the world market. It is vitally important and will only be slowed temporarily.

One way to improve the performance level of our big corporations is to make them smaller. Some are nothing more than government bureaucracies called corporations, and in some cases they are even more wasteful than government.

If we encouraged the breakup of some of the inefficient ones and allowed some of their divisions to start anew, America would be astounded at the results. When the Standard Oil Trust was broken up, all of the newly created companies did well — much better than if they had been left under one giant umbrella.

Special interests dominate Congress, and too many politicians favor people and situations according to how well they are lobbied.

The defense contractors are probably the best example of the power of special interests. Their lobbyists entertain the politicians — wine and dine them and take them on junkets. Some of these contractors are established crooks, and they are stealing the taxpayers' money. If I were a congressman or senator, I wouldn't be caught dead with a defense contractor.

I commented about defense contractors to a high-ranking officer in the Defense Department while we were hunting a couple of years ago. He agreed and said, "Why don't you make a tender offer for a defense contractor? It would do this country a lot of good."

It's a persistent myth that our country's economic vitality depends on the major corporations. In fact, very nearly the reverse is true. From 1981 through 1985 — a period of great expansion — *Fortune* 500 profits actually fell by 17 percent, and jobs in these companies decreased by 12 percent. In fact, small companies have been the lifeblood of the economy, creating 35 million jobs over the past twenty years while the largest of the *Fortune* 500 companies have lost 3 million.

We have entered a new entrepreneurial era. Nowadays, more and more young people want to get out of school and do what I and other entrepreneurs have done. Major corporations in America are not going to be able to attract the kind of talent they need unless they make drastic changes.

The nation's promise is the promise of youth. I have always believed in the ability of talented, motivated young people, and I have seen that promise fulfilled in my own corporate experience. Therefore I am optimistic about the future. A new breed in American business and politics is motivated by the same ideals that made this country what it is, ideals that are sometimes dimmed but that always reassert themselves. This new breed will lead us toward success, and that's a story as old as the country and as fresh and exciting as the discovery of an oil field somewhere in the Texas Panhandle.

# *Epilogue*

## A White Knight

In late 1985, Pioneer, another big independent oil and gas company in Amarillo, announced a restructuring similar to Mesa's designed to enhance the value of its stock. Soon after, the directors received an unsolicited offer from Minstar, Inc., its largest stockholder, to acquire Pioneer. This "bear hug" put the board in an awkward position, for they knew it probably would be changed to a tender offer to the stockholders.

I called Pioneer's president, and we set up a meeting that included both Pioneer and Mesa executives. Mesa had no stock in Pioneer and no intention of making a bid for the company. We had followed Pioneer for years and hoped that someday we would have a chance to talk about combining the two companies. That day had now arrived.

We had a second meeting a few days later, and Pioneer gave us access to the company's internal records. (I might add that they offered this opportunity to other industry companies also.) The Mesa team was already acquainted with Pioneer's assets and had some ideas about how Pioneer might be merged with Mesa. We moved swiftly, and our ideas appealed to Pioneer's management and board; after further negotiations over several days, we jointly announced a plan to issue special Mesa Limited Partnership preference "A" units for Pioneer stock. It was a special limited partnership unit that was tailored to fit Pioneer's assets and stockholders.

We had made an $800 million acquisition, the largest in our history — and it was friendly. Mesa had become a white knight.

The combination of Mesa and Pioneer created the largest independent oil company in the United States. We were now ready to look at deals of any size — well, almost any size.

So in the late summer of 1986, David Batchelder, Sidney Tassin, and Drew Craig gathered in my office on the fifth floor of the Mesa One building. Autumn was on its way. The luminous blue sky held a lot of promise, and we talked in the easy, irreverent way that had come to characterize even our most serious conversations.

Things had never looked better. The MLP had a market capitalization of $2 billion, and during the next six months it would raise another $500 million on transactions already in progress. That was the most financial muscle we had ever enjoyed. Moreover, it was happening when the oil industry was suffering its worst depression ever. It was an endorsement of our management and an indication of tremendous opportunity for those who could predict the future and were willing to bet on their analysis.

The Mesa Limited Partnership was now established as the premier structure for the future in the oil industry.

That morning's *Wall Street Journal* contained a story about Mesa. An analyst had been asked what he thought we would do with our buildup of capital and credit, and he had replied, "What do you *think* Boone will do with that much money?" He meant that we were going to do something, but that something might be different. I have always believed that it's important to show a new look periodically. Predictability can lead to failure.

Back in December 1985, when we formed the Mesa Limited Partnership, I was freed to do some things on my own. The four of us — David, Sidney, Drew, and I — planned to create a new entity called Boone Co.; a joint venture, it would make its own deals away from the MLP. The reputation we had built through the years had enabled us to raise billions of dollars, and it would not surprise anybody for us to do it again.

So the MLP had great financial strength and flexibility, and Boone Co. would also be formidable. It was time to make deals.

"There are good deals all around us," said David.

Drew talked about some of the prospects he had been studying and was quickly accused of having "fallen in love" with several of them.

"Now all we need is a slow backswing," Sidney said.

We knew the companies and we knew each other, so the conversation was short and to the point. Everybody had his say, and when it was my turn I just added, "Let's do it."

# INDEX

# Index